SUBJECT, SOCIETY
AND CULTURE

Theory, Culture & Society

Theory, Culture & Society caters for the resurgence of interest in culture within contemporary social science and the humanities. Building on the heritage of classical social theory, the book series examines ways in which this tradition has been reshaped by a new generation of theorists. It also publishes theoretically informed analyses of everyday life, popular culture, and new intellectual movements.

EDITOR: Mike Featherstone, *Nottingham Trent University*

THE TCS CENTRE
The Theory, Culture & Society book series, the journals *Theory, Culture & Society* and *Body & Society*, and related conference, seminar and postgraduate programmes operate from the TCS Centre at Nottingham Trent University. For further details of the TCS Centre's activities please contact:

Centre Administrator
The TCS Centre, Room 175
Faculty of Humanities
Nottingham Trent University
Clifton Lane, Nottingham, NG11 8NS, UK
e-mail: tcs@ntu.ac.uk
web: http://tcs@ntu.ac.uk

Recent volumes include:

Feminist Imagination
Genealogies in Feminist Theory
Vikki Bell

Michel de Certeau
Cultural Theorist
Ian Buchanan

The Cultural Economy of Cities
Allen J. Scott

Body Modification
edited by Mike Featherstone

Paul Virilio
From Modernism to Hypermodernism
edited by John Armitage

SUBJECT, SOCIETY AND CULTURE

Roy Boyne

SAGE Publications
London • Thousand Oaks • New Delhi

For Maureen and Walter Turnbull

© Roy Boyne 2001

First published 2001

Published in association with *Theory, Culture & Society*,
Nottingham Trent University

SAGE Publications Ltd
6 Bonhill Street
London EC2A 4PU

SAGE Publications Inc
2455 Teller Road
Thousand Oaks, California 91320

SAGE Publications India Pvt Ltd
32, M-Block Market
Greater Kailash – I
New Delhi 110 048

Published in association with *Theory, Culture & Society*,
Nottingham Trent University

British Library Cataloguing in Publication data

A catalogue record for this book is available
from the British Library

ISBN 0 8039 8349 2
ISBN 0 8039 8350 6 (pbk)

Library of Congress catalog record available

Typeset by Mayhew Typesetting, Rhayader, Powys
Printed in Great Britain by The Cromwell Press Ltd,
Trowbridge, Wiltshire

CONTENTS

LIST OF ILLUSTRATIONS

ACKNOWLEDGEMENTS

My colleagues in the Sociology Department of Durham University, in the European Studies Group at the University of Durham, Stockton Campus, and on the Editorial Board of *Theory, Culture & Society*, have provided continual stimulation and encouragement. John Hayward (who deserves a special word for his support, and for his superb work in developing the Stockton Campus of the University of Durham), Adrian Darnell and John Bancroft have provided cover, at critical moments, for my administrative duties in Durham, and I am in their debt. Ruediger Ahrens and the University of Wuerzburg were generous hosts during an extended research visit to Germany. Mike Featherstone, Bridget Fowler, Sarah Franklin, Steve Fuller, Ian Heywood, Scott Lash, John Myles, and Derek Robbins all read parts of the manuscript and made helpful comments for which I am grateful. The responsibility for what lies within is, of course, entirely my own. The National Gallery of Art in Washington, Georg Baselitz, the Prado, the Kunsthalle in Hamburg, the Guggenheim Foundation in New York, the Hirshhorn Museum, and DACS acting on behalf of the Tate Gallery and private collections, gave permission for the reproduction of the pictures which appear in the book. Faber and Faber gave permission for the extract from 'Sweeney Agonistes' to appear. Their help was invaluable.

A version of Chapter 3 appeared in *Symbolism: a Journal of Critical Aesthetics*, Vol. 1, No. 1, 1999. A short version of Chapter 4 appeared in *The History of the Human Sciences*, Vol. 8, No. 2, 1995 and in Chris Jenks (ed.), *Visual Culture*, London: Routledge, 1995. A short version of Chapter 6 appeared in Susanne Fendler and Ruth Wittlinger (eds), *The Idea of Europe in Literature*, Basingstoke: Macmillan, 1999. A version of Chapter 7 appeared in *Angelaki*, Vol. 4, No. 2, 1999.

Finally, I would like to express my thanks to my wife, Nicola, my step-daughter, Clare, and my son, Christopher, who have all been outstanding in their constant support.

PREFACE:
THE FATE OF THE SUBJECT

The story of the subject in Western thought can be approached through Machiavelli's tale of Remirro de Orco. He was the man who forcibly pacified and unified the Romagna at the start of the sixteenth century. Cesare Borgia, known at the time as Duke Valentino, knew that while the inhabitants of the Romagna had been quietened, they were nevertheless liable to nurse resentment and hatred at the way that they had been quelled. He therefore came to the decision that it had become unnecessary to keep faith with Remirro de Orco, despite the fact that this man had been his loyal lieutenant and a fruitful and effective subject acting on his behalf:

> The Duke decided that there was no need for this excessive authority, which might grow intolerable, and he established in the centre of the province a civil tribunal, under an eminent president, on which every city had its own representative. Knowing also that the severities of the past had earned him a certain amount of hatred in the minds of the people and to win them over completely he determined to show that if cruelties had been inflicted they were not his doing but prompted by the harsh nature of his minister. This gave Cesare a pretext; then, one morning, Remirro's body was found cut in two pieces on the piazza at Cesena, with a block of wood and a bloody knife beside it. (Machiavelli 1961: 57–8)

This death of the agent in 1502 exhibits the classic form of the critical paradigm. In abstract, there are six moments: first the subject as untrammelled power, second the emergence of a relatively autonomous agent of that subject; third rejection of the potential consequences of that autonomy, fourth the death of the agent, fifth affirmation of the power of the agent (not now Remirro, but the Civil Tribunal), and sixth the persistence of the subject. What Machiavelli teaches us is to look for the subject behind the agent.

We need not however follow Machiavelli's (and, later, Sartre's) example here and define the subject in terms of the struggle for supremacy. While we do need to hold on to some notion of autonomy if we are to retain a notion of a subject, different forms of autonomy surely exist. In the fields of aesthetics, politics, economics, science, ethics, education, and one might even say, loosely, everyday life, it is not obvious that human actors are only agents acting on behalf of other forces. There will, of course, be plenty of occasions when that will be the case. There will, however, also be times when human subjects take considered actions when loyalties conflict, form critical judgements in the absence of clear rules, attempt innovations without prior approval, and take principled stands which lead them into apparently untenable positions. The ubiquity of such examples presents *prima facie* grounds for arguing that the simple replacement of the human subject by the sociological notion of the agent cannot be justified. Perhaps it will be a matter of seeing these two basic notions as alternatives. At times, even when we do not know it, thought or action may be other-directed, representational, vicarious. This is certainly true. At other times, however, human action is not the action of agents, whether conscious or unconscious, but is seen as an expression of autonomous selfhood. The situation is made difficult because all human action can be seen by others as either agential or subjective, and the actor, him or herself, can never be completely clear which it is or where the balance lies. If we add this hermeneutic indeterminacy to the strength and weight of the formative social forces around us, forces which lead us without realising it to act and think as we sometimes do, it becomes plain that as subjects our constitution is relatively weak. There is however a very great difference between acknowledging this weakness, and acceding to the wholesale critique of the subject that has been common currency within much of the social sciences and some of the humanities since the 1960s.

Suppose, however, that we are living through the death of the subject. If this is the case, we are surely in dramatic and momentous times. Both the objective view of nature advanced especially within science and technology, and the subjective view of human beings as moral subjects, have been enormously productive. Apparatuses of knowledge, law and economy testify to this efflorescence. We might expect, then, that announcements of the transcendence of the objectivity–subjectivity divide will either enshrine a critique of such productivity itself (radical ecology springs to mind here) or offer an equally fecund potential (actor network theory, discussed in Chapter 2, below, may be the best example here). Thus far, however, as I will try to show in the course of this book, denials of either the subjectivity of subjects or the objectivity of objects rest within the general framework of subject and object which remains untranscended. This is not to say that the principles of science and morality (to take the two obvious instances) have not given rise to mistakes, false promises and, certainly, terrors. Nor is it to say that local vectors of the overall subject–object framework are immune to criticism and reformulation.

This book is concerned with the subjective moment that, thus far, remains residual and obdurate even after the fiercest dilutions, deprivations and denials to be found within contemporary social science and postmodern practice within the humanities and the philosophy of culture. What do we mean by the subject? At its core is the idea of an autonomous principle of judgement. A prototype for this principle is based on the idea of single individual human beings who are able freely to decide upon the actions that they take within virtually all social and personal contexts. The site of the decision process, in this view, is the individual consciousness, and although it can be compromised by drugs, emotional turmoil, physical duress, and by the artful manipulations of others, and even though it can never be certain of the authenticity of its own condition, in its normal form it is sufficiently powerful to be autonomous, discerning and, therefore, responsible for its own actions. This view of the subject is a basis of the day-to-day understanding of the self within Western society. It is reflected in contemporary legal systems whether based on English common law, Roman law, or Islamic law. It is also contained in the very structure of our language, with its subjects and predicates, its nominative and accusative cases. The essence of this classical, post-Augustinian view of the subject is that the 'I' is the first cause of its own intentional actions.

There is a clear opposition between contemporary sociological thought and contemporary cultural theory with regard to the question of the subject. Both regard the classical post-Augustinian view as untenable. Sociologists have tended to hold that view in epistemological terms, finding that there is no aspect of human behaviour which can *a priori* be treated as outside the mechanisms of social cause and effect. Cultural theorists have tended to find that the classical view of the subject is an ideological construction, both in theory and in practice. In consequence, and in general, sociological thought repudiates the subject, while cultural theory seeks to understand how the subject is constructed and/or how and where it is placed. In the first chapter of this book, we will look at the first of two major currents within sociological theory: Bourdieu's reflexive field theory. In the second chapter, our topic will be actor network theory. I aim to show, in this first part of the book, that one of the things that unites these exemplars of structuralist and constructivist thought is a shared rejection, on epistemological grounds, of the subject, but that they both, as Machiavelli might lead us to expect, depend upon the principle of subjectivity, even as they have intimated its death.

The second part of the book suggests that the pristine moment of refusal of the sociological consciousness that has defined the contemporary period is to be found in modern art. Paradigmatically, this takes the form of the artist's striving to express something of the subjective, human condition. One might say that the artist tries to puncture, even burn, the institutional layers which lie heavy, like so many sheets on a cold bed,[1] on the subject made supine by the weight of social forces. While the sociologist holds that it is this weight which constitutes the subject, creating the very idea of a moral subject and casting grave doubt upon the artist's project, the artists we will consider try to excavate what is essential to the subject, finding qualities of the subject which are a-social, pre-social and supra-social. They do not aspire to a scientific description of a non-social subject, but rather try to crystallise out the qualities of the subject that endure despite the pressures of social construction and conformity that bear down upon us all.

The varied affirmations of subjectivity that we find in Newman, Baselitz and Bacon give us limited insight into the cultural condition of the contemporary subject, into its modes of possibility as being-in-the-world. The cinema has no particular privilege over literature or philosophy in this regard, but, as the seventh art form, it is both the contemporary mode of leisure and a powerful medium of reflexivity for the subject in the world. This is not, of course, its generally understood function – far from it. So we have to be careful. There is, however, on the evidence of the body of work, accessible work for the most part, that has been produced over the last century, a continuing potential for anthropological analysis and investigation of subjective temporalities which goes far beyond the intentions of the profit seekers, and penetrates into the symptomatology of the contemporary subject.

The cinematic subject cannot be strong, for it, like *Superman* sold for $65 in 1938, then has value only as parody and entertainment. In contrast to the case of sociology, however, the subject for cinema does not disappear entirely from view, nor is it too often made arcane as a result of the brilliant and obsessive hunt for clinching and exquisite essence. The very core of cinema as an art form is the fabulation and illustration of the strength and weakness of the contemporary subject. This subject is not strong enough to forgo accommodation: no matter what form the attempted repudiation of exterior forces might take, whether the attempt to deny one's past or the effort to dissolve oneself in a sealed narrative of private desire, the effort will fail. However, even in the case of a subject entirely overwhelmed by social forces, some element of its own does struggle to endure, an iconic counter-instance even if in death and failure.

It is the overall argument of this book that the humanities and the social sciences are moving too far apart, that the social scientific repudiation of the subject has its counterpart in the Manichaean subjectivism of popular entertainment, and that both risk forgoing the moral narrative subtleties of contemporary life. We fail to appreciate and reinforce these intricacies at our peril, and art, whether on canvas or on the screen, can help with their reproduction.

Note

1 The work of Anselm Kiefer is instructive, not only for his 1974 picture, *Painting = Burning*. His 1992 installation, *The Women of the Revolution*, included fourteen steel beds with mattresses covered with lead sheets.

PART I

THE DENIAL OF THE SUBJECT
IN SOCIOLOGY

INTRODUCTION

Sociology is a contested field. At the point of its great expansion in the 1960s, there were at least four competing approaches within the discipline (structural-functionalism, interactionism, Marxism and phenomenology) and a host of neighbouring disciplines also laid claim to parts of the study of society (history, psychology, anthropology, economics). Significant numbers of empirical sociologists ignored these theoretical disputes, preferring to collect data and analyse it for evidence of trends. During the 1960s, feminist sociology developed into a powerful presence, and cultural studies, fuelled by feminism, Marxism and the anthropology of everyday life, began to grow. Significant strains of feminism, Marxism and cultural studies were informed by developments in French philosophy, and especially by an anti-humanism which rejected the Cartesian first person centredness entailed by *cogito ergo sum* and Sartre's model of *ego* seeking to objectify *alter*. The transcendental structures, to which the anti-humanists, like Lévi-Strauss, Althusser and Lacan, were drawn, were real but intangible: kinship systems, language systems, economic systems, the structure of the unconscious mind. Alongside these currents, but uninflected by French theorising, cybernetic systems theorisng promised to grow increasingly important.

At the other end of the scale from such systems thinking, the work of Harvey Sacks and Harold Garfinkel examined the construction of routine conversational and microsocial interaction, and, as a result of transporting this orientation into the study of the production of scientific, laboratory knowledge, social constructionism emerged to challenge the hegemony of the natural sciences on their own ground. Within the world of empirical sociology, qualitative research grew in importance during the 1970s, as both funding bodies and researchers saw how important it was to understand experiences and motivations from the inside, as it were, if basic trend data were to make any sense. Then, through the 1970s with poststructuralism

and into the early 1980s with the emergence of postmodernism, the transcendental assumptions of the anti-humanists came under attack: hegemonic
principles such as party, proletariat, market, system, structure, progress
were all held to be permanently subject to question and deconstruction.
This blowing apart of the established socio-political canon, at least as a set
of articles of faith, had its parallel in the field of literature with the
emergence of the discourse of postcolonialism, which challenged the
supremacy of white, male writers. Yet, at the same time that the established
order was being dissected and recomposed into local fields, a global cultural
economy appeared to be spreading its reach, tightening its hold, and denying the differences that the new counter-discourses of postmodernism and
postcolonialism were trying to bring to the fore.

To describe the place of the subject across all these different developments is not the task of this book. What is wanted, however, is to indicate
the animus against the subject, and simultaneous reliance upon it, within
sociology in something approaching a representative manner. In order to
do this, it seemed important to select case studies that were closer to the
core of the sociological tradition than to its periphery, thus ruling out
poststructuralist, postmodernist and postcolonial approaches. It also
seemed, for the purposes of this book, that issues raised by overt questions
of identity politics (in areas like race, gender, disability) would divert this
preliminary inquiry, and that while this diversion would almost certainly be
necessary at a later stage, the first thing to do was to lay out some of the
ground.

One of the basic divides in the approach to analysing the social world is
between the view that social structures are relatively fixed and that they
operate at the macro-level of class, gender, generation, tribe, nation and so
on, or that they are relatively fluid, and flow into networks which will seek
to stabilise and grow (making use where necessary of 'imagined' macro-
level phenomena, but, where more appropriate, deconstructing such 'false'
contructs). This divide is, roughly, between a realist and a constructionist
approach. To carry out a preliminary examination of the place of the
subject within contemporary sociology, we will look at the competing perspectives of Pierre Bourdieu, with his notions of habitus and field, and
Bruno Latour, with his concepts of network and actant. Both repudiate the
classical metaphysical certainties of the subject, but, as I will try to show,
both rely on the idea of the subject to establish their projects.

1
BOURDIEU AND THE SOCIOLOGICAL TRADITION

Bourdieu wrote in 1979:

> To escape from the subjectivist illusion, which reduces social space to the conjectural space of interactions, that is, a discontinuous succession of abstract situations, it has been necessary to construct social space as an objective space, a structure of objective relations which determines the possible form of inter-actions. (1984: 244)

Bourdieu makes it plain that the idea of a social situation, conceived as a setting brought about and defined by individual subjects, is to be rejected as a mistake which erroneously devalues the concrete presence and materiality of the real social world by presenting it as merely the aggregation of subjects' actions upon each other. For him, a field (his term for a quasi-autonomous sector of society)

> is not reducible to a *population*, that is to say, to the sum of individual agents linked by simple relations of *interaction* or, more precisely, of *cooperation*: what is lacking, among other things, from this purely descriptive and enumerative evo-cation are the *objective relations* which are constitutive of the structure of the field and which orient the struggles aiming to conserve or transform it. (1996: 205)

Bourdieu quite properly seeks to be consistent. He tells us that he has never failed to treat himself as an object. He has been able to do this because, like any self-critical analyst, he is able to objectify and demystify the appearance of personal autonomy that accompanies his thoughts and actions, and to track the forces that caused them to come into being. In other words, methodological reflexivity reveals the inadequacy of the classical model of the autonomous and responsible subject. For him, rigorous analysis erodes the subject through a relentless process of explana-tion and demystification. Bourdieu tells us that we can 'account for the empirical "subject" . . . by situating him or her at a determinate place in social space' (Bourdieu and Wacquant 1992: 214), and by rigorously, scientifically, detailing the forces focused at that place. Once this is done, there remains, for Bourdieu, nothing left to be accounted for. His view is effectively a sociological version of Locke's thesis that the subject is a *tabula rasa* which is progressively filled up by experience. In the sociological view, as typified by Bourdieu, the space of the subject is given both form and content by social forces, and, what is more, the subject thereby produced is always provisional, an agent of wider forces which may change.

The most important thing for Bourdieu appears to be the concreteness of the dynamically structured world as opposed to the illusions of the subject. What, Bourdieu asks, criticising Sartre's existentialism, are we to make of any social philosophy that pretends that the world offers no resistance to us, or asserts that in bad faith we choose the conditions of our own misery, ignoring the social determination of the very structure of the choices that we can make (1997: 177)? His answer is that we are to treat it, not as the discovery of ontological bedrock, but as a symptom, an outcome of a particular set of experiences, an outcome of causal processes, as a determinate position, without truth value, within a structured field.

Bourdieu takes objectification to be the social scientific method. Proficient social scientists have a range of methodological tools – statistics, ethnographic description, formal modelling (Bourdieu and Wacquant 1992: 8) – available to ensure that analysis relates to the object analysed, and is not corrupted by subjective illusions of permanence and control. The principal controlling strategy which overarches the use of the objectifying tools by social scientists is reflexivity: the rigorous analysis of social science practice by social scientists using all the tools of social science.

In Bourdieu's general view of objectification, the reflexive eye is conceived as, at the limit, an untrammelled, clear-seeing eye. It is tempting to think that reflexivity is actually based on the existential dream of free action which Bourdieu is so set against, and while Bourdieu does not easily fall into this trap, he does so in the end. His argument is that the reflexive consciousness is aware of the forces which determine it and is therefore best placed to exercise the maximum amount of autonomy. This will however be the autonomy of agents within the intellectual field, and not the autonomy of subjects. For Bourdieu, the intellectual field has emerged since the Enlightenment as the field of opposition to dogmatic orthodoxies. When he was asked whether he was putting the sociologist in the place of the philosopher-king, he replied,

> What I defend above all is the possibility and the necessity of the critical intellectual, who is firstly critical of the intellectual *doxa* secreted by the doxosophers. There is no genuine democracy without genuine opposing critical powers. The intellectual is one of those, of the first magnitude . . . I would like writers, artists, philosophers and scientists to be able to make their voice heard directly in all the areas of public life in which they are competent. I think that everyone would have a lot to gain if the logic of intellectual life, that of argument and refutation, were extended to public life. (Bourdieu 1998b: 8–9)

While Bourdieu does not want to see such intellectuals as free-floating subjects, he does, then, want to see them as agents of critique, as opponents of dogma, and as enemies of misplaced certainty. Is it splitting hairs to say that such figures would be, in some sense, autonomous subjects? He said to Axel Honneth and others, in an interview in 1985, 'I want in some way to reintroduce agents . . . I say deliberately agents and not subjects' (1987: 19), and a few years later,

There is action, and history, and conservation or transformation of structures only because there are agents, but agents who are acting and efficacious only because they are not reduced to what is ordinarily put under the notion of individual. (Bourdieu and Wacquant, 1992: 19)

Bourdieu's notion of the intellectual is one of critical agency, discriminating and able to exercise judgement over what is and is not acceptable. How close is the idea of a critical agent to that of a subject doing his or her best to maintain a blend of personal integrity and public responsibility in the face of varying pressures emerging from different fields of power? If there is a difference between subject and critical intellectual agent, it may be that in Bourdieu's schema the critical response is already contained *in nuce* within the field in which the intervention is taking place. The intellectual function, therefore, for Bourdieu, is maieutic not creative. The same may be true of innovation in the fields of art and science, where again the apparently creative action of individual subjects is seen as the action of agents of a field bringing part of its potential into being (Bourdieu 1996: 235).

Agents for whom, or for what? In whose name is such agency exercised? The answer to that question is that social actors, in Bourdieu's sociology, are agents for and within fields. For Bourdieu, a field is a doubly defined social domain. It is defined by the competition for the scarce resources within the field. It is also defined by the precise nature of the resources that are at stake in the field. A field is like a game, although, unlike the latter, a field is not the product of a deliberate act of creation, and it follows rules or, better, regularities, that are not explicit and codified. What is at stake in fields? On the one side, there is struggle for economic goods of various kinds. On the other side, there is the struggle for social capital embodied in forms of prestige, social honour and social access. Between these two sides, there is the struggle for cultural capital, for skills, knowledge and educational distinction.

In Bourdieu's view, it does not follow from this that social actors are mere marionettes. Bourdieu spends a good part of *La Noblesse d'état* examining the way in which socialisation toward field membership takes place, and he establishes that, for the effective functioning of, say, the scientific field, it is very important that its members, the agents at the micrological level, are not produced and reproduced as passive reflectors, since their disciplined activity is required to reproduce the continuing vitality of the field in the context of struggle between fields. However, as Bourdieu has pointed out, in a discussion (Wacquant 1993: 34) of Foucault's theory of power, while individuals are not mere physical entities to be pushed here and there, they do internalise the structure of the external field. The habitus, as a micro-translation of the fluid structures of the objective world, is an interiorisation, a formation of selves.

In broad terms, there are three factors which produce agents within fields as apparently autonomous. First, Bourdieu characterises fields in a relatively fluid way, and the apparent autonomy of social actors partly derives from the fluid multi-determinations of plural field causality. Second, there is one field, or to put this another way, one principle running across fields, the field or principle of power, that when translated from field to agent also produces effects of agent autonomy. The principle of power, internalised by agents, is at root responsible for the agent's structures of motivation and criteria of personal achievement. Third, fields are repositories of practical logic and wisdom, hence agents' practices of reflexivity are invested with efficacy due to that grounded disciplinary wisdom on which they ultimately depend.

What, then, are the principles of action in Bourdieu's thought? The emphasis that we find placed on causality, and its scientific investigation, may lead us to think that the answer must reside in a causally determining historical process. We may consider that social life is to be accounted for, in Hegelian fashion, after the fact, as a process without a subject. We find, however, that the field, which is first candidate to be the bearer of historical movement, is intentionally fabricated as a set of suggestions rather than as a powerful causally unambiguous machine. With the fluidity and freedom of manoeuvre accorded to fields within the real social world restricted only by the power relations within and between fields, we can best conceptualise fields as the social subjects within Bourdieu's system: they are the prime movers. Affirming neither an autonomous rational economic or political individual as subject, nor a Hegelian denial of subjectivity, Bourdieu's thought precipitates a macro-subject between these two positions, in the form of a Machiavellian collectivity:

> in the realm of science as in the realm of politics, one can escape the alternative between the naively Hegelian or Kantian vision of politics only by offering a solution that I would label Machiavellian: just as political virtue presupposes the establishment of a republic such that all citizens have a vested interest in civic virtue, scientific virtue presupposes the establishment of a scientific republic in which social scientists have a vested interest in scientific virtues. (1991: 385–6)

It will be recalled that Bourdieu remarked that he had never failed to treat himself as an object. We now can understand what that might mean in practice. Whether one is talking of scientists or politicians or democratic citizens there appears to be a duty of reflexive awareness; self-consciousness under the imperatives of the field(s) is postmillennial virtue.

Bourdieu's declared intention to 'escape from under the philosophy of the subject' can be located at the current end-point of a venerable theoretical lineage, which he describes as a line from Hegel through Husserl to Mauss (Bourdieu and Wacquant, 1992: 121). This intention to escape from the subject is, in fact, the opening and defining moment of the sociological tradition. The link to Durkheim can be easily established. Durkheim describes the ontological ground of sociology, the very stuff which sociologists analyse, in terms of social facts. These are external to the individual, constraining upon the individual, and more or less general throughout society. This conception can be seen most clearly in Durkheim's view of the basic structural characteristics of any society: population size, geographical area, the form, extent and strength of its various social institutions are all seen as external, general and constraining upon the individual. These are the key causative structural features, and the changes in these independent variables explains much of the variation of the dependent forms of social, political and economic life which we find as we move from one society to another. The implicit critique of the free subject, the individual fundamentally able to choose to navigate any path through the world of social constraints, reaches its maximum rhetorical intensity in *Suicide*, in which Durkheim will explore the reasons for both the relative constancy of the suicide rate within any given society, and the relatively constant variations in the rate between societies. He will do this without any reference whatsoever to the intentions and states of mind of the individuals concerned, and he will seek to draw conclusions which will enable macro-social adjustments of a structural nature to be made which would solve the problem of an abnormal suicide rate. He thought further that a similar approach would be possible to the phenomenon of homicide, and although this work was never done, the complete disregard for individual states of mind and intentions would again have been a feature of the project.[1]

At around the same time that Durkheim was laying theoretical foundations for an anti-subjective science of society which would vigorously reject the concept of the free subject, even viewing any instances of the underdetermined normless individual as representing a pathological condition of anomie, Max Weber was setting down principles for a philosophy of action which seemed to promise the continued relevance of the subject within social science. He asserted that there are four fundamental types of social action: rational instrumental action to achieve a desired end, value-rational action performed because it is the right thing to do irrespective of the consequences, traditional action performed out of habit, and affectual action springing from emotion, which Weber exemplifies by 'an uncontrolled reaction to some exceptional stimulus' (1947: 116). Even though it has been shown that the status of and boundaries between these four types of social action are not clear, with Weber well aware that traditional and affectual action exist at the limit of what can properly be described as social, and with Schluchter's demonstration that instrumental and value-rational actions can become habitualised and/or invested with emotional energies to the point where they become as reactive as the pure types of traditional and affectual action (1996: 248), the principle of the subject, the rational actor as source of decisions about which kind of action would be elected and appropriate in social situations seems to survive, albeit in a weakened form due to the routinisation effects of repetition. However, Bourdieu's work threatens the removal of these vestiges of the unconditioned subject, and it does this through the concept of the habitus, which he will try to show as creating the very structure of dispositions that will produce the decisions to be made by the agent about the kind of action required in all social situations. The habitus is a concept which is oriented to action, but is ontologically prior to action. It is the structure of dispositions, derived from the operative set of social fields, sedimented within agents as an individually functioning *conscience collective*. It is Bourdieu's attempt to settle the Durkheim–Weber dispute, the structure–agency argument once and for all, in favour of sociology, the priority of structure and the repudiation of the subject. It seeks to finish the debate by arguing that the core social process takes place as more or less malleable structures are internalised to create the individual, who then expectorates these structures in the form of choices.

It is important to repeat, at this point, that Bourdieu's neo-Durkheimianism postulates a certain fluidity, a flow and flexibility essential to engagement within a multiply contested world. While Bourdieu did say that habitus is durable, he also emphasised that it is transposable (1988: 786), and in his discussions with Loic Wacquant, he replied to those critics who argue that the concept is essentially a strongly determinist one, by saying that it is an '*open system of dispositions*' (1992: 133, his italics) which is created historically, but then continually subjected to social experience and either 'reinforced or modified' by it. The prime example of the mode of modification is to be found in Bourdieu's depiction and analysis of the petite bourgeoisie. In fact, Jon Elster suggested that Bourdieu's *Distinction* may be seen as a 'generalisation to all classes of the specifically petit bourgeois attitude to the world', going on to say that, 'If in Bourdieu's universe everybody is spending his time looking over his shoulder, it is because everybody is conceived on the model of the petite bourgeoisie' (1981: 11).

Bourdieu invests the petite bourgeoisie with fluidity in two ways. First, it is, as a class, structured by what appears to be a permanent potential for splitting into fractions. The three which Bourdieu identifies are the decliners, the risers and the new. Bourdieu's analysis, in *Distinction*, of the petite bourgeoisie describes these categories in the following way. The 'declining petite bourgeoisie' is made up of craft-workers and small shop-keepers. Their numbers have been in decline for some time, and to the extent that they survive, their values and views come from a past age. The executant, rising petite bourgeoisie consists of clerical workers and junior executives; their attitudes and opinions tend to change as they grow older, with the optimism of youth eventually succeeded by repressive pessimism. The third category is referred to by Bourdieu as the new petite bourgeoisie, and this class fraction 'comes into its own in all the occupations involving presentation and representation' (1984: 359), such as media, marketing, advertising, sales, fashion, and he also adds on junior commercial executives, and the medico-social services (ibid.: 14). The various sections of the petite bourgeoisie are set in opposition to each other, with, for example, the new petite bourgeoisie set against the declining and threatened part of the petite bourgeoisie, such as shopkeepers and sole craft-workers (ibid.: 48). The 'new petite bourgeoisie' is defined as an adaptable vanguard, which in itself means that it enshrines a principle of opposition. In a classic passage, Bourdieu explains his thinking as follows:

> The new petite bourgeoisie is predisposed to play a vanguard role in the struggles over everything concerned with the art of living, in particular, domestic life and consumption, relations between the sexes and the generations, the reproduction of the family and its values. It is opposed on almost every point to the repressive morality of the declining petite bourgeoisie whose religious or political conservatism often centres on moral indignation at moral disorder . . . But it is equally opposed, by the aristocratic pretension of its fundamental choices . . . to the asceticism of the promoted petite bourgeoisie. (1984: 366–7)

Elster's suggestion that the new petite bourgeoisie provides the leitmotif for Bourdieu's entire sociological analysis of French society raises two basic questions. The first of them asks if Bourdieu's principle of transposable habitus could be a generalisation from the fickle inauthenticities and superficialities of the petit bourgeois vanguard. Analysis shows that such a reading is certainly possible. Bourdieu demonstrates that they are defined by a permanent drive to escape social definition:

> Their life-style and ethical and political positions are based on a rejection of everything in themselves that is finite, definite, final, in a word, petit bourgeois, that is a refusal to be pinned down in a particular site in social space . . . Classified [as] déclassé, aspiring to a higher class, they see themselves as unclassifiable, 'excluded', 'dropped out', 'marginal', anything rather than categorized . . . (1984: 370)

He goes on to give an alphabetical list of the variety of interests (eighty-one are listed) one might find amongst the members of this reluctant class fraction. The list stretches from aikido to Zen, by way of gliding, one-night stands and prisons. At the end of the listing, Bourdieu refers to the desperate effort to defy the gravity of the social field. His conception here is reminiscent of Durkheim's famous account of anomie:

> From top to bottom of the ladder, greed is aroused without knowing where to find ultimate foothold. Nothing can calm it since its goal is beyond all it can attain. Reality seems valueless by comparison with the dreams of fevered imaginations; reality is therefore abandoned . . . A thirst arises for novelties, unfamiliar pleasures, nameless sensations, all of which lose their savour once known . . . the futility of an endless pursuit. (1952: 255–6)

So Bourdieu was indeed inclined to use the 'new petite bourgeoisie' as both model and counter-model for his concept of habitus and his repudiation of the subject. This class fraction illustrates the fluidity of habitus, and then, in counterpoint and following Durkheim's notion of anomie almost to the letter, itemises their pointless pastimes. But, now the second question posed by Elster is whether this characterisation is indeed generalised to the whole of Western society, which would then be seen as comprised of non-subjects without any principles of identity of their own. To answer this question, it is necessary to consider more widely the relation between habitus and class, and we can do this by seeing how Bourdieu treats the working class and the haute bourgeoisie.

The seventh chapter of *Distinction* which discusses the working class is, significantly, 'The choice of the necessary', and it opens with emphasis on deprivation and on the self-definition of the working class by the class habitus which leads them to 'resignation to the inevitable' (1984: 372), although one might think that some level of transposition of working-class habitus, perhaps rooted in something entirely opposite to resignation, could be demonstrated by considering changes in working life over, say, the last 100 years. In any event, Bourdieu thinks that intellectuals who write about the working class cannot fully appreciate how their conditions of experience are lived, unless thrown into poverty by circumstance, and even then they are parvenus who will take as much time to adjust as lottery winners do when they try to join the bourgeoisie. One of Bourdieu's examples runs as follows:

> Anyone who doubts that 'knowing how to be served' is one component of the bourgeois art of living, need only think of the workers or small clerks who, entering a smart restaurant for some grand occasion, immediately strike up a conversation with the waiters – who realise at once 'whom they are dealing with'. (ibid.: 374)

Bourdieu's survey information from 166 members of the working class shows that their preferences are derived from their class habitus, constituting an adjustment of taste and values to their objective conditions of existence. A preference for simplicity and functionality in food, furniture, grooming and style of life generally is reinforced by sanctions, by 'calls to order ("Who does she think she is?" "That's not for the likes of us")' (ibid.: 380). Bourdieu, then, describes a formidable enclosure around the working class: 'There is no other possible language, no other life-style, no other form of kinship relation; the universe of possibles is closed' (ibid.: 381). As Elizabeth Wilson put it, in her long review of *Distinction*, 'The working classes thus do not permit the slightest deviations in lifestyle to those who belong to the same class. Such deviations are taken as evidence of ambition and thus a violation of class solidarity' (1988: 57).

This view of the working class is the basis for the understanding of habitus as evidence that Bourdieu is determinist, reductionist and nihilistic.[2] Thus, we have Erik Olin Wright putting the concepts of class and habitus together, stating that, for Bourdieu, 'A class habitus is defined as a common set of dispositions to act in particular ways that are shaped by a common set of conditionings . . . rooted in a class structure' (1997: 394). We also have Jeffrey Alexander arguing that, 'No matter what the ideals of an actor, a group, or an age, Bourdieu's theory of practice suggests that they are bound to be degraded by the strategic will to power that underlies and undermines every dimension of social life' (1995: 129). At this point we can conclude that a view of habitus drawn from the case of the working class would surely be a determinist one. There is no 'open system of dispositions here'. To the extent, therefore, that Bourdieu would wish to generalise the concept of habitus as an 'open system of dispositions' across the whole of society, the working class appears to present an exceptional case. Is this also true of the haute bourgeoisie?

Bourdieu's view of the 'aristocracy of culture' is that their level of reflexive self-awareness is the lowest of all. They are most deeply scored by what he calls the *illusio*, the belief in the game, and this is why contemporary artists are so easily able to play the game of shocking the bourgeoisie. We are here 'in the area par excellence of the denial of the social' (Bourdieu 1984: 11). The values and icons of the haute bourgeoisie are, in their terms, grounded upon timeless essences of truth, beauty and goodness. This is the condition which the habitus bestows on those who are entirely foreign to the realm of necessity. 'Aristocracies are essentialist,' Bourdieu tells us, 'their one inspiration is the perpetuating and celebrating of the essence by virtue of which they are accomplished' (ibid.: 24). Sociologists generally, and Bourdieu in particular, aim to deontologise these class-beliefs, to show that there is a set of rules for a game that can only be played in the absence of economic necessity, and to remove the illusions of timelessness and aura from the symbols and practices that make up the game of legitimate, 'high' culture. For Bourdieu, all essentialist positions taken with respect to cultural objects and attitudes, which is to say, all beliefs in the ultimate value of such objects and attitudes, must fail – because they deny their historical origins. There is therefore no pure artistic gaze, no sublime artistic appreciation, no simple act of creative genius (even Danto [1999: 217], who admires Bourdieu's work, is unsure at this point, asserting that there are autonomous experiences in art) and, to the extent that such admired states of being are allowed to thrive, the differential structures of class habitus formation are performing efficiently and upholding the distinctions between dominant and subordinate classes and class fractions.

A contrast between the aesthetics of the working class and those of the haute bourgeoisie can be drawn in relation to Kantian ethics and aesthetics. Kant took the view that a good action is good in itself, on account of the goodness of the will that embarked upon the course of action, not good because of the desirability of its consequences; in aesthetics he sought to distinguish that which pleases the senses, from that which rewards disinterested contemplation, locating genuine aesthetic judgement in the realm of disinterestedness. For Bourdieu, economic necessity filtered by class habitus provides the working class with a concern for consequences in the sphere of action and, within their marginal aesthetic sphere, with a concern for what pleases the senses. In Kantian terms, the working class is defined by barbarism.[3] The haute bourgeoisie, on the other hand, has the luxury of being able to ignore consequences (although it may be argued that there are specific class fractions of the bourgeoisie which have consequences as its business: the mercantile, military and political fractions, in particular), and the time and inclination to cultivate contemplation, or, in Bourdieu's terms, to relate to the work of culture without ever leaving the realm of culture. Bourdieu puts it like this:

Analogy, functioning as a circular mode of thought, makes it possible to tour the whole area of art and luxury *without ever leaving it*. Thus Château Margaux wine can be described with the same words as are used to describe the château, just as others will describe Proust apropos of Monet or César Franck. (1984: 53)

For Bourdieu, there little doubt that the Kantian philosophy of the subject is modelled on the bourgeoisie and against the emerging working class; Bourdieu's critique and dissolution of the subject dismisses both classes as a model for his conceptualisation, and does so with a certain moral indignation: a repugnance at the self-satisfied unreflexivity of the bourgeoisie, and a sense of sympathy for the necessitarianism of the working class:

> Affirmation of power over a dominated necessity always implies a claim to a legitimate superiority over those who, because they cannot assert the same contempt for contingencies in gratuitous luxury and conspicuous consumption, remain dominated by ordinary interests and urgencies. (ibid.: 56)

His conclusion, for both the haute bourgeoisie and the working class, is that it is the 'immediate adherence, at the deepest level of the habitus, to the tastes and distastes, sympathies and aversions, fantasies and phobias which, more than declared opinions, forge the unconscious unity of a class' (ibid.: 77). The Kantian vanities of the self-possessed subject were also products of the habitus, but what we can see in Bourdieu's work at this point is a move from the bourgeois determination of the subject as the key social principle (with ethics and aesthetics as its intellectual corollary) to its replacement by petit bourgeois determinations of subjectivity, drawing sociology – the petit bourgeois science – in its wake.

In what way then does Bourdieu, through his notion of transposable habitus, generalise the condition of the new petite bourgeoisie to the whole of contemporary Western society? He does so in counterpoint. Neither the working class nor the bourgeoisie can function as a model for a fluid and transposable habitus. Both classes are simply too rigid in Bourdieu's perception of them. If transposable habitus is required for Bourdieu to escape the snare of determinism, and to allow agents within fields to function as their dynamic carriers, the new petite bourgeoisie is the only class fraction which can function as its exemplar.

In a passing comment, John Scott sees Bourdieu's work 'as providing the basis for a framework of analysis complementary to that of class and economic capital' (1996: 193). The question of complementarity is an important one to address if we are to obtain a clear view of the rejection of the subject within contemporary sociology. We have now understood Bourdieu's repudiation of the subject, and its replacement by transposable habitus, as the universalisation of the petit bourgeois cultural condition. What we do not yet have is a clear sight of the position of the agent caught between field(s) and class. Is this, as Scott's comment suggests, a question of parallel forces of field and class, or is one set of forces subordinate to the other? The answer is important since an indeterminate relation between field and class might, behind Bourdieu's back as it were, allow a partially undetermined subject back in. Indeed, perhaps we should expect to find leakage and fissure which allows an uncaused first cause back in at certain points, since Bourdieu's notion of sociological reflexivity demands an outside, a vantage point on the whole to which sociology will, through reflexivity, aspire. As Geldof puts it, 'the true truth . . . can only be articulated by an absolute outside called sociology' (1997: 30),[4] and in asking the question about field and class and their interconnection, in looking to see where Bourdieu is when he formulates that relationship, are we not headed into the outside and the territory of the subject? Let us see.

A first attempt to define the relation between class and field must take us back to Weber's distinction between class and status group. We should recall Weber's definitions:

> We may speak of a 'class' when (1) a number of people have in common a specific causal component of their life chances, in so far as (2) this component is represented exclusively by economic interests in the possession of goods and opportunities for income, and (3) is represented under the conditions of the commodity or labour markets.

Weber went on, in the same passage, to encapsulate the concept of the class situation as 'the typical chance for a supply of goods, external living conditions, and personal life experiences, in so far as this chance is determined by the amount and kind of power, or lack of such, to dispose of goods or skills for the sake of income in a given economic order' (1948: 181). If we add the areas of taste, attitude and opinion as determined by power or the lack of it within a given economic order, and note further that the exercise of this overall style of life and the selection from the available life options given by economic location reproduces the continuity of the economic order, then we arrive at Bourdieu's position. With the supplementary view that such exercise and selection creates an appearance of freedom of subjective self-determination where, in fact, none actually exists, we reach a core aspect of his repudiation of the subject in contemporary class society.

Weber contrasted class and status, saying that 'in contrast to classes, status groups are normally communities' (1948: 186). He defined status as 'every typical component of the life fate of men that is determined by a specific, positive or negative, social estimation of *honor*', and went on to say that 'status honor is normally expressed by the fact that above all else a specific *style of life* can be expected from all those who wish to belong to the circle' (ibid.: 187, original emphasis). Weber thought that class and status were linked in 'the most varied ways', even saying that status honour 'normally stands in sharp opposition to the pretensions of sheer property', but he did think that, 'in the long run', and 'with extraordinary regularity', property is recognised as a status qualification.[5] Here we can see another aspect of Bourdieu's theoretical strategy, which is to shorten the long run to a zero point, to diminish the space within which the 'style of life' can appear to be autonomous from class position, and thereby to remove a realm of apparent freedom for the subject to develop unconstrained by class determinations. His critique of the realms of culture and the subject can thus be understood as a continual exposure of self-deceiving deferrals of the inevitable gravitational pull of class society.

Bourdieu's sociology has been accused of determinism, as we have seen. It has, somewhat perversely – given the importance of transposable habitus – also been accused of reductionism. Alexander offers an alternative view to the one developed so far, but Alexander's reading, perceptive and valuable though it is, does not quite work. In his reading, Bourdieu is presented as a neo-Marxist whose work 'gives full play to the materialism and corrosive cynicism of our time' (Alexander 1995: 129), and 'subjugates both code and action to an underlying material base (reincorporating orthodox Marxism)' (ibid.: 130). For Alexander, Bourdieu's view of subjectivity is determinist and anti-voluntaristic, and his '"Social fields" are far less autonomous from economic structures than has commonly been assumed' (ibid.: 131). Alexander argues that Bourdieu's work ignores the role of social agents, is duplicitous, and instead of allowing actors a degree of interpretive freedom, it attaches them to structures in a fixed way, denying them interpretive freedom and conceiving of them as 'motivated by a structure of dispositions which merely translates material structures into the subjective domain' (ibid.: 135). Alexander argues that it follows from this that Bourdieu cannot account for values:

> Values possess relative independence vis-à-vis social structures because ideals are immanently universalistic. This is so, in the first place, because they have an inherent tendency to become matters of principle that demand to be generalised in 'unpractical' ways. It is also so in a more historical sense, for social differentiation itself involves the growing organisational independence of religious and secular values, and of their intellectual carrier groups vis-à-vis the more particularistic centres of economic and political life. For Bourdieu, however, socialisation does not transmit values that are in tension with life-as-it-is-found-to-be-lived; rather, it produces values that are immediate reflections of the hierarchical structures of material life. (ibid.: 137)

There are a number of problems with this conceptualisation, even though it does capture the basic nature of the sociological reduction of subjectivity to structure.

First, the view of values as universalistic is not entirely compatible with the recognition that social differentiation produces independent value spheres. Second the notion that emerging values demand to be generalised is imprecise, and what is probably meant is that values are already generalised by virtue of their being values. Third, a theory of values which conceives of them as arising out of a tension either between different realms of practical life, or between practical life and some ideal world (which or both is unspecified) is unacceptably indeterminate between critical idealism and relativism. It may be in fact that to secure the critique of Bourdieu's abandonment of the subject, it is a mistake to go outside of Bourdieu's system in this way. The definitions of the outside are always open to challenge, and such challenges deflect the original critical intent. It is better

to remain inside and to pose the questions of how the new petite bourgeoisie is able to resist the specific determinations of the field(s), how it is
able to generate a notion of transposable and therefore weak values, and (a
version of the question animating this book) what forms of genuine
subjectivity this precipitates. It is this set of questions that will enable a
powerful response to the lack of self both in Bourdieu's theory (Alexander,
1995: 143) and in sociology in general.

There are, of course, alternative paths that may be followed. Alexander
also, for example, pursues the question of self within psychology and psychoanalysis. He finds, quite properly, that object relations theory conceives
of the self as gradually crystallising out of the residues of embodied others,
that ego psychology has a related conception of the emergence of the
autonomous individual, and that recent 'European social psychology' has
shown how the internalisation of one set of collective representations can
allow the emergence of autonomous personhood *vis-à-vis* powerful institutions such as class and religion. The problem is that all that can be done
is to set such frameworks alongside Bourdieu's position, to contrast them
rather than to engage them with each other. Alexander writes:

> Bourdieu employs his special kind of sociologized biologism – much as he
> employs habitus more generally – to enforce determination rather than reduce it:
> 'The body [is] an automaton that "leads the mind unconsciously along with it."'
> Socialisation does not depend upon symbolic interaction and a learned ability to
> interpret another's sensibility and intention; it involves, rather, simply the child's
> contact with 'the paternal body and the maternal body.' The result, habituated
> 'practical sense' is 'social necessity turned into nature [and] converted into motor
> schemes and body automaticisms.' (1995: 144)

Most importantly he draws attention to the operation of sociological
thought, to its reduction of subjectivity, but does not quite complete the
task of deconstruction, since he does not go sufficiently inside the corpus to
expose its key weaknesses.

Alexander has also drawn attention to some of Bourdieu's deepest
strategies for assimilating field and agent, in particular to the notion of
unconscious strategisation, which in Bourdieu's scheme of things allows the
priorities of the field to be reproduced in social action without the actor
being aware of the logic of her action, so that action can be 'reasonable
without being the product of reasoned design', oriented to the future without there being a conscious plan, and intentional 'when it is in no way
inspired by conscious concern' (ibid.: 154). Alexander points out that the
problem of Bourdieu's thought here is that the concept of rational action
does not easily integrate with that of normative order; 'like oil and water',
he says, 'they can be placed alongside each other but they cannot mix' (ibid.:
155). In fact, Alexander's comment here is not quite apposite. Rational
action and normative order precisely do mix, not only in the classical
account of the relation between ends (normatively derived) and means
(rationally determined), but also in such fields as Marxism and psychoanalysis, which both conceive of the operation of ideology as the veiling

of operative normative interests in the cloak of rational action. But there is a version of Alexander's point which can be developed, albeit in a speculative kind of way. It concerns the Parsonian distinction between self-orientation and other-orientation, in respect of which it would be true by definition to say that one cannot be on both sides of the divide at the same time, and of which it can be further said that positioning on different sides at different times raises the question of priorities: the subject (whether individual or field) or the determining structure? When there is conflict, what structural or subjective force functions to define what the conflict is and how it will be settled? Alexander suggests that these are the kinds of questions which cultural Marxism, from Lukács to Althusser, had failed to answer. They are questions concerning the limits of relative autonomy from structures and sub-structures. To test out those limits, it has been a recognised move to locate a transcendent standpoint. In Gramsci, for example, it was the organic intellectual; in Bourdieu, and this Alexander does not quite come to, it is the new petite bourgeoisie, the vanguard, the cultural intermediaries, the class fraction which defines itself by its escape from definition.

If there is even a weak sense in which this view can be sustained, then Bourdieu's thought and sociology may be the stronger for it, as both a moral enterprise and an empirical science. With the new petite bourgeoisie established as a locus for subjectivity, a series of questions then arises. Historically, how did this locus of social subjectivity come into existence, and how is it reproduced? Sociologically, what are the characteristics of this transcendent class fraction? Politically and economically, what forces prevent or enable the full realisation by the new petite bourgeoisie of its potential powers? Here we have the opening for cultural studies. The rift between cultural studies and sociology, and between cultural studies and Marxism,[6] or at least one modality of it, turns on the interpretation of the new petite bourgeoisie. This is one of the real ironies of Bourdieu's work: that he uses the petite bourgeoisie to found his basic anti-subjectivist sociological lexicon, and, in order to do this, he feeds off petit bourgeois subjectivity, its autonomies, self-determinations, and evasions of structural capture. While there may be something a little parasitic inherent in the fact that Bourdieu must rely on the richness of the objects of his critique in order to provide variations on his anti-subjectivist fugue, the key point is that his sociology of culture is animated by opposing principles: the anti-subjectivism of the sociological tradition and his (at times reluctant, at times uncompromising) definition of the new petite bourgeoisie as the contemporary social vanguard. This key contradiction may be one of the major sources of the energy and value of his work, allowing him in 1997, for example, to continue his denial of the subject in *Meditations Pascaliennes*, and then, in the same year upon the occasion of his acceptance of the Ernst Bloch prize, to call for resistance to the economic determinations of neo-liberal finance capital (Bourdieu 1998a). It also enables us to distinguish between the sociology of culture and cultural studies. In the latter, the study of culture splits away; also modelled on the new petite bourgeoisie, it reaches different conclusions about the status and significance of subjectivity. Both sociology and cultural studies have been freed from the necessitarianism of the working class and from the auratic conceptions of the haute bourgeoisie, and both have developed through estrangement from the objects of their gaze. In sociology, that estrangement is achieved methodologically and ontologically, while in cultural studies it has been achieved politically and archaeologically. It is the difference between denial and deconstruction.

At this stage, we seem to have reached two tentative conclusions. First, the realm of the cultural intermediary is the ideal home of contemporary subjectivity, much though Bourdieu might hate the idea. Second, a path has been opened to align Bourdieu's thinking on subjectivity with sociological thought in general. There is now one further test which remains to be carried out, and this concerns Bourdieu's direct engagement with cultural studies, and therefore with the deconstruction of the subject rather than with the negation that we find in sociology. Let us begin to conclude, then, with Bourdieu's conversations with Hans Haacke, a German installation and visual artist of international repute, which took place in 1991.

Pierre Bourdieu sees Hans Haacke as a fellow spirit. In his conversations with Haacke, which they worked on extensively over two years, he treats neither himself nor Haacke as an object. In fact he treats both as a site of resistance. As cultural intermediaries, both understand and try to expose the various forms of domination which are exerted on the art world. Haacke knows that art is commodity production and a means to glory for the individual artist, but that it also creates symbolic power that can be used either for domination or resistance. Haacke implies, for example, that Andres Serrano's photograph, *Piss Christ*, is a work of resistance. It showed a plastic crucifix placed behind a bubbling mist of Serrano's own urine. In 1987, Serrano was one of ten people to receive awards from America's National Endowment for the Arts. *Piss Christ* was accused of being offensive and blasphemous. Serrano's response to the allegations made on the floor of Congress was indeed what one might expect from 'an artist of resistance'. He said:

> The photograph, and the title itself, are ambiguously provocative but certainly not blasphemous. Over the years, I have addressed religion regularly in my art. My Catholic upbringing informs this work which helps me to redefine and personalize my relationship with God. My use of such bodily fluids as blood and urine in this context is parallel to Catholicism's obsession with 'the body and blood of Christ.' It is precisely in the exploration and juxtaposition of these symbols from which Christianity draws its strength . . . So let us suppose that the picture is meant as a criticism of the billion dollar Christ for profit industry and the commercialization of spiritual values that permeates our society. (Serrano 1996: 280)

One of the things that characterises Serrano's response here is a looking-glass, one-to-one relationship between an artwork and a social object – in this case, the practices of institutionalised Christianity. That one-to-one relation was also the basis of the accusations of anti-Christian bigotry. It is a relation of the same form as the relation set up by Bourdieu between field and individual, but this time in a conversation between two members of the cultural intermediaries class fraction, the presumption is not of subordination and determination, but of resistance and deconstruction.

Haacke's *Helmsboro County*, 1990 sculpture is a direct comment on Philip Morris's practice of sending out free copies of the US Bill of Rights. Haacke's work incorporates the following statement from their Chairman, George Weissman: 'Let's be clear about one thing. Our fundamental interest in the arts is self-interest. There are immediate and pragmatic benefits to be derived as business entities' (cited in Bourdieu and Haacke 1995: 8). We have here a further example of a simple relation of resistance: on the one side a condemnatory cigarette box installation, on the other side, the self-interested practices of an American tobacco company, which claims to speak for the moral majority while, at the same time, poisoning both their minds and bodies. This was far from the first time that Haacke's art had questioned corporate motive. In his 1978 show in Eindhoven, his triptych, *But I Think You Question My Motives*, cites the Managing Director of Philips in South Africa: 'We are businessmen and look for business opportunities, which is the only factor governing our decisions' (Bois et al. 1984: 183); in 1983, he produced a painting based on a painting which he had found in an Alcan public relations leaflet, about which he said, 'It is a cheerful, sunny picture. Into the bright sky I painted a short caption which announces, in a tone of pride, that the workers at Arvida have an opportunity to contract bone fibrosis, respiratory diseases and cancer' (Bois et al. 1984: 175).

These are powerful examples of critical art: Haacke against the tobacco industry, exposing Philips, denouncing Alcan; and Serrano versus Christian fundamentalism. Direct confrontation is indeed the strategy which Bourdieu's sociology of the contemporary artistic field seems to recommend; and beyond this potentiating political analysis of the field of art, we also find that Bourdieu generalises the duty of resistance for knowledge-workers and culture-workers, saying that there is a 'universalism toward which all intellectuals should struggle' (Bourdieu and Haacke 1995: 68). This universalism is defined in terms of resistance to the hypocrisies of domination. He is disappointed but understanding when this duty toward universalism is abandoned. Consider the dispute over the funding of two exhibitions at the Whitney (*Abject Art: Repulsion and Desire in American Art* and *The Subject of Rape*). The museum directors did not intervene in this too much: but how could they win in this context? As Bourdieu said:

> There is a whole network of dependencies . . . Painters need to exhibit in museums to place their works on the market or to receive public funding. Museums need to be recognised by public authorities in order to have sponsors. And all this creates a set of intersecting pressures and dependencies which, even if there is resistance, continue to exist. (Bourdieu and Haacke, 1995: 11)

It is, however, important here to realise that Bourdieu could understand their abandonment of their petit bourgeois duty to resist as arising out of a rational decision.

There is something else. Bourdieu knows that the artist is capable of moving people (ibid.: 22–3), that forces outside of the class determinations of neo-Marxism or the competition for power deriving from a Weberian perspective are capable of impacting upon individuals; which must mean individuals as subjects rather than as agents, because in answer to the question, in the name of which field principle are you allowing yourself to be affected by the artwork? there is no clear answer, because the question is not the right one to ask. The example he gives is Haacke's installation in Graz, a duplication of the enclosing of the Column of the Virgin Mary which had taken place in 1938. Haacke's installation commemorated those who died under the Nazis rather than, as was the case with the earlier piece of political monumentalising, celebrating Nazi power.

This inversion of Nazi ceremonial, meant as a temporary memorial to the victims of Nazism, was firebombed, provoking outrage. Bourdieu comments as follows:

> in the case of Graz, you compose a work, the work's enemies destroy it, thus unleashing a whole train of discourses that force a deployment of critical intent. These works make people talk, and, unlike those of certain conceptual artists, for example, they do not make people talk only about the artist. They also make people talk about what the artist is talking about. Through facts and actions, you prove that it is possible to invent unprecedented forms of symbolic action which will free us from our eternal petitions and will put the resources of the literary and symbolic imagination at the service of symbolic struggles against symbolic violence. (ibid.: 29)

Haacke's work was enhanced immeasurably by the actions of the fire-bombers, but the aleatory and contingent fate of the final work impresses upon us even more clearly the inadequacy of the field–habitus couplet as the foundation for understanding subjective action and response. What is more, this is an inadequacy that Bourdieu himself recognises when he is working within the field of culture.

The danger in reading Bourdieu is to allow his variations on the same theme to overwhelm. He insists that it is crucial to recognise that art historians and philosophers of art refer continuously to art's absence of function; they speak of the primacy of form over function, and of the disengaged nature of art as art, and they must not be allowed to keep ignoring the socio-historical location of the work and of its reception. He tells us over and over again that aestheticism privileges the analyst's decontextualised subjective experience of the work of art, and therefore that aestheticism universalises the particular, translating particularity into transhistoric normativity. He argues that ignoring the historicity of both the work and the gaze at the work means that there cannot possibly be anything approaching an adequate view of aesthetic experience. However, if the sociological consciousness was the consciousness typical of the

twentieth century, is it not now the case that the petit bourgeois consciousness has become typical? So does not Bourdieu, and indeed sociology
in general, completely miss the point? Which is that 'we' know all the stuff
that he says, both intuitively and in our practice much of the time, and
when it is not in our practice – when we talk about colours and line and
aesthetic innovation – then frankly what we are doing is wilfully allowing
ourselves to be distracted, it is an indulgence: art is luxury, it is self-
indulgence, but Bourdieu seems to think we do not know that, and of
course we do. We are not the cultural dopes sociology takes us for. In other
words the range of habitus is probably much more aware and artful than
Bourdieu takes it to be. His analysis may work in the case of religion (but
even then there are many exceptions), and it may work for art for many
also, but it is not the general condition that he claims. This seems to leave
us with a final irony: that Bourdieu has seized upon a class fraction to
develop sociological concepts which will apply to the rest of the society, but
not by definition to that petit bourgeois class fraction, but he is doing this
at exactly the moment when the cultural condition of that class fraction is
in the process of being generalised across the whole of the society.

What we find, then, when Bourdieu enters the world of the cultural
intermediary is a strategic withdrawal from his anti-subjectivist view.
Perhaps we can see this as a switch from sociology into cultural studies, a
move from epistemology to politics. Indeed, it is hard to see how a petit
bourgeois politics of culture would be other than a politics of resistance,
one which called for those forces of the subject resistant to field determinations to be consolidated in an effort to make a difference to them. We
will not find out what those resistant forces are, however, by denying their
existence as soon as we leave the arena of culture. Haacke comments, at the
end of his interview with Bois, Crimp and Krauss, that while 'nothing can
escape eventual absorption . . . the informational aspect probably makes it
immune, at least for a while' (Bois et al. 1984: 200). It is this, even if
temporary and a matter of remission, immunity from structural determination that Bourdieu will allow (indeed must allow if what he says is to get a
credible reception) when he is inside the field of contemporary practice, but
refuses *qua* sociologist.

In sum, Bourdieu's arguments against the subject are somewhat dis-
ingenuous in two important respects. The critical intellectual, whether
artist, academic or journalist, is required to be and allowed to be immune
to, or at least distanced from, the interior determinations of the powerful
fields which have made him or her what they are. This will not mean that
the critical intellectual is an absolute prime mover, since the critical positions to be adopted are already enshrined as possibilities to be articulated
within the fields concerned, and as new possibilities for critical articulation
emerge, in a process of *autokatakinesis* (Dyke 1999: 199), then intellectual
production can and should be dynamically reactive. Bourdieu's ideal
intellectual is therefore a moral witness (perhaps to be contrasted with the
existential witness whom we will encounter in the art of Francis Bacon,

later in the book). Although he or she is not a prime mover, this does not mean that the question of the Prime Mover is entirely absent from Bourdieu's thought, because we encounter it in the notion of the field itself, which is seen by Bourdieu as a kind of Machiavellian collectivity, effectively modelled on the classical subject, with all its mythical power (especially its creation of new possibilities), but without its breadth of responsibilities. Perhaps this is an accurate picture, in abstract, of contemporary society, with the subject's powers of creation and responsibility split apart, but it may seem a little perverse that the witnesses have no excuses while the prime movers have no need of reasons.

Notes

1. The motiveless murder, which Joel Black describes as a 'modernist invention' (1991: 93), and which also links to the phenomenon of serial killing (Stratton 1996) is disturbingly commensurate with Durkheim's sociological vision here, being in some senses its logical supplement. It is also worth noting that Sara Knox's *Murder: a Tale of Modern American Life* emphasises that the 'tale of murder must somehow necessarily be about the storyteller's own distance from the murderous subject. This is the case even when the author/mediator and the author/murderer *are* identical' (Knox 1998: 4–5, italics in original).

2. It has to be recognised that Pierre Bourdieu's work here is over twenty years old. Does the idea of necessitarianism still hold up? A large amount of empirical work would be needed to give a substantial answer to that question. However, the exquisitely sensitive taste sensors of contemporary French cinema appear to register that the idea of necessitarianism is still powerful. For example, Agnès Jaoui's film, *Le Goût des autres*, the most popular film in France in March 2000, again affirms (in counterpoint) that the strong default position is that taste is determined by class. It would make an interesting research project to track the numerous European cinematic examples of representation of the valorisation of what is available in 'underclass' cultures.

3. Bourdieu cites from Kant as follows: 'Taste that requires an added element of charm and emotion for its delight, not to speak of adopting this as the measure of its approval, has not yet emerged from barbarism' (cited in Bourdieu 1984: 42).

4. The quotation from Geldof continues, 'or – and this amounts to the same thing – one called Pierre Bourdieu'.

5. Dyke argues that the social sciences have tended to be dominated by static, linear and typological approaches, which accounts for their inability to prosper, as sciences of what are now coming to be recognised as non-linear dynamic systems. Weber's sociology, in particular, however, may be construed as a counter-example. Not only might his methodology of the ideal-type, as a permanently revisable analytical tool, be appropriate to non-linear dynamic systems permanently on the edge of change, his analyses (for example) of economic change in different societies recognise the importance of apparently quite minor differences for the creation of different patterns, well before the advent of non-linear systems thinking.

6. Cf. Judith Butler who writes against the 'explicitly Marxist objection to the reduction of Marxist scholarship and activism to the study of culture' and against 'the tendency to relegate new social movements to the sphere of the cultural, indeed, to dismiss them as being pre-occupied with what is called the "merely" cultural, and then to construe this cultural politics as factionalising, identitarian and particularistic' (Butler 1998: 33).

2

ACTOR NETWORK THEORY: THE PLACE OF THE SUBJECT WITHIN CONSTRUCTIONIST SOCIOLOGY

The search for an adequate characterisation of sociology *vis-à-vis* the subject is not achieved by confrontation with the work of Bourdieu alone. We cannot characterise sociology in general as anti-subjective simply on the basis of Bourdieu's inheritance of the triple legacy of Marx, Durkheim and Weber. We have seen that in the battle with Weber, Bourdieu is conceptually victorious with his notion of habitus, and we have also seen that he claims the Machiavellian tradition for himself with the implicit declaration (retreated from only when caught unawares within the field of culture) that fields are the true social subjects. In contrast to this, there is a contemporary marriage of Weber and Machiavelli, of agency and the strategic accretion of advantage, which we might contrast with Bourdieu's neo-Durkheimian position. We find this in that version of social constructionism which has come to be called actor network theory. On the assumption that at the core of sociological thought will be its reference to a minimal set of structures, it should tell us something about the status of the subject within sociology if we can go to the variant of sociological thinking where that set is at its sparest. This will add considerably to our picture of the treatment of the subject within sociological thought.

For actor network theory (ANT), the perspective developed by (among others) Michel Callon and Bruno Latour, the difference between micro-actors and macro-actors is a matter of density and durability, qualities that are achieved (or lost) over time by the forging of contingent alliances. Callon and Latour have some disagreement with Bourdieu's view that social forces are not to be seen as aggregates. Speaking of Hobbes's Leviathan, the macro-actor 'created' by the social contract, they say:

> The sovereign is not *above* the people, either by nature or by function, nor is he higher or greater, or of different substance. He is the people itself in another state – as we speak of a gaseous or a solid state. (Callon and Latour 1981: 278)

They know that the social contract is a mythical device without much historical credibility, but argue that this false instance would have been, had it really taken place, a single case of a more general process which is referred to as translation. 'By translation we understand all the negotiations, intrigues, calculations, acts of persuasion and violence, thanks to which an actor or force takes, or causes to be conferred on itself, authority to speak or act on behalf of another actor or force' (ibid.: 279). John Law puts it well, when he notes that actor network theory sees actors as relational effects within a world of temporarily ordered bits and pieces, in which the contingently achieved actors either grow or shrink through their success or failure in securing the translation of further bits of this contingent order into their own terms. 'Translation,' Law explains, 'is a play to achieve relative durability, to make verbs behave as if they were nouns' (Law 1994: 103). Actor network theory holds that sociologists cannot assume *a priori* that one level (say the level of the field or class) is more important than, or (as in Bourdieu's case) has completely displaced, another, since it is precisely differences in level and scale, and their contingent causes, that will elude us if we do so assume. The methodological corollary to this is that sociologists should treat all actors (micro- and macro-) as if they were the same size, treating them with the same analytical tools, and asking in each case how the translation processes had worked to produce the contingent ordering of apparently different scalar phenomena under examination. Failure to reject the commonsense assumption that some actors are bigger than others, and therefore deserve more attention and special theoretical treatment, is actually itself a piece of the translation process, part of the story of how macro-actors get to appear bigger and how they maintain their size. There is, Latour explains, 'a background/foreground reversal: instead of starting from universal laws – social or natural – and taking local contingencies as so many queer particularities that should be either eliminated or protected, it starts from irreducible, incommensurable, unconnected localities, which then, at a great price, sometimes end in provisionally commensurable connections' (Latour 1997b).

One of the first exercises within this tradition of privileged human subjectivity denial concerned the scallops of St Brieuc bay. Could they be farmed? Callon's investigation of their story sought to hold fast to three methodological principles: first, 'no point of view is privileged and no interpretation is censored' (Callon 1986: 200); second, a single vocabulary of translation is to be used which will cover all aspects of the case under examination; third, the abandonment of all *a priori* division between natural phenomena and social organisation. The drama concerned scallops, scientists and fishermen, and was a matter of negotiation between the actors representing these three groups. The scientists had discovered that the Japanese were successfully breeding scallops: the main questions which arose (dressed in Callon's single vocabulary of translation) were as follows. Could representatives of the French scallop population be persuaded that their community might expand in the same way as had that of their Japanese cousins? The fishermen were accustomed to landing what they could catch, but would their representatives be prepared to exercise restraint so as to allow the scallop community time to act out their preferences? Would the scientists properly integrate into this hybrid community of knowledge-workers, crustaceans and sea-farmers? Or would they reap their publications and run? For Callon the outcome was not pre-ordained (as Latour was to put it later, 'Instead of constantly predicting how an actor should behave, and which associations are allowed *a priori*, ANT makes no assumption at all, and in order to remain uncommitted needs to set its instrument by insisting on infinite pliability and absolute freedom' [Latour 1997b]).

The striking innovation of Callon's paper was the treatment of the scallops as actors. The problem was to get them to anchor themselves, in their larval state, to objects called 'collectors' (not thematised as actors, but they could have been):

> If the scallops are to be enrolled, they must first be willing to anchor themselves to the collectors. But this anchorage is not easy to achieve. In fact the three researchers will have to lead their longest and most difficult negotiations with the scallops. (Callon 1986: 212)

As in the case of the more conventional, internationally reported, political negotiations which take place in meeting rooms, hotels, palaces and embassies, there are outside forces working to avoid particular outcomes. In St Brieuc Bay there are predatory forces – starfish – and disruptive forces – currents[1] – and sundry other parasitic and environmental agencies which disharmonise the negotiations. But the researchers are prepared to give a great deal of ground in their negotiations with the scallops; they will go to great lengths to find out what it will take for them to resist these other forces, and they offer one concession after another.

The negotiations appear to be successful:

> How many larvae anchor themselves on the collectors? . . . The anchorage is equivalent to a vote and the counting of anchored larvae corresponds to the tallying of ballots. When spokesmen for the fishing community are elected the procedure is the same . . . From the fishing community which is just as silent as the scallops in the Bay, a few individuals come forward . . . The votes are counted . . . analysis of these results leads to the designation of the official spokesman . . . Although no vote is taken, the agreement of the scientific community is also based on the same type of general mechanism: the same cascade of intermediaries who little by little reduce the number of representative interlocutors. The few colleagues who attend the different conferences or seminars speak in the name of all the researchers involved. Once the transaction is successfully accomplished, there are three individuals who, in the name of the specialists, speak in the name of the scallops and the fishermen . . . The social and 'natural' reality is a result of the generalised negotiation about the representativity of the spokesmen. (Callon 1986: 215–16, 218)

After a first season which confirmed that the negotiations appeared to have worked, troubles break out. The initial representatives, it turned out, did not command the confidence and loyalty of their constituents: the scallops refuse to continue to anchor themselves, the scientific institutions revise their funding programmes, the fishermen abandon restraint, and take their winnings from the first season: 'brutally, and without a word, they disavowed their spokesmen and their long term plans' (ibid.: 220).

In Callon's case study of St Brieuc Bay, the closure of negotiations was short-lived, the network established insufficiently robust. Contrast this with the analysis by Latour of Pasteur's negotiations with the anthrax virus. Here the outcome was shown to be much more stable and far-reaching. This story begins with a simple assertion, that activities in a laboratory in Paris and day-to-day life on a farm, some fifty kilometres away in Pouilly-le-Fort, are a world apart. What Latour will show is how Pasteur, the media, the laboratory, the scientific establishment, the farming community, livestock and microbes all came to be linked together in a network which remains impregnable to this day.

In 1881, there is great media and scientific interest in what Pasteur is doing in his laboratory. This is not surprising. In the 1850s at the University of Lille his work on fermentation had made the outstanding contribution to the understanding and prevention of the souring of both milk and wine, which he showed to be due to the activities of bacteria. If the sugar solutions used in the production of wine were initially subjected to high temperatures, the bacteria responsible for the spoiling of wine were eliminated; and if milk was subjected to high temperatures (the process which subsequently became known as pasteurisation), it would subsequently keep for very much longer. In 1865, he was responsible for saving the French silk industry, which was threatened by the silkworm disease known as *pébrine*. Through breeding experiments, Pasteur showed that the disease was hereditary as well as contagious, and his work resulted in the adoption of the careful sorting process, whereby disease-free eggs became the basis for the growth of a new generation of *pébrine*-free silkworms. This scientific work meshed brilliantly with the economic sectors related to wine, milk and silk. By 1881, Pasteur was not a mere human subject (and, as we are beginning to see, in the actor network perspective, no human subject is merely a human subject – all are more or less durable, more or less extended networks) but was already a highly elaborated network. As Latour says, the 'interest of outsiders in lab experiments is not a given: it is the result of Pasteur's work in enrolling and enlisting them' (Latour 1983: 143), as Law might put it, translating them from verbs into nouns.

In 1881, everyone 'knew' that anthrax was a major problem for cattle farmers. A whole system of local knowledges and expertise had grown up over past generations. This system took into account all kinds of local variations:

> the soil, the winds, the weather, the farming system, and even the individual fields, animals and farmers. Veterinary doctors knew these idiosyncrasies, but it was a careful, variant, prudent and uncertain knowledge. The disease was unpredictable and occurred according to no clear pattern. (ibid.: 145)

This complex, folk-epistemological setting was, as Latour points out, hardly conducive territory for the incursion of a mono-causal, laboratory-science approach. What does Pasteur do? He extends his laboratory (which we will now see is not a simple bounded space, but a network which can be extended or contracted in time and space) to include the farm at Pouilly-le-Fort:

> No two places could be more foreign to one another than a dirty, smelling, noisy, disorganised nineteenth-century animal farm and the obsessively clean Pasteurian laboratory . . . But . . . They learn from the field, translating each item of veterinary science into their own terms, so that working on their own terms is also working on the field. (ibid.: 145)

Pasteur is now able to take the farm back with him to his laboratory in Paris, where his negotiations with the anthrax bacillus are more successful than was to be the case with the scallops in St Brieuc Bay. He farms the microbes. So, in 1881, if you want to negotiate with anthrax, you do not go into the countryside – you go to Paris.

But the local variations are still a key issue:

> Especially puzzling for all practitioners and farmers, is the *variation* of the disease. Sometimes it kills, sometimes not, sometimes it is strong, sometimes weak. No contagionist theory can account for this variety. So Pasteur's work, although interesting, could soon become a curiosity or more precisely, a laboratory curiosity. (ibid.: 147)

At this point, Latour draws our attention to the new suite of skills that is being developed in the laboratory. Not only are microbes being farmed, but Pasteur has formed such a good relationship with their representatives that he can now make them reveal their tricks. As in the confessional, they tell him what they are capable of. 'The result is that laboratories are now able to imitate the *variation of virulence*' (ibid.: 148, original emphasis), and Pasteur can grow bigger now, since he can translate the language of local variations into a laboratory language of variation. Furthermore, there are two further extensions that he can make. One is back in time, to the discovery of the process of vaccination, made some eighty or so years earlier, when a relation of repulsion was discovered between cowpox and smallpox. The second link is to the relation of repulsion discovered between weak and strong strains of chicken cholera. As Latour puts it, Pasteur now has a lever with which to move the world.

It is not the purpose of this exposition of Latour to retell his account of Pasteur's transformation of cattle husbandry, although it should be said that the story does not stop at this point, but goes on to examine the negotiations that take place between the agricultural interests and Pasteur's laboratory, which turn on the demand that the farm must be, at crucial points, inside the laboratory. Nor do I want to echo Latour's double message (although I do not doubt it) that laboratories do not have fixed insides and outsides, and that microbiology labs have played a much greater part in transforming the social world than most sociologists realise. What I do want now to focus on is the significance of this work for the contemporary idea of the human subject.

The strategy that Callon and Latour adopt to help them retain a view of all actors as isomorphic is to treat actors as networks, and they find that what counts is the extent and durability of these networks. This is not just a question of contracts and alliances, but is also a Machiavellian affair, a matter of castles and laboratories, bacteria and fishing boats:

> What make the sovereign formidable are the palace from which he speaks, the well-equipped armies that surround him, the scribes and the recording equipment that serve him . . . Instead of dividing the subject with social/technical, or with the human/animal, or with the micro/macro dichotomies, we will only retain for the analysis *gradients of resistivity* and consider only the *variations in relative solidity and durability of different sorts of materials.* (Callon and Latour 1981: 284, italics in original)

In the case of the scientists, scallops and fishermen, the network becomes less than formidable: the scallops are poorly prepared to fight off parasites and predators, the scientific 'recording equipment' is insufficiently sophisticated, its laboratory setting is unable reliably to incorporate the marine environment, and the interpretations of the 'scribes' dissolve into competing accounts of excuse and failure. Pasteur, on the other hand, enlists more and more forces into his network which is extended into an international monument, served by an enormous, well-equipped and clearly scripted educational and manufacturing apparatus.

We do not have to step far into this sociology of translation to recognise a defining sociological moment: the denial of privileged status to the human subject. Indeed, we can also see how Bourdieu's fields (although denied the permanently privileged status Bourdieu would like to accord them) can be construed as subjects, as, in other words, macro-actors. However, Latour's repudiation of the classical human subject is a careful denial. The human subject is conceived to be an actor on account of his or her acquisition of material forces: 'only thus can one "grow"':

> An actor grows with the number of relations he or she can put, as we say, in black boxes. A black box contains that which no longer needs to be reconsidered, those things whose contents have become a matter of indifference. The more elements one can place in black boxes – modes of thought, habits, forces and objects – the broader the construction one can raise. (ibid.: 284–5)

In fact, the way that actor network theory denies the subject, at the same time as providing a powerful critique of Bourdieu's neo-Durkheimian sociology, is not, as Bourdieu does, to dissolve subjectivity, but to place the components of subjectivity (values, feelings, cognitive, aesthetic, ethical and musical capacities, innovativeness, curiosity, susceptibility to feelings of awe, fear, pride, hauntedness, repulsion, and attraction, impulses to murder or charity, and our sense – even if it sometimes betrays us – that we belong to ourselves) inside just one small corner of a black box (as Latour says of actor network theory, 'the self and the social actor of traditional social theory is not on its agenda' [1997b]). The 'size' of an actor is then determined by how much is held in the box and how well it can be kept there. The outcome of competition between subjects is determined by 'who can muster on the spot the largest number of well aligned and faithful allies' (Latour 1990: 23), which means the largest number of forces prepared to be corralled. Once boxed, these forces are taken for granted unless and until they begin to leak out. Thus we have the actor network theoretical approach to the classical human subject, effectively that it is boxed away, and of no further relevance unless it should begin to leach through the walls, *osmotically pulled by another network*. As Law puts it:

> Agency and size (together with machines, social entities, and every other kind of object to which one can point) are uncertain effects generated by a network and its mode of interaction. They are constituted as objects to the extent, but only to the extent, that the network stays in place . . . agency and other objects, together with the dualisms that infest the modern world, are all relational achievements. And since they may be undone, this is a sociology of contingent ordering, a sociology of verbs rather than of nouns. (1994: 103)

Latour denies the fundamental dualisms of subject and object, individual and society, social and natural, which he sees as underlying modernism. His most graphic illustration of the position is contained in his diagrammatic characterisations of modernism (Latour 1993) as the episteme of purification: from the simple distinction between nature and society in Hobbes, through Kant's separation of the *a priori* and *a posteriori*, intensified with Hegel's notion of history as the unfolding of the original contradiction of the alienation of spirit, followed by three attempts at termination: phenomenological difference, Wittgensteinian incommensurability of language games, and postmodern repudiation of metanarrative. Here is a list of some of the figures that modernity has erected as representative of the post-Renaissance subject: the *tabula rasa*, the free agent, the class-for-itself, the other, the cogito, the dialogic relationship, intersubjectivity. These inventions of Locke, Sartre, Marx, Foucault, Descartes, Bakhtin and Schutz (not alone, of course, since all 'their' figures are interdiscursive creations) are all, for Latour, 'asymmetrical' (Latour 1993: 135). They are the complement of the pure object of the sciences. Their essence for these thinkers, and for many more, at least partly resides (even though some might protest that this is not the case) in the absolute difference between the rock and the hard place, between the thing and the subject. Latour's view is that we cannot grasp the human unless we restore to it its element of quiddity, its 'share of things'. He argues, 'So long as humanism is constructed through contrast to the object that has been abandoned to epistemology, neither the human nor the nonhuman can be understood' (ibid.: 135).

All the attempts to purify are miscast, because at the most basic level the epistemological basis of modernity was miscast. As the title of his book declares, Latour thinks that actually *We Have Never Been Modern*. From the beginning all has been mediation, and attempts at purification were always already outmoded and scholastic. In more recent times, the modernist version of truth based on the primacy of nature first gave way to the revisionism of the 'strong programme' of the sociology of science, which saw truth explained by social principles, and now gives way to the generalised insight that both nature and society are to be explained from the standpoint of the networks created between them. As Stephen Ward has noted, Latour's approach seeks to transcend the 'objectivistic expectations of traditional epistemology, the relativistic conclusions of postmodern theory, and the Durkheimian "special case status" of social explanations' (Ward 1994: 89). What is the consequence of this approach for the human subject?

The actor comes to be defined vectorally: 'What is an "actor"? Any element which bends space around itself, makes other elements dependent upon itself and translates their will into a language of its own' (Callon and Latour 1981: 286). In these terms, the computer, for example, is an actor. Latour's view, essentially, is that the subject is eternally and irreducibly constructible. If the computer, for example, can be an actor, bending space around itself, making other elements dependent upon it, translating their will into a language of its own; if the human has to be understood as an intertwining of will and object(s), then, to take one instance, the existential definition of freedom defined apart from inert nature will not stand. The thick liquids of human freedom cannot be separated from what Sartre called the practico-inert. The human subject is inevitably and permanently hybrid. This does not amount, for Latour, to the death of the human, but it does mean that the human is not a stable form:

> We should be talking about morphism. Morphism is the place where techno-morphisms, zoomorphisms, phusimorphisms, ideomorphisms, theomorphisms, sociomorphisms, psychomorphisms, all come together. Their alliances and their exchanges, taken together, are what define the *anthropos*. (Latour 1993: 137)

The human subject is not endangered or compromised by technology, the cyborg does not threaten to obliterate what it means to be human, nor does the greatest of organisations promise the terminal decline of the human subject as an inhabitant of the realm of freedom and future extensions of hybridity, since, according to Latour, the loss of essence is merely an imaginary evil. How could things be otherwise if the essence of the human subject is change, alliance and hybridity? The true threat, he suggests, comes from those who seek to reduce the essence of the human subject to some simple set of principles, making 'humanism a fragile and precious thing at risk of being overwhelmed by Nature, Society, or God' (ibid.: 138). For Latour, the project of excavating what remains of the subject after taking the sociological critique fully into account would probably make no sense, but if it did have a vestige of intelligibility, then it would begin from the recognition that 'modern societies cannot be described without recognising them as having a fibrous, thread-like, wiry, stringy, ropy, capillary character that is never captured by notions of levels, layers, territories, spheres, categories, structure, systems' (Latour 1997b). These latter terms, he argues, represent network effects rather than ontological, topological or political essences.

The position which is outlined here replaces the modernist asymmetry between subject and object, in which the human subject is a paranoid construction always under threat from the other side of the divide, with a symmetrical world in which machines are not simply machines, organisations not simply organisations, and human subjects not simply human subjects. Machines, organisations, goods and subjects are all hybrid quasi-objects. They exist between 'hard' nature and 'free' society. A computer system is 'much more social, much more fabricated, much more collective, than the "hard" parts of nature' but at the same time it is not a member 'of a full-fledged society' (Latour 1993: 55). The human subject is also more social, fabricated, and collective than 'hard' nature, and, for Latour, its position within society is inevitably dependent on its hybrid construction, which is, as is the case for all networks, capable, just like Pasteur's laboratory,[2] or, as in the St Brieuc's Bay case, of collapse.

We might say, perhaps with a misplaced sense of the dramatic, that the critique of actor network theory emerges fully formed on 10 February 1990, at a meeting hosted by the University of Bath which brought together some of the main participants from the field of the sociology of scientific knowledge (SSK). At issue was the past history and future direction of post-Mertonian sociology of science, and a central element of the debate concerned the work of Bruno Latour and his colleagues. Harry Collins and Steven Yearley had some very clear thoughts on the matter. Their view was that since the mid-1970s there had been four key moments in the sociology of science. The first of these concerned the relativist thesis that truth is a socially organised consequence of social behaviour. This constituted a liberating moment. Scientific knowledge could be seen, not simply as the attempt to discover the exact nature of the physical world, with the progress of science measured in terms of increasing verisimilitude, but as a social, an interactional, achievement. Studies of how scientists actually behave in laboratory and other settings would demonstrate how scientific truth is accomplished, and the explication of the social processes involved need make no extended reference to the technical problematic (of physics or chemistry, etc.) that the social actors shared, beyond acknowledging that it was there, and that this problematic too would have been a social accomplishment. The second moment was that of discourse analysis which focused on the organisation of communication between scientists. Conceptually, discourse analysis is fairly clearly a development within the relativist paradigm. It was, however, felt by some, Collins and Yearley among them, that discourse analysts thought their work to be superior, that earlier work was not truly representative of what scientists did, and that 'discourse analysis touched bedrock' (Collins and Yearley 1992a: 304). The third moment is that of reflexivity, which problematises the position of the sociologist, and establishes that a philosophical problem of the sciences – how do we know that our representations, photographs from an electron microscope, for example, truly represent reality? – applies just as much to what social scientists have to say. It was Collins and Yearley's view that each of these three developments claimed epistemological priority over other approaches. They conceptualised this as 'epistemological chicken', with each personification prepared to stay longer on the relativist road than the one before, despite the traffic bearing down on them. Alongside these three moments, the sociology of scientific knowledge has also witnessed a fourth emergence in the form of the work of Callon and Latour, and most of the 'epistemological chicken' paper (1992a) is devoted to a critique of their work.

Collins and Yearley think that what distinguishes this fourth approach is that while the relativist/discourse analysis/reflexive approaches are human centred, actor network theory has no centre. As they put it, 'From this viewpoint it is just as natural to ask how natural objects represent us as to ask how we represent natural objects' (ibid.: 310), and while they admire the rhetorical flair of the approach, they believe that it actually says nothing new at all, in fact that it is regressive. Their clearest demonstration of what they regard as radical vacuousness is presented in their analysis of Callon's St Brieuc Bay paper about scallops, which is methodologically founded on the commitment to treating human and non-human actors 'symmetrically'. With some aplomb, they write:

> Though as we will see, the scallops of St Brieuc Bay are to be treated as actors on a par with the fishermen, the creation of symmetry is very much in the hands of the analysts. The analysts remain in control the whole time, which makes their imposition of symmetry on the world seem something of a conceit. Would not complete symmetry require an account from the point of view of the scallops? Would it be sensible to think of the scallops enrolling the scallop researchers so as to give themselves a better home and to protect their species from the ravages of the fishermen? Does the fact that there is no *Sociological Review Monograph* series written by and for scallops make a difference to the symmetry of the story? (ibid.: 313)

To add to the suggestion that Callon does not even come close to following his own precept of symmetry, and that he could not follow that precept in any event, Collins and Yearley also try to demonstrate that the innovative language employed merely paraphrases what any traditional historian of science would have written about the case study. One of their three examples, for them demonstrating the real nature of Callon's translations, runs as follows:

> [Callon] The researchers are ready to make any kind of concession in order to lure the larvae into their trap. What sort of substances do larvae prefer to anchor on? Another series of transactions is necessary to answer the question . . .

> History of science version: The researchers are willing to try anything. What sort of substances do larvae prefer to anchor on? Another series of experiments is necessary to answer the question. (ibid.: 315)

With Callon's approach duplicating the perspective of the traditional historian of science, Collins and Yearley find themselves forced to ask why anyone should take seriously what he has to say. Callon would have an answer based on the principle of allowing no *a priori* distinction between the actants in his case study, treating, in other words, scallops, fishermen and scientists *symmetrically*, but, for Collins and Yearley, he cannot develop it, since he has nothing approaching a methodology for taking the scallop point of view:

> There is only one way we know of measuring the complicity of scallops, and that is by appropriate scientific research. If we are really to enter scallop behaviour into our explanatory equations, then Callon must demonstrate his scientific credentials. He must show that he has a firm grip on the nature of scallops. There is not the slightest reason for us to accept his opinions on the nature of scallops if he is any less of a scallop scientist than the researchers he describes. (ibid.: 316)

The scientific method need not be the only strategy for attempting to fulfil the requirements of symmetry, but it is hard to imagine any other approach that could succeed in taking the scallop point of view. The consequence, for Collins and Yearley, is that actor network theory, if followed through rigorously, forces the analyst to surrender epistemological hegemony to science and technology. For them, however, this surrender is neither necessary nor desirable.

The rejection of actor network theory in this critical response is twofold. The imperative to treat actants as equivalent is rejected, and is to be replaced by the reinstatement of a human-centred approach. This socio-logical, human-centred approach is an amalgamation of Cartesianism and Wittgensteinianism, as the human subject is conceived as inherently capable of switching between language games: 'a well-educated person is not just a faithful specialist but one who knows how to take another's point of view – even to invade another's world of knowledge' (ibid.: 302). The second aspect of the rejection provides space for sociology in general, and for a sociology of scientific knowledge in particular. This, for Collins and Yearley, follows from the adoption of the human-centred, paradigmatically plural but permeable, ontology that they advocate. They ask, how can we understand relations between humans and 'intelligent' machines? Rejecting the actor network answer that we treat them symmetrically with other actants, they compare the different frames of reference within which work is done on such machines:

> The builders of intelligent machines have one method: they try to model human beings; the scientists, technologists and philosophers work hand in hand using another method: it is called natural science. What sociology of scientific knowledge provides is a third method, no longer subservient to accounts of the work of the scientists and technologists but rooted in a special understanding of social life. (ibid.: 321)

If this rejection of actor network theory, and its concomitant call for the preservation of the genuine contribution that sociology can make to the understanding of science, has not been entirely successful, despite its clarity and power, it is because it places the subject back in play – a move which contradicts the founding moment of sociology, its denial of the subjective principle, a denial of even a vestigial element of freedom for the subject. Thus Woolgar writes:

> Given that there are different epistemological natural attitudes, Candy [a short-hand term for Collins and Yearley] say that we are free to use whatever version is appropriate for the purpose at hand. But once we recognise the constutive function of language, the strength of the argument that we are immersed in our language games, this idea of freedom of choice is laughable . . . Do Candy suppose that we are so free of the constraints of conventions of language? (Woolgar 1992: 331)

And Callon and Latour make the same point in replying to Collins and Yearley:

> Alternation is supposed to be the answer, but it is the most damning solution of all. This 'Don Juanism of knowledge,' as Nietzsche called it, cannot posture as a highly moral position. Don Juanism is a convenient way of avoiding the constraints of marriage and forgetting in one frame every tenet that was learned in the other . . . We prefer not to alternate at all. (Callon and Latour 1992: 355)

What this debate about actor network theory comes down to is the status of the subject in sociology. Callon and Latour, with scrupulous rigour, take the sociological view that subject and object positions are contingently determined, that the 'Great Divide' between nature and society is contingently constructed, that the language games of which we are a part are discursively and relationally extraordinarily powerful. They do have the single privilege of the sociological point of view which allows them to see that they, as social actors in this encompassing context, are partially responsible for reproducing the very conditions that they describe. This reflexively acute sociological knowledge at least allows for the possibility of building a strategy, at the end point of which might arise the possibility of genuine social transformation out of a condition which is little less than deplorable. One only has to think of the social 'realities' of war, pollution, plural forms of discrimination, and poverty to make some sense of their moral impulse. The strategy which actor network theory is in the process of constructing involves fabricating an approach that denies the primacy of the human subject, and treats humans and non-humans as *a priori* part of an undifferentiated universe. This is a strategy of de-differentiation, and it requires a viewpoint and a vocabulary which hardly exist. Both morally and intellectually, it is an impeccable position. Collins and Yearley, on the other hand, are less than convinced by the sociological imperialism which Callon and Latour espouse. For them, the commonsense split between nature and society is an ontological given, and if the application of science by technology has led to disasters of one form or another, this is not because of false epistemological premises, but because of the social organisation of science and technology within its greater social, political and economic context. The risk of losing the capacity of understanding the social organisation of science and technology, of misrecognising the colonisation of discourse by the politically and economically charged utilisation of scientific concepts and technological possibilities, is, for Collins and Yearley, serious. It is the risk of giving up the (admittedly weak when faced with the panoply of strong and entrenched interests) power of rational demonstration.

We have here a case of what Jean-François Lyotard called a differend: each side of the dispute is divested by the other of the means to argue.[3] It is, in such a case, illegitimate to say that if we can see both sides of the debate, then we might incline toward the Collins and Yearley position, since the principle of such a meta-alternation is precisely what they argue for. What can be said, however, is that there is a version of undetermined subjectivity that can be found on both sides. In actor network theory, the sociological analyst, searching for a new vocabulary and determined to treat human and non-human in the same terms, is an originating force, a subject position in the classical sense; we find a similar case in Bourdieu's field sociology: in both cases there is a sociological immunity from the critique of the subject maintained within the sociological perspective concerned, although there is implicit recognition also in both cases that the forces focused on the sociological standpoint are enormous and weakening. In the critique of actor network theory which we have been considering, the subject able to alternate between frames of reference need not do so as an emissary of the Gods, but is inevitably pulled by the forces within each frame. In all of these cases, the vestige of subjectivity that remains, despite the attempt in some cases to deny it, relates to permanent abilities to resist, to connect and disconnect, even if these abilities are externally shaped or subdued much of the time.

The theme of residual capacity for resistance through multiple connection strategies as evidence of the abiding relevance of the subjective moment, even despite the sociological anathematisation of the subject, can also be found in the politically inclined critique of actor network theory advanced by Donna Haraway. On first inspection, her critique of Latour is straightforward, but closer examination reveals great depths. Even though she, like Latour, is engaged in the development of what she calls a 'reflexive artifactualism' (Haraway 1992: 295) which will extend the notion of the actor beyond the human, and which sees nature as a 'co-construction among humans and non-humans' (ibid.: 297), she finds that Latour has 'too narrow a concept of the "collective," one built up out of only machines and scientists, who are considered in a very narrow time and space frame' (ibid.: 331). Second, she asserts that for Latour, '*any* consideration of matters like masculine supremacy or racism or imperialism or class structures are [*sic*] inadmissible because they are the old "social" ghosts that blocked real explanation of science in action' (ibid.: 332). Haraway develops the first criticism into an argument against the politics of representation in general, and at the same time allows us to deepen our critical response to Callon's St Brieuc Bay study and Collins and Yearley's response to it. Following a discussion of Joe Kane's review of Alexander Cockburn's *Fate of the Forest*, and a brief mention of a question asked by some pro-life groups, she writes:

> Who speaks for the jaguar? Who speaks for the fetus? Both questions rely on a political semiotics of representation. Permanently speechless, forever requiring the services of a ventriloquist, never forcing a recall vote . . . for a political

semiology of representation, nature and the unborn fetus are even better, epistemologically, than subjugated human adults. (ibid.: 311–12)

Whether it is the scientist or the sociologist or the campaign group which acts as representative, the result is the same: the disempowerment of those who might be seen to be 'closer' to the voiceless entities, whether pregnant women, forest tribes or fishermen: 'Both the jaguar and the fetus are carved out of one collective entity and relocated in another, where they are reconstituted as objects of a particular kind – as the ground of a representational practice that *forever* authorises the ventriloquist' (ibid.: 312). For Haraway, the practice of representation requires that actants are silent, pliable, stripped of their powers, that, in other words, their ontological status as beings-in-the-world is denied. This is easier to slip by even the watchful critic in the case of machines and crustacea, but the full force of Haraway's critique becomes most apparent when dealing with 'higher' animals including humans (whose capacity to resist will allow them to repudiate Bourdieu's sociological ventriloquism, for example).

Haraway's second criticism, that Latour (amongst others) does not address how phallocentrism, racism and other forms of discrimination get built into the networks which he examines, is one that I am sure Collins and Yearley would agree with, at least in spirit. The kind of claim that they make for the sociology of science is precisely that it should be at its strongest in dealing with matters of social organisation, social structure and practices of exclusion. However, Haraway's critique is not aimed at Latour alone, but clearly is meant to include such co-workers in the sociology of science as Collins and Yearley themselves, for, in Haraway's eyes, there has been little attempt within recent sociology of science to benefit from the powerful discourses focused on the reproduction of structures of difference and inequality which have emerged from feminism over the last quarter of a century:

> For all of their extraordinary creativity, so far the mappings from most SSS scholars have stopped dead at the fearful seas where the worldly practices of inequality lap at the shores, infiltrate the estuaries, and set the parameters of reproduction of scientific practice, artefacts and knowledge. (ibid.: 333)

Indeed, it would not be unreasonable to say, along with Haraway, that at the same time as one finds little acknowledgement of the issue of gender difference in Latour's work, one also will look in vain there for the kind of sensitivity to cultural differences that is such a mark of Haraway's own work, as evidenced in her account of Japanese primatology (Haraway 1989: 244ff.). The reason for the susceptibility of actor network theory to such comments is that it is by design and intention incorporationist: Pasteur will incorporate the farm into his laboratory, the scientists will try to persuade the scallops into their network. The rights of farmers to maintain community traditions or the rights of scallops to their ecological niche will be disregarded by the macro-actor struggling to grow. The key to the political abrogation which Haraway implies is the inability of any Machiavellian perspective, such as actor network theory, to allow a set of competing, countervailing and even incompatible values to contribute to strategy. The result would be indeterminacy and perceived weakness, not desirable attributes for the Prince. As Haraway put it more recently, 'Latour wants to follow the action in science-in-the-making . . . technoscience itself is war, the demiurge that makes and unmakes worlds . . . all trials and feats of strength, amassing of allies . . . nature is multiply the feat of the hero' (Haraway 1997: 34).

The presence of resistant subjectivity, of weak subjectivity, is incarnated in Haraway's concept of the modest witness, and it will enrich our understanding of Latour and actor network theory if we detour this way a little. What is a modest witness? To begin with, a modest witness is finite and faulted, not transcendent and pure. Even from such a limited perspective, it can be seen that there is something troubling when the modest witness looks at scientists, for they too claim to be modest witnesses, but since they inhabit the culture of no culture, as Haraway (following Sharon Traweek) puts it, they locate their modesty in relation to the transcendent purity of the operation of nature. The modesty of the scientists meant that they deferred to the authority of nature and none other. Haraway knows, however, that this 'modesty' was constructed, and would recognise, I think, that a Latourean perspective on how the modest male scientist came to grow larger would tell us a great deal. Learning from Barbara Potter, she tells us:

> Mediaeval, secular, masculine virtue – noble manly valor – required patently heroic words and deeds. The modest man was a problematic figure for early modern Europeans, who still thought of nobility in terms of warlike battles of weapons and words. (Haraway 1997: 30)

So perhaps the men of science should not be seen as quite so modest. In achieving their brand of modesty, they overcame the legacies of the past, and in doing so, as both Potter and Haraway point out, they constructed a particular kind of gender-specific modesty. In Latour's terms, they put women in a black box:

> How did the masculine practice of modesty, by appropriately civil (gentle)men, enhance agency, epistemologically and socially, while modesty enforced on (or embraced by) women of the same social class simply removed them from the scene of action? (ibid.: 29)

Haraway's answer to this question is that submission to the authority of nature required completely transparent subjectivity. To be a credible witness to nature's workings required that the witness be in no way contaminated by nature:

> The kind of visibility – of the body – that women retained glides into being perceived as 'subjective' that is, reporting only on the self, biased, opaque, not objective. Gentlemen's epistemological agency involved a special kind of transparency. Colored, sexed and laboring persons still have to do a lot of work to

become similarly transparent to count as objective, modest witnesses to the world
rather than to their 'bias' or 'special interest'. (ibid.: 32)

Because of this, as Haraway puts it, they are 'evacuated of agency'. The
very largest part of the world's population was defined to be excluded from
the subject pole of the power–knowledge relationship, principally because
they could be seen – yet, did not Descartes, with what we can now see as an
astonishing lack of prescience, say that he would be mad to think of himself
as having a body made of glass? In truth, the glass body, Haraway tells us,
was the Enlightenment ideal.

Haraway's complaint against work in the sociology of science is that
despite all the constructionist epistemology, sociologists of science have
tended to see gender as a 'pre-formed, functionalist category, merely a
question of preconstituted '"generic" men and women' (ibid.: 26). Not only
has this constituted an epistemological blind-spot, in particular allowing an
unquestioned male subject to operate as a norm in the background to work
which might at the same time, as with Latour, declare uninterest in the
category of the subject, it has also meant that the critique of transparency
which SSK does elaborate is incomplete, since it only operates at the
objective pole. To complete the critique of transparency in the face of
nature, what is needed is to pose Haraway's question about the possibility
of the non-transparent modest witness. All witnesses must be dirtied by
culture if the sacred premise of science that it has no culture, or at least no
culture that cannot be discounted given the appropriate methodological
safeguards, is denied. As Haraway asks, how can we 'queer the modest
witness this time around?' (ibid.: 35). The point of the question is to allow
'the political back into realignment so that questions about possible livable
worlds lie at the heart of our best science' (ibid.: 39), and, we might add, at
the heart of our best sociology. The question, put this way, challenges the
unacknowledged interpellation and subject-construction that lies within
actor network theory, which, at the same time that it denies the privilege of
the human subject, reconstructs it in traditional ways.

Although she was not specifically responding to the project of translation
into a single discourse followed by ANT, nevertheless, when she says that
she finds 'the discourses of natural harmony, the non-alien, and purity
unsalvageable for understanding our genealogy in the New World Order
Inc.' (ibid.: 62) she is clearly challenging the apolitical continuism that she
finds in the work of Latour and others (ibid.: 43). What is the crucial point
of challenge against this continuism? It is that the world we inhabit is a
'vastly underdetermined drama' (ibid.: 67). Not, let us be clear, that she
challenges the fundamental position of actor network theory, that actors
need not be human – she makes that clear when she discusses the
Oncomouse (the first patented animal, a genetically engineered rodent used
for cancer research), which she sees as a 'murine smart bomb' which is 'in
the strongest possible sense, a cultural actor' (ibid.: 83), and she admires
Latour's denial of the scientistic dichotomisation of nature and culture. But

she is not, as Latour seems to be, a relativist,[4] arguing that constructivism is about contingency and specificity but not epistemological relativism' (ibid.: 99)[5] hence arguing that 'biology is a subject in civics' (ibid.: 103, 117), with all the commitments to democratic and personal values that are thereby implied, and with a certain scepticism, perhaps a distaste for the Machiavellian opportunism exemplified by the emergence of commodified bioethics ('a regulatory industry' [ibid.: 220]) over the last twenty years (ibid.: 109). The modest witness, for Haraway, attests to the real powers of agents: it is a recognition of the obduracy of the objective world, and the local knowledge relations working between them within the horizon of democratic values, and in recognition that there is something immanently excessive about both subjects and objects. For Haraway, the black box of categorisation and psycho-political control is never sealed. As she puts it, 'Yearning is fed from the gaps in categories and from the quirky liveliness of signs' (ibid.: 128). The modest witness is an ethical creation, a moral subject, fuelled by such yearning (in contexts of 'friendship, work, partially shared purposes, intractable collective pain, inescapable mortality and persistent hope' [ibid.: 265]) and inspired to action by the projects which rise out of locally emergent knowledge. It is from this standpoint that we can understand Haraway's project, which is to 'excavate something like a technoscientific unconscious, the processes of formation of the technoscientific subject, and the reproduction of this subject's structures of pleasure and anxiety' (ibid.: 151). This is a trajectory beyond scientific monism, but also beyond postmodern nihilism and SSK relativism, since she considers it beyond disputation, having 'the status of matters of fact' (ibid.: 267), that citizens of (as she puts it) New World Order Inc. are seduced, interpellated, enchanted into reconstituting themselves as technoscientific subjects. But such reconstituted subjects, while denied the powers of instrumentalist master narratives, nevertheless can and will engage in struggle for 'liveable techoscientific corporealisations' (ibid.: 172). The metal shoulders of the technofoetus do not shrug.

A series of criticisms have been levelled at Latour's work. Collins and Yearley have argued that Latour re-establishes the hegemony of science by embracing the objectivity of objects. Making a similar point from within a different problematic, Donna Haraway (1992) has argued that Latour deals with just men and machines, and Mark Elam regards Latour as a neo-imperialist, asserting that the hybrid quasi-objects he celebrates can be compared to colonial projects. For Haraway and Elam, in particular, his 'Give me a laboratory and I will move the world' becomes 'Give me a power base and I will rule the world.'

It is not the purpose of this analysis to draw out all the criticisms that might be made of Latour's conception of the politics of hybridity (although to secure democratic control over the pace of recombination in an era of multiple hybrid human subjects would surely require additional constitutional guarantees – the territories of law, ethics, and economic regulation spring immediately to mind – from which would follow the need to reconceptualise a number of areas from the standpoint of Latour's position). Rather what I have sought to do is to show that structural sociology, as exemplified by the work of Bourdieu, and constructivist sociology, as illustrated by actor network theory, both in their different ways reject the classical subject. Additionally, it is not my intention to argue that the sociological view that we have been discussing has nothing to offer. On the contrary, both the positions of Bourdieu and of Latour are enormously fecund, allowing us to interrogate cultural trends and political possibilities incisively and with great insight. However, as representatives of a sociological tradition which owes its very birth to the attenuation if not denial of the human subject, both exemplars illustrate relegation of the human subject, with its properties, powers, internal organization and fate placed in the far margins of social scientific concern. What is important about the work of Donna Haraway is that she has sought to embrace the critique of privileged standpoint subjectivity, without repudiating subjectivity *tout court*. In her idea of the modest witness, we find weak, but uncageable, subjectivity, in counterpoint to her abiding notion of a liveable world.

Notes

1. For an example (from a theorist whose work has been influential on Callon and Latour) of an approach treating currents as subjects in communication with other subjects, consider the following: 'Winds create flows of air in the atmosphere; rivers make flows of water across land; glaciers make solid rivers, cutting their way across mountain and valley; rain, snow and hail are flows of water through the air; marine currents are flows of water within water; volcanoes are vertical flows of fire, from earth into the air, or into the sea, one element passes through others and they, conversely, pass through it. It supports or it transports. These reciprocating fluidities create such a perfect mixing that few places lack at least some knowledge of the state of others. They receive this knowledge by means of messages' (Serres 1995: 26).

2. A key extension of identity can be provided, he suggests, by the establishment of a new constitution which will provide for the government of things and the government of humans, in the light of the fact that they are inseparably intertwined, and that the subjects within society emerge between these poles. There are four constitutional guarantees, Latour tells us, which would be appropriate to a society of hybrid subjects. The first is a restatement of the determining ontological position, that the production of both societies and natures is common and non-separable. For the purposes of practical illustration, Latour will use a concept like 'hard' nature, and while this carries no ontological weight in his universe of irreducible hybridity, it does found a strategic politics, and hence the second guarantee, of 'continuous following of the production of nature, which is objective, and the production of society, which is free' (1993: 141). This second guarantee introduces elements of monitoring and audit into the very heart of this political ontology, affirming a principle of and a commitment to surveillance – in the notion of 'continuous following'. This component, duplicating Bourdieu's notion of the Machiavellian collectivity, is cemented in place with the fourth guarantee (below). Nature is objective and transcendent because no one created it, while society is immanent, providing us with the freedom that accompanies the workings of our own constructions. Latour does not claim, indeed quite the reverse, that the distinction is absolute, but he does suggest, in this call for (the continuation of) a regime of surveillance as a fundamental part of his new constitution, that in practical terms it is really quite basic for the practical regulation of his non-modern society. As he puts it, 'The moderns were not mistaken in seeing objective nonhumans and free societies. They were mistaken only in their certainty that that double production

required an absolute distinction between the two terms and the continual repression of the work of mediation' (ibid.: 140). From these two guarantees, he redefines freedom as the capacity for recombination. This, his third guarantee, raises to the level of the constitution Lévi-Strauss's notion of *bricolage* as a right, which is to be unfettered by outmoded choices between nature and culture, local and global, cultural and universal. The only constraint on the right of recombination is to be found enshrined in his fourth, and final, guarantee, that 'the production of hybrids, by becoming explicit and collective, becomes the object of an enlarged democracy that regulates or slows down its cadence' (ibid.: 141). Latour does not make explicit, nor does he really address in his thoughts toward a new constitution, the fact that within his system the human subject as a network is just as liable to failure as the network of fishermen, scallops and scientists which Callon described.

3. 'A case of differend between two parties takes place when the "regulation" of the conflict that opposes them is done in the idiom of one of the parties while the wrong suffered by the other is not signified in that idiom' (Lyotard 1988: 9).

4. Latour's relativism can be clearly seen in his recent view that that we should not use the term 'network' any more (Latour 1997a) because of its tendencies in these days of the web to refer to instantaneous and transparent communication. The word 'actor' is also to be jettisoned. His view is that social ontology does not reduce to the agency–structure divide but is more a matter of circulation founded on the dissatisfactions which attend focus on both the micro and the macro levels: dissatisfaction with one leads to the other in a never-ending circulation. This circulation provides actants with their 'subjectivity, with their intentionality, with their morality' (1997a). Circulations are summed up into local focuses. Actant and network, then, are two facets of the same phenomenon, and currently the crucial distillate of his position is that 'by following circulations we can get more than by defining entities, essences or provinces'. For Latour, what this second wave of science studies gives us is a 'theory of the space and fluids circulating in a non-modern situation' (1997a). In this context, 'Subjectivity, corporeality is no more a property of humans, of individuals, than being an outside reality is a property of nature.' It is fundamentally 'a circulating capacity, something that is partially gained or lost by hooking up to certain bodies of practice' (ibid.). While it is not clearly the case that repudiation of subjectivity in itself implies moral relativism, when that position is supplemented with an abiding unconcern for social values and with the key notion that macro-structures and networks are only ever contingent, then the case for his position equating to uncompromising relativism is overwhelming.

5. 'science itself is now widely regarded as an indigenous, and polycentric, knowledge practice . . . Such a claim is not about relativism, where all views and knowledges are somehow "equal," but quite the opposite. To see scientific knowledge as located and heterogeneous practice, which might (or might not) be "global" and "universal" in specific ways rooted in ongoing articulatory practices that are always potentially open to critical scrutiny from disparate perspectives, is to adopt the worldly stance of situated knowledges. Such knowledges are worth living for' (Haraway 1997: 137–8).

PART II

KEEPING TO THE SUBJECT: SUBJECTIVITY IN MODERN ART

INTRODUCTION

I have suggested so far that the denial of the subject is constitutive of sociology.[1] Rather than extend the discussion further into sociology, I want now to compare the situation of sociology with that of other forms of inquiry into the human condition. In particular, I want to examine the *mélange* of biography, mythology, style, technique, history and desire that animates the world of contemporary art, especially as it focuses on the question of the subject. In that school of art known as abstract expressionism, we find a perfect case study illustrating the tensions between figure and ground, actor and *mise-en-scène*, agent and field, the figure of the human subject against the background of transcendent ideas which can only be hinted at, but which nevertheless put the merely human, and indeed the merely social, in its place. The exemplary work to which I will refer is the series of fourteen paintings by Barnett Newman, collectively titled *The Stations of the Cross*. This serial attenuation of classical subjectivity both acknowledges and undermines the pretensions to centrality which underlie the Western concept of the human subject. The acknowledgement is contained in the subject of the paintings, precisely the role-model of human subjectivity for the many millions of people brought up in the Christian tradition. The undermining of self-centring and classical subjectivity is achieved in a number of ways: the repetitiousness of seriality, with its implications of the de-privileging of subjective freedoms and of the defining homogeneity of the field of operation (expressed so clearly, in this same century, in Schoenberg's twelve tone scale);[2] the abandonment of naturalistic representation; the submission to aleatory outcomes achieved within the constraints of the media rather than within the limits of skills and vision (this same submission will, as we shall see, also be a feature of the work of Baselitz and Bacon); the removal of aesthetic meaning from events and individuals and its attachment solely to the pure essence of ideas such as death, tragedy and love – in Newman's view the great background against which the human subject is silhouetted. It is quite ironic that this form of painting came to be called 'subjective', although in the sense that it repudiated representations of the object, it can be seen how this happened. It was however not an active subjectivity imposing itself within a territory it was coming to understand and manipulate; it was, rather, a passive subject striving merely to stand still long enough to allow the imprint of unknowable but defining forces to emerge through it. It bears a family resemblance to Bourdieu's notion of the agent, both conceptions pointing to the subject as a bearer of content of transcendent scale. Although, unlike Bourdieu who, in denying the subject its own brea(d)th, thought to have done with the thing, Newman pursues it along its length.

It is then, I will suggest, possible to follow Euclid and set subject alongside 'breadthless length'.[3] In pursuit of a tool to open up a discussion of the subject, without yielding to the temptations of a theory of human nature whilst resisting the complete annihilation of the human subject aspired to by social science, the figure of a mark in the cosmos, without breadth, but composed of an infinite number of points of potential connection, is a place to begin. Is it a coincidence that one of Barnett Newman's first 'zip' paintings, from 1946–7, was titled *Euclidian Abyss*? He said of it, 'I removed myself from nature, but I did not remove myself from life' (Newman 1992: 255), and in this same interview with David Sylvester, he spoke of the importance of conveying to those who saw his work a sense of their separateness and individuality. He strove, as he said, to convey space and place as both mystery and metaphysical redolence (ibid.: 257), but also, as he said, just two months before he died, to the filmmaker Emile de Antonio, he had wanted his work to demonstrate a certain openness, the potentialities and future connectivities of an open world (ibid.: 308). In the examination of Newman's *Stations of the Cross*, we will try to explore some interrelationships of linearity, mystery, separation and the subject, and will address the question of humanism.

If the human subject in the work of Barnett Newman is comparable to the inhabitants of Plato's cave, making shadows in a rigorous search for understanding about the existential condition, in the work of the German artist, Georg Baselitz, one might say that the cave-dwellers have reached the outside only to be broken to bits, or, at best, to have been thrown into a state of perpetual disorientation. As Baselitz put it in 1994, 'I don't need angels' (Waldman 1995: 250). Fracture and inversion have been his themes. Exhibitions of Baselitz's work, at the New York Guggenheim in 1995, at the Michael Werner Gallery in the same city in 1997, and at the Berlin Guggenheim in 1999, have tended to emphasise a historical interpretation of his work, whether in regard to his own personal history (a series of 'Family Pictures' begun in 1996), the history of Europe (Slav and Turkish elements emerge in his work from 1997 on) or to the history of art (pictures inspired by Caspar David Friedrich created in 1998). He has, then, not yet been fully recognised as a theorist of the contemporary subject. However, compared with Newman's confident and determined self-deployment as a conduit for timeless ideas, Baselitz also has much to tell us about the contemporary subject. He was particularly concerned about the privileged gaze of the artist-subject (echoing, in ways yet to be fully explored, the question of reflexivity in the social sciences). This concern led to the technique for the production of his fracture paintings described by Baselitz in notes for the 1995 Guggenheim catalogue, as follows:

> There's a surrealist's game, with a folded piece of paper . . . A person begins a drawing on the folded paper and the next elaborates on it, and so on. Then when the paper is opened you see a mysterious picture. So I tried to work with this principle in mind . . . I did more and more experiments, strongly influenced by surrealism – from the idea, the agenda, of surrealism, not from its style or form. Paintings resulted that I called fractured paintings, broken paintings, shattered paintings. (see Waldman 1995: 57)

As Diane Waldman noted in the same catalogue, 'What Baselitz did was he cut and spliced the figures and joined them together so that the figure no longer read as a coherent whole. And he also merged the figure with the background so that it became harder and harder to distinguish figure from ground.' The concern to undercut his own controlling mechanisms of production and interpretation then led subsequently to the feature for which he is best known, that of inversion. He describes the context in the 1995 Guggenheim notes for his 1974 painting, *Nude Elke*:

> Why did I begin painting upside down pictures? I can only say that, aside from creating something interesting, and from wanting to produce a shock, aside from that, gradually it happened that the objects I used in the picture, people and trees and dogs, began to lose their goal, their direction. They ended up on the upper edge or moved down from above, but there was still always a ground. Then with this experiment it occurred to me, that this was a lot of nonsense, to be operating in a way that assumes that in a painting there is a direction – up, down, right, left. What one calls direction is a convention, an agreement that we've made. And of course once you've discovered this, that's the point where as a painter, as an artist, you can take these conventions and do something against them, against these agreements . . . And then it is very exciting for the one doing it, for the painter himself, when he's stumbled upon such a boundary and breaks through it. I found myself in a state of excitement, and I thought, erroneously, that from then on – it was 1969 – it would never again be a problem for me to paint pictures. I thought, now, I can paint the entire history of art in a new way, upside down. And at first I tried that, I tried it for one year, but I noticed that the difficulty of painting pictures was still great, it didn't get any easier. The problem of painting was still there even though the impetus was much happier. (Baselitz 1995a)

So Baselitz realised that inversion was a trick, a way perhaps of subverting the conventions of artistic vision, but that it did not remove the privilege of the artist-subject, the individual subject who will take on the conventions. Instead, confrontation with conventions makes the artist-subject reflexive, since the conventional framework of the artist's encounter with the object matter is now at least partly on display: the problem of the painter has moved from the subject as conduit, which we find in abstract expressionism, and also in Bourdieu's account of the working class, to the subject as reflectively implicated in a varying relationship between material technique, conventional perspectives, and the object. If there is a parallel here to be drawn with the conception of the subject in sociology, it is with Bourdieu's understanding of the sociologist as best placed to evade the overdetermin-ism of a simple field–habitus model. In other words, Baselitz's employment of inversion is precisely parallel to the sociological use of method.

If Newman is concerned with the idea of the subject, finding it essential to express its potential in a revolutionary pictorial language, and if Baselitz is concerned with the conventions of the subject, seeking to break with holistic and other-determined ways of representing the subject, Bacon's approach is more forensic and pathological. He asks what is the subject, as a body, as a head.

In the essay which Allon White wrote on Deleuze and Bacon, still unpublished at the time of White's early death, we find an attempt to understand the art of Francis Bacon in terms of the category of abjection. We can find a link between this powerful view of Bacon and a view of Baselitz (and indeed a great deal of modern art) as engaged in reflexive practices. White wrote:

> Abjection denotes acute fear and disgust of a pathological kind, obsessive and recurrent . . . triggered by the 'abominable and filthy' . . . abjection describes the panicky, twisting aside and away from those things which burn and mutilate our self-possession . . . Reactive, almost reflexive on account of uncontrollable nervous discharge, the abject feels split between a self and internalised otherness which s/he attempts to dispel . . . The abject is split between subject and object, neither fully an independent self nor completely determined by the objective realm. (White 1993: 166–7)

In White's interpretation, the category of abjection, when applied to Bacon's work, refers to a realised, reflected-upon indeterminacy between self-control and suppuration, between meat and mental alertness, and – taking a view of the subject in the pictures as often supplemented by prosthesis – his overall view is that Bacon's work 'develops a particular modality of what might be called 'the prosthetic grotesque' (ibid.: 171). No doubt, White would have developed some of his ideas further, and I wish not to seize upon any one of them (indeed there is something of a critique of this reading of Bacon in what follows) but rather to summon up the distinctly post-Cartesian tone of the piece, which in the same way as Baselitz's comments on inversion, and found in spades in Newman's quest for the absolute, affirms that, even if blown to bits or abjectified by decay and discharge or dwarfed by the immensities of the enveloping field, the subject still persists in some fashion. Weakened, no doubt, but still, poten-tially, a subject. In White's reading of Deleuze, Bacon is the contemporary artist who has given us a vision of subjectivity as nerve cadences in meat.

What we find, therefore, in Chapter 3 is an exploration of strong conduit-subjectivity by Barnett Newman. This is followed by Baselitz's account of a condition which I have referred to as fragmented subjectivity. With Francis Bacon we can find, disturbingly, the concept of the subject which might even, if harshly, be said to be most appropriate to sociological discourse, the subject as meat.

Notes

1. As the discussion of Latour intimates, this can certainly be extended to anthropology. It may also be true of psychology. The case of economics is rather different, since its microeconomic foundations are set in the ground of rational choice. This difference indicates the crucial importance of theories of the subject for understanding the tensions which traverse the social sciences as a whole.

2. As Georgina Born puts it, 'Serialism as it was originally conceived focused on the organisation of pitch. This approach involves the construction of a twelve note series or row using all twelve chromatic notes of the scale in a fixed order before the series can be started again. To generate material for a piece, four basic structural transformations of the series are produced: the original form, backward (retrograde), upside-down (inversion), and retrograde-inversion. The four transformations can then be transposed to start on each of the twelve chromatic notes, so giving forty-eight permutations that provide the seeds of the composition. Serialism implies the principle of the homogeneity of the chromatic space' (Born 1995: 48).

3. Any line has an infinite number of points along its length, although Euclid refers, in *The Elements*, only to the two points at each extremity of the line.

3

BARNETT NEWMAN: EXISTENTIALISM AND THE TRANSCENDENT SUBJECT

At the dawn of deconstruction

Jacques Derrida's move in the opening pages of *De la Grammatologie* is now entirely familiar. He took a related pair of concepts – speech and writing – summoned up the venerable Socratic tradition (in a characteristically spiky way, by quoting Nietzsche) wherein speech is prime and had always come first, and then in the counter-intuitive move we now know as the key to deconstruction, he demonstrated first that the traditional pairing has always been a matter of subordination of what supposedly comes after to what supposedly is first, and second that it is possible to resist that relationship of subordination and to expose its flawed histories and assumptions. He wrote of the Bible that it was received not primarily as a work of writing, that it was 'not grammatological but pneumatological' (Derrida 1976: 17). As Derrida went on to say in this text, 'The beginning word is understood, in the intimacy of self-presence, as the voice of the other and as commandment.' His argument was going to be that there was no pure moment of self-presence, no moment at which an original voice declared itself without intermediary. To assume otherwise, to follow, in other words, the philosophical tradition from Plato to Heidegger, was to abandon social and human responsibility for the horrors done in the name of making the other the same, in the name of forcing all to hear the same voice, which, for Derrida had never been heard as pure voice and which, in any event, had to be taken on trust or swallowed by force:

> The subordination of the trace to the full presence summed up in the logos, the humbling of writing beneath a speech dreaming its plenitude, such are the gestures required by an onto-theology determining the archeological and eschatological meaning of being . . . as life without difference . . . Only infinite being can reduce the difference in presence. In that sense, the name of God, at least as it is pronounced within classical rationalism, is the name of indifference itself. (1976: 71)

One may of course object that we are bathed in differences and that quite a few of them hardly appear as testament to Derrida's underlying thesis that the violent denial of difference is the secret to the history of the West. One example of this is simply the extraordinary variety of names for every different thing imaginable. But, for Derrida, proper names were never proper names. The process of naming locates what is named in a classificatory system. Names do not signify uniqueness or difference, even if

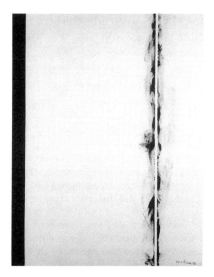

Barnett Newman, *First Station*, 1958

Ecce homo. Behold the man. It has been ordered that he will die. It is a beginning and contains and leads what is to follow. 'The gloomy and sublime thunder-cloud of the wrathful Jehovah was brooding continually. Only here was the rare and sudden piercing of the gruesome and perpetual general day-night by a single ray of the sun' (Nietzsche 1974: 189).

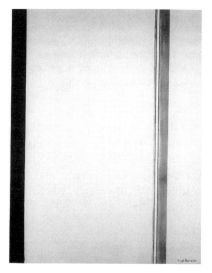

Barnett Newman, *Second Station*, 1958

A second ray of sunlight crossing the first (did Norman Adams know why he painted the cross yellow in his version of the *Second Station?*). The promise of their intersection is for the redemption of the world. At this point Newman had no notion of what he was doing, but already he refuses the wound which is made when one line cuts into another. Just two months before his death, he told the world that his zips create totalities, they do not divide them (Newman 1992: 306).

difference is the semiological basis of classification. To be more precise, they perpetuate the myth of original transparency in which a duplicated essence is self-labelled for all to see, at the same time as they are held within the confines of a classification that forms a tree structure (a ubiquitous form critically discussed by Deleuze and Guattari in their introduction to *A Thousand Plateaus*) with an origin at the seed of the original voice. Perhaps the place where we can see this most clearly is in Derrida's reading of Lévi-Strauss's *Tristes Tropiques*. The Nambikwara of central Brazil did not tell their names to outsiders, an aspect of their social organisation of which Machiavelli would surely have approved, but Lévi-Strauss managed to find out most of the names of the tribespeople by befriending the children and playing them off against each other. The children were admonished, and that appeared to be the end of it. Some time later, Lévi-Strauss was asked by the chief for a writing pad, and for some assistance in using it. The Nambikwara had neither writing nor did they do any drawing apart from the odd squiggle scratched in the dirt. Yet the chief knew there were possibilities here for the reassertion of his status and power:

> I handed out sheets of paper and pencils. At first they did nothing with them, then one day I saw that they were all busy drawing wavy, horizontal lines. I wondered what they were trying to do, then it was suddenly borne upon me that they were writing or, to be more accurate, were trying to use their pencils in the same way as I did mine, which was the only way that they could conceive of, because I had not yet tried to amuse them with my drawings. The majority did this and no more, but the chief had further ambitions. No doubt he was the only one who had grasped the purpose of writing. So he called me for a writing pad, and when we both had one, and were working together, if I asked for information on a given point, he did not supply it verbally but drew wavy lines on his paper and presented them to me, as if I could read his reply. He was half taken in by his own make-believe; each time he completed a line, he examined it anxiously as if expecting the meaning to leap from the page, and the same look of disappointment came over his face. But he never admitted this, and there was a tacit understanding between us to the effect that his unintelligible scribbling had a meaning which I pretended to decipher . . . As soon as he got the company together, he took from a basket a piece of paper covered with wavy lines and made a show of reading it, pretending to hesitate as he checked on it the list of objects I was to give in exchange for the presents offered me. (Lévi-Strauss 1976: 388)

Derrida reads these two incidents, the artful discovery of the proper names and the collusion with the chief over the simulation of reading and writing, as confirming a foundational prejudice of Western society, that there was once a pristine civilisation uncontaminated by dissimulation and secrecy; and that this originary instance was corrupted by contact with an outside, whether in the case of the enemy who should not know the names used within the tribes or in the case of the anthropologist with his pencils and child psychology. Both examples duplicate the Edenic structure which Derrida denies. He denies this notion of a pristine innocence because the potential for its defilement was always already inside, always already a part of the experience of innocence itself. The very facticity of humankind deconstructs the image of a pure God. In a reversal of the ontological argument, that God is first cause, Derrida shows that the first singularity must already have been multiple, and that the first inside must already have been a part of its outside. His demonstration that writing, for the Nambikwara, did not come like a bolt from the blue, that, in other words, the Nambikwara was already a political society, with names to be hidden and a chief with an eye for the consolidation of his power, is an explicative variation on the denial of the original uncontaminated, unmediated voice.

It is but a short step to turn Derrida's critique of the original voice, the proper name and the myth of pristine innocence into a repudiation of singular subjectivity, which would never speak to itself to say exactly, and without external determination, how things are, whose name would therefore be a conceit, and whose pristine innocence or alienation really referred to a time that never was. Barnett Newman, had he heard this would have massively, fundamentally, disagreed. The original voice, for Newman, was

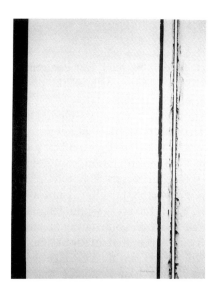

Barnett Newman, *Third Station*, 1960

'Consider this first fall of Jesus under his cross. His flesh was torn by the scourges. His head was crowned with thorns; He had lost a great quantity of blood. So weakened He could scarcely walk. He yet had to carry this great load upon His shoulders. The soldiers struck Him rudely, and He fell several times' (St Alphonsus 1965: 9). Boris Pasternak intuited that the function of the fall (mentioned in not one of the four Gospels) was to endow Christ's virtue with life and humanity, to scramble slightly the edges of its line. As Yury Andreyevich Zhivago says to Larissa Fyodorovna Guishar, while they are together in Yuryatin, 'I don't like people who have never fallen or stumbled. Their virtue is lifeless and it isn't of much value' (Pasternak 1988: 359).

a cry, and it expressed solitude and anguish. The *Stations of the Cross* tell of this voice, in its exquisite abandonment:

> Man's first expression, like his first dream, was an aesthetic one. Speech was a poetic outcry rather than a demand for communication. Original man, shouting his consonants, did so in yells of awe and anger at his tragic state, at his own self-awareness, and at his own helplessness before the void . . . Man's first cry was a song. Man's first address to a neighbour was a cry of power and solemn weakness, not a request for a drink of water. (Newman 1966: 158)

The *Stations* speak of a defining subjective condition, not merely solitude, but solitude reimposed after the solemn promise that there would be no abandonment: subjectivity denied but then restored in an act of betrayal, at the point when the flame is weakest. The pathos of the *Stations* derives from a defining, a social betrayal:

> The earliest written history of human desires proves that the meaning of the world cannot be found in the social act. An examination of the first chapter of Genesis offers a better key to the human dream. It was inconceivable to the archaic writer that original man, that Adam, was put on earth to be . . . a social animal . . . Adam, by eating from the Tree of Knowledge, sought the creative life to be, like God, 'a creator of worlds' . . . and was reduced to a life of toil only as a result of a jealous punishment. (ibid.: 159)

'Do not the *Stations* tell of one event?' (ibid.: 188) Newman asks. The event that is a life, but that is also all lives, and which is summed up in the

question, *Lema*? To what purpose? Newman cites the following words from
the book of the Hasidim (*c*.200 BC), the *Pirke Abot*:

> The ones who are born are to die
> Against thy will art thou formed
> Against thy will art thou born
> Against thy will dost thou live
> Against thy will die. (ibid.: 188)

and he does so as a witness. Not quite a modest witness, but certainly a
witness for a subject in that utterly typical context in which all the power
and the glory appears to be on the other side.

The cry from the First Station can well be seen as a moment of
intersubjectivity. This surely would be Derrida's position, that subjectivity
would always already be intersubjectivity, and that the cry would be a call
to re-establish an intersubjective bond. Such an interpretation is, of course,
confounded by the story of the Passion, since Christ's cry is not addressed
to those about him, but to the Absolute. Newman's position is not at all
social, and we can see the warrant for that. But if the cry is within language,
formed by the rules of language, surely we must be confronting an intersubjective moment? Must not subjectivity be structured like a language?
Things are not so clear. If the framing of the cry within language is the
work of the listener, of the poet or the priest, there is every chance that this
overlay misrepresents the moment at the First Station, treating it as formed
when it may be *formless*.

To be clear, such a view as Newman's belief in the solitary and tragic
subject – a whole to itself, but struggling to realise that wholeness due to its
supplementary condition as part of another entity – would repudiate any
simple idea of human nature, would reject assertions that a distinction like
form and content would allow insight into the condition of the subject at its
zero point, and would certainly take the view that the ascription of value to
such an instance would be an *a posteriori* social affair. Although they were
concerned with the material, we are in the same field already explored by
Rosalind Kraus and Yves-Alain Bois in their reading of Bataille:

> The type of matter Bataille wants to speak about is what we have no idea of,
> what makes no sense, what 'has no rights in any sense and gets itself squashed
> everywhere like a spider or an earthworm'. (Kraus and Bois 1997: 29)

It is to be admitted that Newman did not strive towards the base,
towards the lowest point. Quite the reverse – although he was capable of
seeing this in others as he did when he commented on Giacometti's first
show in New York in 1948, saying that his figures 'looked as if they were
made out of spit – new things with no form' (cited in Hess 1972: 36). But
his effort to confront the moment of formless subjectivity is palpable. His
use of line, like Gunther Forg's parallel attempt to travel the Stations by
means of the formless black reliefs which can be seen in the Ludwig
Museum in Cologne, involves a certain sacrifice of the conventional

Christian model of the subject only to reach for something of limitlessly less content, yet of wider and higher import, of scarcely any breadth, but of inestimable length.

Line before figure

Barnett Newman's work emerged out of moral crisis. It was a crisis that was not restricted to him alone. He put it like this in 1967:

> You must realise that twenty years ago we felt the moral crisis of a world in shambles, a world devastated by a great depression and a fierce world war, and it was impossible at that time to paint the kind of paintings that we were doing – flowers, reclining nudes, and people playing the cello. At the same time we could not move into the situation of a pure world of unorganised shapes and forms, or color relations, a world of sensation. And I would say that for some of us, this was our moral crisis in relation to what to paint. So that we actually began, so to speak, from scratch, as if painting were not only dead but had never existed. (Newman 1992: 287)

The plural 'we' of whom he spoke were, by and large, the group of painters who became known as the abstract expressionists. Newman was not their theorist. Indeed there were major differences of views, with Robert Motherwell, for instance. Jackson Pollock, who was friendly with Newman, referred to his work as 'boring' although he was similarly dismissive of Rothko, Gottlieb, Kline, Still and de Kooning (Naifeh and Smith 1992: 632), and, by the middle of the 1960s, commercial success probably had some part to play in the invective issuing from Still and Rothko and aimed at Newman (ibid.: 763). Nevertheless, Newman championed this 'new art' widely and sought to come to some kind of understanding of what, in particular, it was that he himself had been producing. In his writings a number of themes stand out: the metaphysical aspects of personal existence, the tragedy of the human self, the creative-emotional-intellectual make-up of the artist, the quasi-parental controls of the European art tradition against which it was necessary to revolt, his belief in the spirituality of the art of non-Western civilisations, and his belief in the utter validity of a core self. As he put it, in regard to the last of these themes, 'The self, terrible and constant, is for me the subject matter of painting and sculpture' (Newman 1992: 187). His work is a leading (in both senses of the term) example of the celebration and preservation of subjectivity which is formative of the humanities.

His commitment to the human subject can also be seen in silhouette, in terms of the positions that he ruminated on and fulminated against. He was anti-communist, anti-fascist, anti-totalitarian, anti-isolationist, anti-genre, anti-blind traditionalism, anti-purist and ferociously anti-nihilist ('I have always hated the void,' he said [1992: 249]). He knew, and in part helped to form the New York Museum of Modern Art line, from the impressionists' struggle with colour through the post-impressionist engagement with shape, leading to the cubists' exploration of the picture plane, culminating in the return of the subject matter of painting, first in the Freudian shallows of surrealism and then in the spiritual and metaphysical depths of subjectivism in modernist abstraction as it came to develop in post-war America. In relation to all this work, he was clear that all worthwhile art had to be transcendental, personal and charged with emotion. In his view, no socially determined art could aspire to this. He was disappointed in all forms of objectivism, whether they took the form of Mondrian's dogmatic translation of landscape into geometry, or the cautious art criticism that would only describe colour, dimension and form. For Newman, an objective approach to the subjective field of art, even, or perhaps especially, if carried out by a virtuoso, would effectively lead to a rule-bound, colour-by-numbers art, where 'The feeling of objectivity toward these subjective factors has been transferred to the painting itself so that it has become a gadget, a fancy object, with the result that beauty has become a similar objective fact to the end that painting has been reduced to a kind of manufacture' (Newman 1992: 142). In sum, great painting or sculpture would be defined not by its formal qualities, but by what it does, by virtue of the line established between the beholder and the artist. He would, had he engaged with it, have found the structuralist, death-of-the-author temper of Parisian theory in the 1960s anathema.

He was, then, an expressionist and a romantic. As the latter, he thought that painters should play their part in the creation of modern myths, much as ancient art appeared to him to be about summoning up the Gods. He had reservations about classical Greek art, which did not rival its literature in advancing the tragic conception inherent in the Egyptian tradition, but his attitude to painting and the painter was Homeric: 'shall we artists make the same error as the Greek sculptors and play with an art of over-refinement, an art of quality, of sensibility, of beauty?' he asked, replying, 'Let us rather, like the Greek writers, tear the tragedy to shreds' (Newman 1992: 169). Thus Newman's art was not a quiet exercise in clerical subversion, nor a bedazzled quest to penetrate the inner and outer mysteries of the given world; rather it was rooted in the urge to create. He saw the Edenic myth as the story of the first artist because Adam ate from the tree not primarily in order to know, but in order to create and thereby give expression to himself. This Newman took to be a fundamental human impulse. The roots of this expressionism are, finally for Newman, metaphysical, and it is for this reason that he distanced himself from the German expressionist tradition (about which more in the next chapter) which, for him, illustrated that European art has been tied to sensation (ibid.: 162), an emphasis which has tended to close off the expression of ideas (ibid.: 155). While the German expressionists tended to present the world and its objects through the quasi-objective lens of social history, the American expressionists of Newman's time were, on the whole, more concerned with ideas that might express transcendental experience. He found this same concern in a completely different art history:

Barnett Newman, *Fourth Station*, 1960

Mary meets Jesus. Newman had still not quite concluded his overall conceptualisation by the time *Fourth Station* was painted in 1960. He was almost there, however, and so it is perhaps not entirely out of order to contrast this painting with Willem de Kooning's *Woman I*, painted between 1950 and 1952. The two men were both in the famous 'Irascibles' photograph of the New York School artists, taken in 1951, and then they shared a two-man exhibition in 1962, at the Allan Stone Gallery in New York. Writing about de Kooning, in 1951, Newman finds his work crucial for its advocacy and exemplification of ambiguity (Newman 1992: 123). There is some indication that this critical approval was not easily reciprocated. The next year, Newman notes, 'De Kooning has moved from his original position that straight lines do not exist in nature. Geometry can be organic' (ibid.: 241). De Kooning's *Woman I* is iconic, powerful, visually deconstructed, but wholly daunting; a model for Mary *against which* (in the double register of line and figure) Newman can now be seen to have been working. This unlikely linkage also works in the opposite direction, since, as Claire Stoullig points out, de Kooning posed the issue of the Crucifixion 'at the very moment he developed his early series of "Women"' (Stoullig 1992: 127). From here it is but a short step to agree with the feminist critique of phallocratic Christianity and to think of the *Fourth Station* as somehow the key. It is only after this point in the series that Newman painted knowing what the precise subject of the series was.

The Kwakiutl artist . . . The abstract shape he used, his entire plastic language, was directed by a ritualist will toward metaphysical understanding . . . To him a shape was a living thing, a vehicle for an abstract thought-complex, a carrier of the awesome feelings he felt before the terror of the unknowable . . . Not space cutting nor space building, not construction nor fauvist destruction; not the pure line, straight and narrow, nor the tortured line, distorted and humiliating; not the accurate eye, all fingers, nor the wild eye of dream, winking; but the idea-complex that makes contact with mystery – of life, of men, of nature, of the hard black chaos that is death, or the grayer, softer chaos that is tragedy. (Newman 1992: 108)

Newman thought that the basic truth of human life was tragic. However, he attempted to find ways of showing that truth through a certain use of line and colour. If we want to look further into the *Stations*, and to explore a little more the notion of subjectivity that may be at issue there, we should perhaps think about the notion of line, about Newman's 'zips'. Cézanne is perhaps the place to start, for Newman took Cézanne to be 'the first artist to comprehend that in nature there are no lines . . . that nature is a collection of cubes, cones and spheres . . . mass instead of contours' (ibid.: 82–3). Newman understood precisely what was his opposition to Cézanne on the strict question of the line, and how he transcended Cézanne's understanding. He sought, of course, to transcend the impressionist and post-impressionist focus on nature, and he disagreed with Mondrian's oversimplification that the world is made up of lines, but on the question of line itself he was continuously in search of fuller understanding. He was not, he said, a painter of lines, but of pictures. He agreed with Clyfford Still's comment that Newman's '"vivid blaze" was no "portrait of a line" but that [he] had found something "big and a way to make vivid this *new* thing"' (ibid.: 232), but also thought that 'a straight line is an organic thing that can contain feeling' (ibid.: 241), that he could 'make an area of canvas come to life with the one line' (ibid.: 278), that line can be 'a thing' (ibid.: 299) which, he inferred, could be invested with created energy and meaning, and could act as a totalising and unifying rather than a dividing force – his example here is his first 'zip' painting, *Onement I*, 1948). In answer to David Sylvester's suggestion that his zips were fields between other fields, Newman replied, 'Yes. A field that brings life to the other fields, just as the other fields bring life to this so-called line' (ibid.: 256). So, Newman saw himself as grossly misrepresented if referred to as a 'stripe' painter, principally because his zips were much more than mere lines. They were unifying moments inside this painter's pictorial expression of his intellectual-emotional engagement with the tragedy of the human self. But still one feels that Newman did not get to the heart of the matter, that the question of line still remains partly unanswered.

Let us continue with a counter-example: Derrida's work on Husserl and his *Origin of Geometry*. This text raises the question of line, but leads us to issues concerning 'the status of the ideal objects of science' (Derrida 1978b: 25) and tries to show that the ideal object has its material source in inexactitude, that 'by a practical necessity of daily life, certain shapes and certain processes of transformation could be perceived, restored and pro-gressively perfected; for example, rigid lines, even surfaces, and so forth' (ibid.: 123). Newman would have been uncomfortable with this position. He said, 'the edge of the UN Building is a straight line. If it can be made, it does exist in nature' (241); even Cézanne, Newman noted, had the sensation of the edge (122) It seems, however, that Derrida chooses not to con-template the independence of line: for him line is always already figure, the figure of enclosure. An enclosure to be filled by colour. As Derrida puts it in one of his essays on painting, 'first the full encircling ring, the black line, incisive, definitive, then the flood of broad chromatic scales in a wash of colour' (1987: 172). His focus is upon the line as edge between inside and outside, a frame around a picture (unlike Newman, who, at least until he

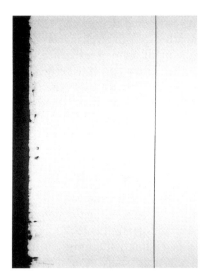

Barnett Newman, *Fifth Station*, 1962

Lyotard had this to say: 'A painting by Newman is an angel. It announces nothing; it is in itself the annunciation . . . there are no allusions' (Lyotard 1991: 79–80). Thomas Hess, Newman's friend and biographer, said that Newman did not tell stories, did not transmit messages, was never allegorical. While, for Lyotard, the work is unclouded, certain and innocent, it also presents an exemplary poverty; something also said of Jesus Christ. The *Fifth Station* is the point at which Simon, the Cyrenian, helps Jesus to carry the cross; it is also the point at which Newman knows he is making the same movement. It is the moment when Newman realises that he too has picked up the cross.

began to make the series of prints entitled *18 Cantos*, saw himself 'as one of the first painters to reject the frame' [cited in Schor 1996: 18]), not the picture itself, not something to be seen in the mode of the chief waiting for something 'to leap from the page'. For Derrida, line 'gives itself up to analysis' (ibid.: 174), and he will write of the lines across a divided Europe (Derrida 1992), of line subordinated to text, meaning and enclosure.

Derrida's opposition to vocal primordiality is one that Newman could, in a certain way, share. Both are advocates of an open society, and Newman could surely have drawn, as others have, impetus for resisting totalitarianism from what Derrida did in providing philosophical resources for resisting the power of the 'I say unto you.' I suspect, however, that this is about as far along the same path as we can make Newman and Derrida go together. For Newman, it is plain that there is an origin: alone, abandoned, even (unlike the man on the *Via Dolorosa*) unsignifying and unlamented at the end. For Derrida, such humanism cannot be sustained, and he alluded to what he thought were the flaws in humanism in his 1968 New York lecture entitled 'The Ends of Man'.

The difference between Derrida and Newman on the question of line can be illuminated by asking about their concept of the human. Suppose that Derrida's lecture had been redesigned to address Newman directly, what might it have said? In broad terms, it would have taken the form of 'Yes . . . but'. Opening with that version of the Categorical Imperative which insists that humans are never to be treated as means alone, that they must always be considered at least to some extent as ends in themselves, as in other words sources of ultimate value, and then underlining and updating that position with a reminder of Sartre's view that the ultimate ends of human existence derive from that existence itself, Derrida starts with an inside and an outside: an inside operating according to the rules of rationality, and an outside in the form of the existence that precedes and defines the essence/ inside. This beginning would seem sympathetic with Newman's post-representational engagement with the tragedy of human existence. His abstract art is finely attuned to the dilemma of falsely concretising what is essentially re-makable at every instant, this realm of ends, and Newman's insistence upon evocation and against depiction is entirely understandable, and appropriate as an existential affirmation and defence of subjectivity, the line a matter of subjective potentiation, neither the secret of division nor the already enclosed figure of a character. In short, the line as place, as *Makom*, as the place where the subject stands. At this point, however, Derrida injects a note of doubt, pondering that 'man' is a recent invention, and may last only as long as a figure drawn in the sand at low tide. Newman's response, however, is 'Of course!' His focus on and conjuration of tragedy, his examination of abandonment and death, his location both inside and outside of a defining narrative of ending and transfiguration, illustrate precisely that the postulation of the historically contingent and even evanescent nature of 'man' makes absolutely no difference to the validity of interior, autonomous and formless (in the way that line is unformed into figure) subjectivity as a (if not the) key category for understanding and responding to the human condition. Simply put, there may be lines that will resist the erosion of the tides.

Derrida's next move in this counterfactual engagement is to deconstruct the idea of humanism. This will add to the emphasis on the temporariness of the figure of 'man' on which Newman may be thought to rely. If humanism is understood in Sartrean terms of existence preceding essence, and as linking to two crucial issues, that of the isolated, anguished individual and that of the de-essentialized socially constructable values of care and democracy, then it is perfectly proper to emphasise values such as democracy and this to some extent will devalorise the interior moment of subjectivity. However, Derrida appears tempted to do a little more, and affirm that humanism was entirely destroyed some time ago. If Derrida and others are right in saying this, then a contemporary reading of Newman's project of apprehending the human in its tragic dimension is almost impossible. This may be why there are no such contemporary readings.

We can revisit this death of humanism by considering Derrida's case carefully. He writes:

> The humanism which marks Sartre's philosophical discourse in its depths, however, is very surely and very ironically taken apart in *Nausea*: in the caricature of the Autodidact, for example, the same figure reassembles the theological project of absolute knowledge and the humanist ethic . . . It is in the dialogue with the Autodidact that Roquentin levels the worst charges against humanism, against all humanist styles; and at the moment when Nausea is slowly rising in him, he says to himself . . . 'I don't want to be integrated, I don't want my good red blood to go and fatten this lymphatic beast: I will not be fool enough to call myself "anti-humanist." I *am not* a humanist, that's all there is to it.' (Derrida 1982: 115)

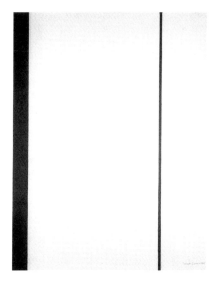

Barnett Newman, *Sixth Station*, 1962

In 1943, Adolph Gottlieb, Mark Rothko and Barnett Newman published a joint statement. It agreed with the position of Clement Greenberg who had argued that allusion to three-dimensional space in painting was illegitimate, that the proper basis of painting was the encounter of colour with the two-dimensional flatness of the stretched canvas, but the joint statement asserted that this technical position needed to be supplemented, and the nature of that supplement was to be the tragic and the timeless. They wrote: 'We are for flat forms because they destroy illusion and reveal truth . . . We assert that the subject is crucial and only that subject matter is valid which is tragic and timeless.' The *Sixth Station* is where Veronica hands Christ a cloth to wipe his face.

What are the charges against humanism which Derrida refers to? Note first when they are probably made: a week after Ash Wednesday. Confessions have been made, but Christ is still in the wilderness. The day begins with Roquentin squashing a fly. It is lunchtime, in a restaurant. The year is 1932. Roquentin and the Autodidact are going to eat together. They skirmish a little, but pull back and remain separate. They are distracted by new arrivals. They exchange thoughts about sculpture and painting. The scene is elaborated from Roquentin's point of view, and he is intense. This intensity deepens and finally breaks with Roquentin's laughter. He is taken by the thought that all around him people are doing things like eating and talking and making love, all of this to extend and nourish their existence, but that none of it has any meaning or purpose. The Autodidact reacts to this. For this 'provincial humanist' the mere existence of other people provides sense and purpose. He explains: 'in the internment camp, I learnt to believe in people'. He had been regularly locked up with two or three hundred people in a dark room, with the rain falling outside, and had come to love his fellow inmates to the extent that this room became a holy place: 'I slipped into it all alone and there, in the darkness, at the memory of the joys I had known there, I fell into a sort of ecstasy' (Sartre 1965a: 165). Roquentin holds back his anger. The Autodidact continues. He does not believe in God, but something does happen at Mass; it is the communion of souls. Then he confesses that he has joined a socialist organisation. The Autodidact is waiting for a stronger reaction than the nod of apparent approval that he gets. Roquentin's response is kept to himself, and is as follows:

> While he speaks, I see all the humanists I have known reappear . . . The radical humanist is a special friend of civil servants. The so-called 'left-wing' humanist's chief concern is to preserve human values; he belongs to no party because he

doesn't want to betray humanity as a whole, but his sympathies go towards the humble; it is to the humble that he devotes his fine classical culture. He is generally a widower with beautiful eyes always clouded with tears; he weeps at anniversaries. He also loves cats, dogs, all the higher animals. The Communist writer has been loving men ever since the second Five-Year Plan; he punishes because he loves . . . The Catholic humanist . . . speaks of men with a wonder-struck air. What a beautiful fairy tale, he says, is the humblest life . . . Those are the principal types. But there are others . . . the humanist philosopher who bends over his brothers like an elder brother who is conscious of his responsibilities; the humanist who loves men as they are, the one who loves them as they ought to be, the one who wants to save them with their consent, and the one who will save them in spite of themselves, the one who wants to create myths, and the one who is satisfied with the old myths, the one who loves man for his death, the one who loves man for his life, the happy humanist who always knows what to say to make people laugh, the gloomy humanist whom you usually meet at wakes. They all hate one another: as individuals, of course, not as men. (Sartre 1965a: 168–9)

Roquentin finds these varieties of humanism repellent because they are so utterly dishonest. All assert an abstracted love of 'man', but depend upon skilled avoidance of existence. The impassioned desire for man camouflages an absolute preference for distant romanticism over close experience. When the Autodidact realises that Roquentin is unimpressed by his infelicitous declaration of his general love for man, he plays out a standard response and accuses him of being a misanthrope. It is at this point that Roquentin refuses to play the game, declaring, 'I am not a humanist, that's all.' He poses difficult questions for the Autodidact, about whether he 'loves' this particular example of 'man' and what it might be about him or her. The Autodidact is easy meat, has no answers. The nausea at the desperately naked and viscous nature of existence, once shorn of its idealised ornamentation and once seen for the unadorned existence that it is, overcomes Roquentin. He leaves the restaurant, sees a priest admiring the sea, which to the priest 'speaks of God'. But 'the *real* sea is cold and black, full of animals; it crawls underneath this thin green film . . . The sylphs all around me have been taken in, they see nothing but the thin film . . . I see underneath' (ibid.: 179).

Now, this dismissal of humanism by Sartre is not a dismissal of the subjective moment, it is a repudiation of crass humanist idealism. More generously, one might say that it is a repudiation of saintliness as a credible foundation for a general ethics. When reflecting upon his critique of humanism as presented in these celebrated pages, Sartre had this to say:

There is another meaning of humanism. Fundamentally it is this: man is constantly outside of himself; in projecting himself, in losing himself outside of himself, he makes for man's existing; and, on the other hand, it is by pursuing transcendent goals that he is able to exist; man, being this state of passing beyond, and seizing upon things only as they bear upon this passing beyond, is at the heart, at the centre of this passing beyond. There is no universe other than a human universe, the universe of human subjectivity. This connection between transcendency, as a constituent element of man . . . and subjectivity, in the sense

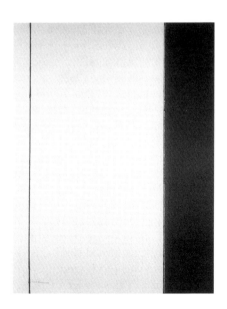

Barnett Newman, *Seventh Station*, 1964

At the *Seventh Station*, Christ falls a second time, yet goes on to comfort the women walking alongside. Countless millions have reacted with awe and wonder to the ordeal on the *Via Dolorosa*, and the story of the Passion is also the second origin of European art. As the life of Christ empowered and sustained the Renaissance, this second origin of European art stands alongside the Greek classical tradition. These rival sensibilities of beauty and the sublime were of great moment in Barnett Newman's thinking. He said, 'I believe that here in America, some of us, free from the weight of European culture, are finding the answer, by completely denying that art has any concern with the problem of beauty . . . if we are living in a time without a legend or mythos . . . how can we be creating a sublime art?' (Newman 1992: 173) Here is the mythos.

that man is not closed in on himself, but is always present in a human universe, is what we call existentialist humanism. (Sartre 1965b: 61)

The Sartrean critique of idealist humanism does not really bear upon what Derrida refers to when he writes, 'after the war, under the name of Christian or atheist existentialism, and in conjunction with a fundamentally Christian personalism, the thought that dominated France presented itself essentially as humanist' (1982: 115). In other words, one of the key attacks 'very surely and very ironically taken apart' just does not present the slightest difficulty for a reading of Newman as a humanist, or of his zips in terms of subjective potentiation, as bearing upon 'the state of passing beyond'.

He was not entirely sure how he thought about these 'lines'. At one point he thinks they are not lines at all. He dislikes the term 'stripe'. His first *Onement* made little sense to him for months, but he did come to recognise that it was 'full', that the line made something come alive, that it created a totality. For Newman it was a metaphysical event, without connection to figurative depiction (unlike, therefore, Derrida's understanding of line) but somehow connected to the self. He wrote, 'I hope that my painting has the impact of giving someone, as it did me, the feeling of his own totality, of his own separateness, of his own individuality, and at the same time of his connection to others' (Newman 1992: 258). He could not understand the disdain for the self that was becoming clearly visible in the worlds of art and culture by the mid-1960s. As Derrida noted in 1968, 'the current questioning of humanism is contemporary with the dominating and spellbinding extension of the "human sciences" within the philosophical field' (Derrida 1982: 117). This is of a piece with the sociological denial of the subject, and what we are seeing with Newman is a resistance to that influence, and, what is more, it is that resistance, articulated through post-representational engagement with the self and its transcendent projects, which enables us to see that the dismissal of humanism in the 1960s was far less complete than we had ever suspected. Heidegger in his *Letter on Humanism* (1978) thought that humanism was the problem, that what mattered was to be clear about what thinking was. It was not, he argued, an instrumental matter, however tempting the thought that thinking should be rationally allied to action and thereby should receive its meaning in the notion of praxis. Nor is it – perish the thought – a matter determined from a socially constructed elsewhere. It was, for Heidegger, writing in the aftermath of the Second World War, neither instrumentality nor sub-ordination to a higher wisdom of whatever kind: instead thinking itself is an expression of what it is to be human. Not thinking in order to do some-thing, but thinking as the key to understanding the unadorned simplicity of human being at its root. For Heidegger, humanism was too bound up with elaborated and over-abstracted concepts to approach this order of Parsi-falian simplicity. Heidegger's critique of humanism does not leave the field of humanism. It merely crops it to its soil. From Heidegger through Sartre and thence to Newman, the inquiry into subjectivity is increasingly pared down toward an inner essentiality. Derrida, of course, fastened on the idea of presence involved in this movement and showed it to be suspect. He did so, however, within a style we might label the ontology of lack, deriving particularly from Freud but also from Kant, since subjective presence to itself is, for him, never complete; it is always linked to an outside, to otherness, yet, in the final analysis, that outside, that other, can never be tied down, it is finally always secret. There is, of course, no reason why humanism should require plenitude, unless to sell one substantive variation (Christian, ecological, scientific, etc.) or another. And perhaps subjectivity may be possessed of a secret resource. Blanchot, as we will see later in this book, seemed to think so at times. However, neither the lack of plenitude nor the thought of a secret will denegate subjectivity as a key constituent of renascent humanism. Sartre, Heidegger, Newman were figures for a period which is returning.

Seriality

Derrida took us back to the point of origin of meaning, and threw into question the powerful but subterranean assumption that singularity and transparency of meaning had issued from one golden throat. The story of hermeneutics was then a reprise of the dismissal from Eden, and was about the loss of that original clarity. The whole history of the world thus could be read as a series of failed attempts, whether noble or ignoble, to re-establish the lost language of the first moment. Failed repetition results in

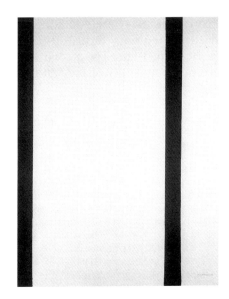

Barnett Newman, *Eighth Station*, 1964

It is not without significance that the theme of the *Eighth Station* is Christ's act of comforting. Not for the first time there is an act of identification. Newman seeks to re-establish the Renaissance sublime, the life of Christ as sustaining theme, in the middle of the twentieth century. Yet he also wishes to proceed without illusion. Wilfully to install the Renaissance sublime as successor to the machine aesthetic of cubism seems redolent of withdrawal, reversion and escape into the past. Two words of Hebrew, however, the subtitle Newman gave to the series of fourteen paintings, suggest that Newman's intent was to confront the present, to mourn the loss of comfort and meaning, to pose an unanswerable question and even to find comfort in its very unanswerability: *lema sabachthani* – 'Why have you forsaken me?' You comforted them? Where am I to look? The only answer Newman can countenance is that it must be necessary in some way to look *beyond*.

difference, ranging between family resemblances and non-contiguous aberration and malformation. The loss of some volume from the original voice entails a certain increase of significance in the marks of difference. What was silent and prior to the message, the sheer fissure of the mark, a line in the sand or along a geological fault, is about to speak. Marks of identification and distinction form series. Lines, formerly neither mute nor authoritative, will group together, enclosing not on account of their curvature, their intrinsic properties, but on account of their calls to others. The loss of origin and the advent of difference lead away from the mono-clonal context of the origin toward the singularities of multiple subjects. The creation of serialities is a form of opposition to the post-foundational situation of negative entropy in which we find ourselves. If Derrida is less than enthralled by singularity and line, perhaps his attention is drawn to lines one after another, to the phenomena of seriality and repetition. It is certainly true that he exposed the key role of repetition in the reproduction of the voice. The repetition of something that never took place, being haunted by the ghost of a body that had never lived (Derrida 1994), is a constant theme in his work. Indeed, he worries at the phenomenon of seriality, like a dog with bones:

there are the *25 Variations on the Idea of Rupture* . . . the *18 Mausoleums for 6 New York Taxi Drivers*, there are the *20 Variations on the Idea of Deterioration* . . . the *17 Examples of Alteration of a Sphere*, then there are the *VI Spheres*, the *7*

Dismantlings, the *15 Latin Incisions* . . . the 19 drawings of *The Use of the Necessary*, the 34 drawings of *The Four Season Sticks* . . . (Derrida 1987: 204–5)

He tells us that the number 'comes to corrupt in the title the authority of the name'. But this is a notion of number that is already textual. It is not the notion of number that arises with the second line. The second line, which inaugurates number, did not corrupt the authority of the first line, for that line had no authority, only length.

Barnett Newman, *Ninth Station*, 1964

At the age of twenty-four Barnett Newman's plan to become an artist of independent means was ruined by the Great Depression. He had deferred his desire to be solely an artist twice already. He had completed his college education, and then he worked in the family business. Now the Wall Street crash meant a third denial. Newman would work to save a collapsed clothing business and practise as a teacher of art until virtually the outbreak of the Second World War. Newman's third fall did not, however, cause him to deviate from his path. Already, in 1926, angered by the unavailability of the collection of post-impressionist paintings kept cloistered by the Barnes Foundation in Merion, Pennsylvania, he had scribbled the following on paper bags in a Greek take-away: 'Modern theory holds that art is a combination of line and colour that makes up pictorial form . . . Appreciation . . . consists in a contemplation and grasp of [this] form . . . This manifests a nominalistic attitude toward art which makes of art an accidental, almost arbitrary phenomenon, void of significance . . . Barnes [and T.S.] Eliot tell us in true nominalistic style that the artist creates form. This is a falsehood that has created much mischief . . . The artist emphatically does not create form. The artist expresses in a work of art an aesthetic idea which is innate and eternal' (Newman 1992: 58).

Derrida's reflections on seriality extend beyond commentary, and in a kind of Wittgensteinian move, into use. Writing between 12 and 14 December 1977, his first point has four parts; his second point is made on 15 December. He commences a second list on 1 January, running to seven numbered points. The next day another list is started; it is extended to six points by 8 January, with sub-lists of four and three respectively attached to items four and five, and with a six-part list attached to the last item. The last six-part list invites us to consider different perspectives, and I will say they are invitations to look at lines in different ways. First, we may look at lines according to their techniques of production: 'charcoal, more or less broad pencil, graphite lead' (Derrida 1987: 244), finger-drawn, stick-scratched, clawed. Second, we can think of the perspectives: 'top or bottom, left or right', but, as Derrida asks, 'In terms of what "truth" are these angles to be ordered?' Third, we should consider the material onto which the marks are inscribed: stone, sand, metal, ice, wood, fibre or flesh, of what 'size, value, thickness . . . colour'. (In parenthesis, we might note that the three dots elide the two words, 'and even', from the translated text. 'Et meme' – a symptom of glimmering recognition that line is scratch and not enclosure, that it marks but does not territorialise, that it bespeaks no inside or outside to be coloured by the blood of empire.) Fourth there is the question of the pathology of the line: was it made by a serrated edge, a blunt instrument, a scalpel? We are at the dissecting table, looking for things present and absent. Fifth, we want its measurements, and lastly we would like to know when it appeared and if it will happen again. This analyst's inventory is drawn up at the end of an essay which formed part of a catalogue for an exhibition entitled, 'The Pocket-sized Tlingit Coffin and the 61 Ensuing Drawings' (the catalogue actually featured 127 drawings based on the coffin: 'One hundred and twenty-seven times like a salvo of black-edged missives' [ibid.: 245]). It is a sub-classification of the sixth item in a list. The topic of this sixth item is classification. For Derrida, seriality is a matter of classification. Subjects will be typecast. Classification is occasioned by repetition, which means sanction, approval, enclosure, territoriality and the colours on the map. It means that unenclosed subjectivity is a contradiction in terms. It means also that to approach subjectivity one has to approach the issue of seriality. Without classification there can be, Derrida implies, no recognition. Nothing could possibly jump out at the chief from the page. The lines the chief looked at were unclassifiable; thus their only impact could have been rooted in falsehood or credulousness. To reverse this condition, and privilege line as *Makom* over text, meaning and classification was the goal of Barnett Newman, and his desire was for something to jump from the white canvas once line has been inscribed there.

In addressing this possibility, that line may have a form of existence prior to textuality and classification, we are not only thinking *contra* Derrida, but also *contra* Lévi-Strauss, since it is a question also of the behaviour of the chief who overcomes disappointment to fold the lines into a story of secrets: 'More probably he wanted to astonish his companions, to convince them he was acting as an intermediary . . . that he was in alliance with the white man and shared his secrets' (Lévi-Strauss 389), a question of attempting to construct him in a way which is not entirely Machiavellian. Is the choice which governs abstract expressionism that between disappointment and priesthood? In answer to that question we will try to find a path out of this seemingly tight enclosure, and we have known, at least since Gödel, and probably for ever, that no system is ever entirely hermetic.

Barnett Newman, *Tenth Station*, 1965

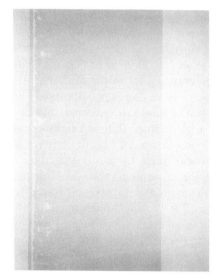

Jesus is stripped of his garments. The act of rending creates lines and reveals lines. What is inessential is ripped away to show yet another layer of inessentiality. The operation is not a scientific one, even though the impulse to remove the covering and analyse what lies beneath is itself the kernel of the scientific approach. Nor is it seen as a total act: most depictions of the Crucifixion show Christ on the cross still wearing a loincloth. This modesty in the face of brutality has been the norm in the history of art. Gerard David's depiction of the skinning alive of Cambyses, in his *Judgement of Cambyses* (1498: Groeninge Museum, Bruges), shows a meticulous brutality but still the loincloth remains, even as the skin is peeled from the victim's left leg, and as surgical incisions are made in his right arm and from sternum to the base of the stomach. There are protocols to be observed, a realm of illusion to be maintained, illustrated most clearly by the papal approval given to the line of fourteen metaphors which we know as the *Stations of the Cross*, authorised by Clement XII in 1731.

Let us assume that the second line is not essentially a matter of repetition. It would follow from such a starting point that the phenomenon of seriality might not be analytically exhausted by notions of classification and repetition. The second line is certainly capable of being described as the second in a series, as part of a class of lines, or as the first of a new class of lines. It is also, however, conceivable as a response to something which is neither mute nor endowed with authority, as the beginning, in other words, of a conversation with the *Other*. For Newman there was a certain task which was for him both an absolute duty and one which would never be finished, since it would raise itself anew again and again. This task was described in, amongst other places, Newman's short article in *ARTnews*, at the time of the first exhibition of the complete *Stations of the Cross*, at the Guggenheim in 1966:

> Neither did I have a preconceived idea that I would execute and then give a title to. I wanted to hold the emotion, not waste it in picturesque ecstasies. The cry, the unanswerable cry, is world without end. But a painting has to hold it, world without end, in its limits. (Newman 1992: 190)

As conversation with the *Other*, as reinvigoration of the mythos, as containment of feeling and emotion without illusion, the *Stations of the Cross* is precisely not a simple matter of a series of anecdotes. In 1962, he wrote:

The central issue of painting is the subject matter. Most people think of subject matter as what Meyer Schapiro has called 'object matter.' It is the 'object matter' that most people want to see in a painting. That is what, for them, makes the painting seem full. For me both the use of objects and the manipulation of areas for the sake of the areas themselves must end up being anecdotal. My subject is antianecdotal. An anecdote can be subjective and internal as well as of the external world, so that the expression of the biography of self or the intoxicated moment of glowing ecstasy must in the end also become anecdotal. All such painting is essentially episodic, which means it calls for a sequel. This must happen if a painting does not give a sensation of wholeness or fulfilment. That is why I have no interest in the episodic or ecstatic, however abstract. The excitement always ends at the brink and leaves the subject, so to speak, hanging there like the girl in *The Perils of Pauline*. The next painting repeats the excitement, in a kind of ritual. One expects the girl to be saved finally, but she is again left hanging on the brink, and so on and on. This is the weakness of the ecstatic and the episodic. It is an endless search for a statement of personality that never takes place. The truly passionate exists on a different level. (Newman 1992: 250)

Barnett Newman, *Eleventh Station*, 1965

Fixed by nails to the cross. The Gospels do not dwell on the question of the physical pain, and we have no real indication of what Newman thought on this topic. The portrayal of the Crucifixion in the Isenheim altarpiece in Colmar does feature the nails, which are given bold heads. However, in the series of thirteen studies based on this work by Picasso, which he did in 1932, at Boisgeloup, there is hardly a nail in sight. Except, most notably, in the drawing of 7 October, which features a steel bolt on a trajectory from a drilled shoulder-blade, we find the bolt is paralleled with a safety pin projected from the loincloth. Francis Bacon knew and admired this drawing, but in his studies of the Crucifixion we find that the body is the total focus, upstaged by neither cross nor nails, and, particularly in the right panel of the 1962 triptych, presented as flesh, ribcage and scream. The absence of the physical in Newman's work is underlined in the surgically bleak acephalous crosses of his sculpture *Here II* (Calas 1995).

Jean-François Lyotard thought of the duty to remember the Holocaust in the same way. It is more than a question of making sure that the details appear in the history books, and that the history books are set as part of a national curriculum. To approach the matter only in that way would be to locate an episode within a series. It would be like programming the machine, and once the machine is programmed, it can be forgotten until it goes wrong. This creates a gap when the work of remembering stops. When the machine needs attention, who will remember why it was built like that in the first place? Mimesis and repetition, then, is not enough. There has to be engagement, invention, some creation, a kind of reliving even though the time has past. This must mean an inevitable and deep pluralism, an aesthetic duty to try to step outside of the established classifications to converse with the *Other*. We have the gap between now and then, between us and them, between me and you, between him and her. Measuring the distance between the lines, listing their number and their types, posing equivalence and non-equivalence, was clearly the utter antithesis of what Newman was seeking to accomplish. In considering the Holocaust, Lyotard posed the crossing of the divide, the breaching of the gap, as an event in its own right: not merely as a ritual observance and temporal thing to fade out of thought, but as an other ever to be unforgotten. Newman's line was fierce creativity as a duty in the light of chosen sacred spheres from past and present. As Lyotard put it, 'The West is thinkable under the order of *mimesis* only if one forgets that a "people" survives within it that is not a nation (a nature). Amorphous, indignant, clumsy, involuntary, this people tries to listen to the Forgotten' (Lyotard 1990: 94). And if this leap from Newman to the Holocaust seems somewhat fanciful, the glass-cased prayer shawls to be seen in the exhibition areas at Auschwitz, with their black lines on raw wool, are interstitial members of the *Stations of the Cross*. Just as there are infinitely more members of the set of numbers lodged between those rational numbers we can determine, so too there is an infinity of worlds between the Stations.

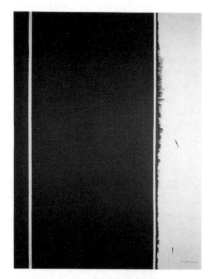

Barnett Newman, *Twelfth Station*, 1965

The tenth chapter of Philippe Ariès's, *The Hour of our Death* (1981), is entitled 'The age of the beautiful death'. It opens with an apparent approval of the enyclopaedists who 'had blamed the clergy and the church for concealing beneath its strange and frightening machinery the "narcotic sweetness" of death, and for changing its nature, a nature that romanticism would redeem and exalt'. If redemption and exaltation are the criteria which define the treatment of death within the romantic movement from the late eighteenth century forward (cf. Edmund Burke's comment on Milton's description of death in *Paradise Lost* as 'dark, uncertain, confused, terrible and sublime to the last degree'), then there is a case to be made that the papal approval of the *Stations of the Cross* constitutes a clamorous herald of Shelley's 'high Capital, where Kingly Death keeps his pale court in beauty and decay' (*Adonais*, 1821).

The supplementary structure of abstract expressionism

Bill Viola's installation, *Room 4, St John of the Cross* (1983) depicts a small room with an earth floor, the smell of which is a part of the work. He writes, 'the Spanish poet and Mystic St John of the Cross (1542 to 1591) was kept prisoner by the religious establishment for nine months in 1577. His cell had no windows and he was unable to stand upright. He was frequently tortured. During this period St John wrote most of the poems for which he is known. His poems often speak of love, ecstasy, passage through the dark night and flying over city walls and mountains.' The room is enclosed within a small box in the centre of a larger room, and on one of the walls of the larger room there is a series of pictures depicting the changes and weather extremes in a mountainous region. On the table in the small room there is a video monitor with a picture on it of a mountain at peace and in good weather. Inside the small room we find St John of the Cross murmuring Latin prayers in an attitude of religious fervour and devotion. There is a jug of water on his table. A glass nearby. The contrasts between the religious incantation murmured and the flashing storms on the

Barnett Newman, *Thirteenth Station*, 1965/66

The *Thirteenth Station* sees Jesus removed from the cross. The anointing of a body with various oils just before or after death is known as unction. The stone of unction in Jerusalem is a hybrid place which has become sacro-profane, as various people (bag-people, as Richard Hecht calls them) bring an extraordinary variety of artefacts – rings, teacups, books, lipsticks, fountain pens, rosaries, shoes and shrouds – and lay them on the stone, to invest them with its healing and forgiving power. The stone has to be regularly cleaned with the same sort of substance that would have been rubbed into Christ's dead body, and this is done most days during Easter week.

video wall set up an intense contradiction between the solitude of the prisoner in all bodily functions, and the freedom and wild responses of his mind. The aesthetic value of this installation resides in its foregrounding of the contradiction between subjectivity and context. The contradiction is presented in its entirety within the artwork. This is not typically the case with abstract expressionism since it presents works which are, in Melanie Klein's vocabulary, part-objects. They require interpretation not to say what they are but to complete their being. It is, of course, possible to respond to them without making that gesture of co-building. In particular, this is what Lyotard did when writing of the *Stations of the Cross*, when he argued that 'The work of Newman belongs to the aesthetic of the sublime' (Lyotard 1991: 84) and that their power resides in the relief that the terror that they evoke is held at bay. He writes of Newman's work that it is not

> concerned with the resurrection in the sense of the Christian mystery, but with the recurrence of a prescription emanating from silence or from the void, and which perpetuates the passion by reiterating it from its beginnings . . . It is fitting that it should not offer anything that has to be deciphered, still less interpreted. (ibid.: 88)

Barnett Newman, *Fourteenth Station,* 1965/66

Participating pilgrims used to experience the time of Christ, which was eternal and radiated from the overarching metanarrative of progress and salvation. Newman's work came from that. If we have moved from the aura of the metanarrative to the everything-included package tour (hostilities permitting), then Newman's work greets that development with enormous sadness. It may be appropriate that the *Fourteenth Station* is sealed into darkness by a boulder, which on the following day has been moved, leaving emptiness behind.

Lyotard was surely right when he saw these works as inimical to inter-pretation, but he did not thoroughly grasp that they need to be added to, that the sublime response is not a second line which follows naturally from the first, but that it is a willed engagement with the first. Let us suppose, problematic though it might be, that terror and relief is a naturally sublime response of delight at being safe from the worst storm that there ever was, and also that a sublime response to art of a certain huge scale is possible without much or even any engagement. If we ask whether the *Stations of the Cross* have that *automatic* power, the answer is surely not. To make of them the Niagara Falls of abstract expressionism, they need to be supple-mented. When Lyotard agrees with Burke that the sublime sensation is 'privation at one remove' where the soul has achieved safety from the threats of darkness, silence and death, he fails to emphasise that the soul has to construct those threats in the first place by completing the part-object which is confronted. It is the nature of that completion that matters as much as the nature of the part-object which is completed. This is why T.J. Clark's interesting and valuable attempt to see abstract expressionism in terms of a positive notion of vulgarity – 'what we shall value most in the painting is the ruthlessness of self-exposure, the courting of bathos, the *unapologetic* banality' (Clark 1997: 64) – does not quite recognise what the Viola installation shouts at us, that the canvas is only part of it.

The supplement, however, exerts a penalty. As Derrida pointed out, the supplement is undecidable. It is both addition and replacement. Whether the supplement is a set of considerations about, say, the artist's life, or about a fourteen-part metaphor given papal approval in 1731, it is clearly possible that it may overwhelm the original work, like a parasite feeding and giving nothing back. This can happen most easily in the case of institutional supplementation in areas like religion, politics, and the commercial culture industries, but it is a permanent threat in every context, combated only by repeatedly drawing attention to the contingent connections made between the vivid context deficiencies of abstract expressionism and the supplements that may levy a high price for their works of completion. For Newman, the advent of the supplement is both fulfilment of potential and the birth of tragedy.

4

GEORG BASELITZ: FRAGMENTED SUBJECTIVITY

The unimaginative subject

The divide between the subject and the world is immemorial. It has been approached in many ways: in religions, mythologies, sciences, fairy tales and philosophies. In the last of these, for example, the conceptual heart of Michel Foucault's *Les Mots et les choses* (*The Order of Things*) is the concept of the episteme which, aspiring to be a determining framework of epochal proportions, tries to establish the way that the subject and world have been interrelated since the Renaissance. In this conception, the world is subject to radical shifts, and the human condition would follow them, finally coming to be, in the modern era, a restless and shifting affair, with the human sciences described by Foucault as undevelopable. In *The Order of Things* the human world typical of modernity is an analogon of Bourdieu's rising petite bourgeoisie. It will not be pinned down, its very condition being to have no permanent condition. Because of this judgement at its terminus, *The Order of Things* has been seen as a failed philosophy. As much is announced in its celebration of structural impermanence in modernity, and also in Foucault's determined avoidance of notions of epochal rupture and closure in his comparative treatment of the classical Greek and early Christian self in his late work. This is, of course, not the only attempt to specify the causal ground of human ontology. Darwinian, behaviourist, neurological and sociological theories also try to reduce the subject to its causal antecedents. In each case there is considerable controversy about these theories and their demonstrations. At this point, we can start from the principle that there will not be a simple unidirectional relationship between subject and the world, a theorem elaborated in various ways (in the sociological theory of structuration for instance) since Marx wrote that people make history but not in circumstances of their own choosing.

In Jacques Derrida's concept of the supplement, we have the basis for an alternative understanding of the relation between subject and the world, in which one will always usurp and replace the other which will subsequently always return alongside, eventually to usurp in its turn: a relationship without origin, in which the core process is undecidable between supplementation as replacement and supplementation as addition. Does this not leave us exactly where we were with actor network theory: that is, staying closely focused on the subject, its essence is connectability – even if every connection leads to potential dissolution? This line of thought leads us now to be fascinated with the question of the subject's supplementation by various social and physical processes, by the technological object, as with cyborgs, prostheses and the discourse of cyberpunk, or by the interpellations issued by social movements connected to major axes of social difference.

Without even looking back to the thought that commences, 'In the beginning was the line', or, yet again, the commonsense view that the condition of the subject relates to issues of need and desire within the world, it can be seen that the relation between subject and world is difficult. One response here is to say that the attempt to locate and dissect the very core of the relation is misguided, that since the subject forms the world at the same time as the world forms the subject, we are actually dealing with a unity that is, at root, ineffable. For those of a positivistic frame of mind, the notion of an internally necessary yet fundamentally unanalysable unity between subject and the world is a sure sign that a mistake has been made. This would not be a small mistake, capable of being rectified by some small addition here or subtraction there. It would be a fundamental mistake, the whole quest for some enlightenment, with regard to the relation between subject and the world, being misconstrued and meaningless. The view that the long lines of theologians, philosophers, artists, storytellers, mythmakers and song-writers, who have suggested that there is something other about the relationship between the subject and the world, are mistaken, is powerfully expressed in the school of thought known as ordinary language philosophy, and, more recently, in contemporary philosophy of mind. Let me take these two cases, one by one.

It is coincidental that one of the best critiques of ordinary language philosophy, Ernest Gellner's *Words and Things*, shares its title with the work by Foucault mentioned above. Gellner's portrayal of ordinary language philosophy and its view of the world begins with a picture that might have appealed to the early Wittgenstein: 'the world is just what it seems (and as it seems to an unimaginative man about mid-morning)' (Gellner 1968: 23). The standard-bearer for ordinary language philosophy was this 'unimaginative man at about mid-morning'. This apparently non-problematic model subject (an unspeakable distance away from Sartre's Roquentin) would know that the world around him was solid, that tables could be thumped, that orders were orders, and that any gap between appearance and existence meant you were dealing with a crook. J.L. Austin, however, whose work ordinary language philosophy for the most part was, owned up to the enormous gulf in this anti-system of commonsense philosophising, when he considered what would occur when something out of the ordinary happened to our representative unimaginative subject. Isaiah Berlin tells of a discussion, about counterfactuals and identity, with Austin and others (probably in 1937) as follows:

> the principal example that we chose was the hero of Kafka's story *Meta-morphosis*, a commercial traveller called Gregor Samsa, who wakes one morning to find that he has been transformed into a monstrous cockroach, although he

retains clear memories of his life as an ordinary human being. Are we to speak of him as a man with the body of a cockroach, or as a cockroach with the memories and consciousness of a man? 'Neither', Austin declared. 'In such cases, we should not know what to say. This is when we say "words fail us" and mean this literally. We should need new words. The old ones just would not fit. They aren't meant to cover this kind of case.' (Berlin 1973: 11)

This 'unimaginative man at about mid-morning' is something of an auto-maton, a sociologically acceptable practitioner of dull orthodoxy who knows both the world and his place in it. Now, Gellner suggested some years later that Wittgenstein's *Tractatus*, as a 'poem to solitude', presents a picture of human beings as homogeneous, without framework, links or overlap, meaning that 'Collectivity, community, culture [become] deeply irrelevant to our culture (Gellner 1998: 70). The mass condition and homogeneity of the unimaginative subject, unheeding of differences and the contingency of frameworks, taking the stolidity of community for granted to the extent that it becomes an unnoticed background and therefore a psychological irrelevance, a matter without impact because its impact has ever been the same, is sustained because words do not fail us, because we have never woken up to find skin become carapace (cf. Alasdair Gray's *Lanark* whose main character suffers from 'dragonhide'), and because we are mostly shielded from the disruptions of a war-torn night followed by a tribal dawn.

At this point, there are a number of possibilities. If this conception of the subject is right, social changes during the twentieth century and earlier have not been enough for words and this concept of the commonsense subject to fail us. So we would say that the whole range of 'All that is solid melts into air' formulations have exaggerated matters to this extent, that words have not failed us. Bringing the matter right up to date, we would say that technological, industrial, economic, military, political, scientific and cul-tural events and changes taken all together do not amount to the situation of Gregor Samsa when he would have found that his categories failed him. This is a serious and defensible position to take. It is sociologically impeccable. The unimaginative subject has been gradually accustomed to changes. When they have come as sudden shocks, then maybe words have failed for a short time, but not for long: social institutions do function to deal with even great change. They may show signs of strain; they may evolve; they may decay, but they do not tend to fail catastrophically and irreparably. Inherent in the 'unimaginative man' concept of the subject, which is actually a non-concept, or a version of the sociological denial of the subject, there is, then, the view that socio-historical development up to this point has been subjectively non-ruptural, that events like the colon-isation of America, the development of capitalism, the experience of world war and the emergence of consumer society have not been, at least from the point of view of the experience of the subject, epochal shifters. How this might be explicable has been explored (without this being fully realised) in the philosophy of mind.

Let me start with the case of Mary, a thought-experiment of the Australian philosopher, Frank Jackson. Mary has been developed a little since her first appearance in 1982, but at the beginning she was a brilliant scientist who was working in the neurophysiology of vision. The particular thing about Mary was that, brought up only to see shades of grey, she was then forced to do her work in a black and white room using a black and white television monitor. From that room she finds out everything it is possible to know about the physical events that take place on those occasions when people use colour terms like red and blue, so that she gets a complete set of behavioural and neurophysiological data which enable her to understand what goes on when people use colour terms. The question that Jackson poses is whether Mary will learn anything new when she is let out of her room. His answer is that she will, and the significance of this answer, for Jackson, is that it demonstrates that qualitative experience cannot be entirely rendered in physicalist terms (or, to stretch the point, that experience is not entirely reducible to discourse). Paul Churchland, an uncompromising physicalist, points out that Jackson's conjecture and conclusion repeat the terms of an earlier attempt to deny physicalism by Thomas Nagel, who asked what it might be like to be a bat. Since bats get around by using sonar, and since echo location is not a skill that humans possess, Nagel argued that it is just not possible for us to know what it is like to be a bat, since we do not have access to the first person (as it were) experience of a bat. Again, we have a conceptual construction recognising the possibility of ruptural otherness.

Churchland's rebuttal of the arguments of Nagel and Jackson takes the following form: it may be true that a human cannot know what it is to be a bat, but the reason for that is that humans lack the necessary synaptic connections; and it may be true that Mary has a deficient understanding of colour, but that is because the appropriate synaptic connections were not made because of Mary's environment. For Churchland, neither of the arguments succeeds in showing that there is a realm of existence other than the physical (or, otherwise put, he denies that these arguments show the presence of a rupture in the very being of the human subject). What is interesting about Churchland's position, and indeed the position of most of the protagonists in contemporary debates in the philosophy of mind, is that they are not interested in denying the subject, but are trying to know it rather better than we do at the moment. While they appear mostly to maintain that our 'unimaginative' constitution, with its implicit definitions of the ordinary and its adaptations to the extraordinary, is ultimately an experiential representation of brain states, this has not led them to deny the importance of consciousness. In fact, quite the reverse has happened, with consciousness taking a central place in recent developments in the philosophy of mind. Churchland writes:

> An assumption common to many thinkers, not just to Nagel and Jackson, is that
> the neuroscientific, computational, physicalist approach to human cognition is in

some essential way hostile to the notion of consciousness, and to the unique, first-
person perspective that any creature has, onto itself and onto the world at large.
Although the assumption is widespread, nothing could be farther from the truth.
The explanation of consciousness, both animal and human, is one of the central
hopes of current research in cognitive neurobiology . . . And reconstructing the
intricacies of each creature's unique cognitive perspective on the world is part of
the lasting explanatory obligation that cognitive neurobiology is eager to accept.
(1995: 202)

The position may appear somewhat ironic: a reductionist cognitive
neuroscientist is seemingly more prepared to accept a category of the
subject, at least as a unique first-person perspective, than the sociologists
whose work we have examined. But any such appearance is deceptive.
Churchland's 'subject' is precisely the 'unimaginative man at mid-morning'
who if synaptically reprogrammed[1] could become 'the unimaginative
woman, with different synaptic connections, at mid-afternoon'. Not only
does such a formulation parallel the sociological condition in which the
subject becomes an actor playing out a programmed script, it also repeats
and enables the actor network theoretical postulate that bat actors and
human actors differ only in their network configurations. If sociologists,
drawn by their discipline to deny the relevance of subjectivity, having
stepped away from their traditional philosophical foundations in Kant and
Hegel, were to imagine that a new philosophical underpinning were needed,
then the contemporary philosophy of mind would do very nicely.[2] That, in
general, such a reductionist underpinning philosophy is largely rejected in
the social sciences, despite the parallels which can be drawn between the
philosophy of mind and sociology, is due to the commitment *in both spheres*
to emergent relational realism, to the recognition that abiding connections
can produce new *sui generis* levels of reality; in the cases under discussion
these are the levels of mind and society.[3] However, while the neuroscientists
and philosophers of mind demonstrate that the puzzling nature of the
relation of consciousness to its material substratum is their central concern
(there will be more to say about this when we come to look at the art of
Francis Bacon), there is much less of a concern within sociology for the
connections between subjectivity and social process.

The situation is, then, a contested one. If events and processes like the
institutionalisation of slavery in ancient Greece and the extermination of six
million Jews in the Second World War are seen to rupture and displace the
'unimaginative man', to make this character an anachronism, then the
philosophy of the subject has two tasks: to try to understand the changes in
the subject and to see what, if anything, subsists beneath them. If, however,
the view is taken that such changes are, with relative efficiency, dealt with
by the social shaping of the 'unimaginative man', then the issue of the
subject may be, as I am sure J.L. Austin would have been tempted to point
out, meaningless. One of the main themes of the humanities has been to
resist the social and scientific imposition of meaninglessness, and this has
been done, very largely, by focusing on the works of single individuals:

writers, painters, composers. Here we find that the two levels of subject and society, of individual and mass, are kept together in a permanently self-revising synthesis of a kind that sociology has eschewed more vigorously than even the evangelical reductionists of the philosophy of mind.

Expressionism

In 1911, Wassily Kandinsky said that 'The desire of the future will purely be the expression of the inner meaning' (1977: 30). For the artists who formed a group in Dresden in 1905, calling themselves *Die Brücke* (the Bridge), expression of inner states was both the method and the point of painting. This was not narcissism. When he portrayed himself, as he memorably did in *The Drinker* (1915) and in *Self-Portrait as a Soldier* (1915), Ernst Ludwig Kirchner did so in such a way as to express the world through himself. He wrote of *The Drinker* (see page 76): 'I painted it in Berlin, while screaming military convoys were passing beneath my window day and night' (Dube 1972: 46).[4] The painters of *Die Brücke*, including also Otto Mueller, Erich Heckel and Karl Schmidt-Rottluff,[5] all sought to express their subjective experience of their contemporary world. They were somewhat critical of academic traditions within art history, and their taste for the more direct appeal of African and Oceanic primitivism can be seen at many points. While they recognised the power of elemental natural forces, and although what we now refer to as expressionist literature and film might emphasise the dark side of such forces, Mueller and the early Kirchner expressed a potential for harmony between man, woman and nature. This does, however, come to contrast with the disturbing atmosphere, created by darkening colours, the angularisation of curves, and the geometrical disposition of emphatic figures, which emerges from many paintings, such as Heckel's brooding portraits and landscapes, and Kirchner's Berlin street scenes of 1913–14. As Kuspit puts it, 'Expressionism in general is a kind of abstracting that is deliberately aggressive against reality' (1988: 10).

There were many similarities of approach and temper between works which were being done in the second decade of the twentieth century in Dresden, Munich and Berlin (not to mention Scandinavia[6] and Belgium[7]), with the key link being the representation of the world as it was subjectively seized and the communication of its spirituality through the medium of the freed artist. As Wolf-Dieter Dube, discussing Kandinsky's *Mountain Landscape with Church* (1910) and comparing Munich and Dresden, points out, 'The concentration on the impression made by nature, rather than on the physiognomy of nature itself, was intended in both cases to intensify expression' (1972: 111). There was, however, something else. According to the influential interpretation of Kasimir Edschmid, as expressionism developed its practitioners began to look beyond the impressions to find rather greater significance in their depictions of the world (Roskill 1992: 84). This thesis is attractive but somewhat flawed. The search for transcendence

Ernst Ludwig Kirchner, *The Drinker* (1915)

through the realisation of spirit was there from the beginning, but it was an interior affair. Never social, it was a matter of inner potentiality. As Bahr put it in 1914, 'This is the vital point – that man should find himself again' (Bahr 1992: 119). When Edschmid gave his Berlin lectures in 1917, to search for something that transcended the expressions of militarism, hardship and death, to find some way of genuinely going beyond the trials of embattled life, never to return to them, must have been enormously tempting. Yet it would also have signalled a profound betrayal,[8] a turning away from inner life in one of three directions. The first was toward the artistic scholasticism represented by Kirchner's work from 1929–33, influenced as it was by Picasso's mid-1920s 'classical' period (and repeating, to some extent, the terms of the earlier influence of *Les Demoiselles d'Avignon* on his Berlin *Strassenbilder* of 1913–14). The second direction to be taken was back toward impressionism, the movement against which *Die Brücke* came together, and this turning back toward landscape and light can be seen in Heckel's watercolour landscapes from 1924 through the rest of his life. The third direction is the one which is most usually cited, and is toward what was called the 'new objectivity', exemplified in the position of Otto Dix that the object painted or sculpted had to become primary. Despite the fact that Dix wished to preserve the transforming role of the artist dear to expressionism, the subordination of the artist to what is outside pointed the way to the propaganda battles within German art in the 1930s.

By the end of 1925, subjectivity had been further impressed by politics. Max Beckmann's subjective reactions are portrayed in a mode which we might describe as that of the diabolical caricature. Again, though, and the same will be true of the work of Lovis Corinth and Georg Grosz, the work depicts the artist's apprehension of the world: for Corinth, in a series of memorable paintings, the world and its subjects have slid out of focus; the complexities of corrupt politics drip from Grosz's brush.

It is against this history, presented as though through one small chink in the fence, that we must consider the work of Georg Baselitz, which has been referred to as neo-expressionist. Baselitz himself has rejected this label. His quest for greater levels of intensity (Pagé 1996: 13) takes him, he thinks, beyond a simple engagement between interior and exterior:

People were starting to say that my works had a link with German Expressionism. In fact this only applies to the way I handle the canvas, my manual use of the
canvas. I have never had any relationship with Expressionism. In fact I have
always wondered why it was so alien to me. The reason is that the Expressionists
use a method that illustrates our environment. They use what exists; they extract
from it an illustrative method of making a painting . . . I have always invented the
objects and the various figurations that I wanted to show. I have never had a
model. That is something that has remained entirely alien to me, something that
does not suit me at all. (Baselitz, cited in Waldman 1995: 149–50)

Baselitz thinks that this is something over which he has no control, that the
more he might try to capture something in an intentional kind of way, the
more his work would escape and set itself up as something irremediably
different (Darragon 1996b: 19). Another way of understanding this would be
to say that, for Baselitz, his own work is of a plastic and not a narrative
order (Shiff 1996: 41). Nevertheless, despite Baselitz's distaste for the incor-
porations of academic art history ('What's so great about the enforcement of
a style?' he asks [cited in Waldman 1995: 226]), and despite his strongly held
aversion to narrative and depiction, the link to expressionism does make
some sense,[9] because, no doubt without intending this, Baselitz has been one
of Europe's foremost, if unrecognised, commentators on the contemporary
condition of subjectivity.[10]

Baselitz and the fractured subject

The 'fracture paintings' of Georg Baselitz were produced between 1966 and
1969. They raise, from the very first, the opposition between expression
and reality. The first painting to examine is *B for Larry* (see page 78) and
immediately the issue is clear. Are we looking at an exploded subject, at a
subject blown into discrete and incompatible bits? Is that what *B for Larry*
shows us? Or do we actually misrecognise what is there because it is partly
concealed by camouflage? In this painting, the image is chopped up and
partly obscured. What form of exploration might this be? What is the
trajectory of the subject in works such as this?[11] This is not an isolated
painting, not the only work where the issue of camouflage arises. Calvocoressi
wrote as follows:

> colour organised in non-descriptive bands or blocks, interpenetration of figure
> and landscape, and superimposition of line. The resulting camouflage effect is
> best seen in some of the fracture paintings themselves, where the image of a
> forester, dog, or cow is chopped into disconnected and incompatible segments, or
> is partly obscured by objects such as logs and branches, or by arbitrary strips of
> colour. (Serota and Francis 1983: 14)

Camouflage distorts and conceals what is essentially whole. It hides the
enemy. In these fracture paintings, what is revealed and what is hidden? Is
Baselitz exploring the fragmentation of the unified, one-dimensional,
ultimately totalitarian subject? He shares the legacy of twentieth-century
German history (he was brought up in East Germany), so would it not be

Georg Baselitz, *B for Larry* (1967)

attractive to him to suggest to us that the absolute subject, the one whose orders had to be obeyed, whose ideal follower is the unimaginative man at mid-morning, is gone? Or is it just much more complex? Are we confronting only the appearance of fragmentation? As we look closer, is what appears exploded merely camouflaged? Does the work suggest that the one-subject, one-destiny, one-truth, with all else as barbarism and lies, is just in hiding? Is it waiting to spring out from the undergrowth?

A clue is available: the picture *Die grossen Freunde*. Baselitz produced families of pictures in 1965 and 1966: heroes and partisans whose heads were too small for their bodies, whose clothes were in disarray, whose displacement and bewilderment at their surroundings was clear for all to see, with prominent hands often palm outwards in a gesture almost of supplication. Some of these pictures were exhibited in Hamburg eight years later under the title of *Ein neuer Typ*.[12] The picture which stands at the very head of this group, as its culmination and inspiration, is *Die grossen Freunde* (see page 79). This painting is the beginning of a second mode of exploration into the nature of the subject. In its own way, it expresses fragmentation, fracture, and a view of contemporary subjectivity as divided (the Berlin Wall had not long been in existence). The 'Friends' are ego and id, 'I' and 'me', the least complicated presentation of the anti-Cartesian post-Enlightenment subject. The confidence levels of this individual depend on staying in touch, but the linkage is already broken, and we see no hand in hand, only the actuality of withdrawal and the possibility of future reconnection. When *Die grossen Freunde* was exhibited in 1966, it was accompanied by a manifesto entitled 'Why the picture "The Great Friends" is a good picture':

> The picture is an ideal picture, a gift of God, impossible to ignore – a revelation. The picture is the *idée fixe* of friendship, drawn forth from the Pandemoniac redoubt and well on the way to dropping back into it – in accordance with biographical decree. It is ambiguous, because the canvas has behind it more than could have been meant. The principles of the picture, colour, structure, form, etc., are wild and pure . . . The painter has looked up his own trouserleg and painted his economy onto the canvas. It is good . . . It is hale and hearty, because it does not contain all the signs that would indicate the contrary . . . The picture is free from all doubts. The painter has, in all due responsibility, held a social parade. (part cited in Muthesius 1990: 83)

Georg Baselitz, Die grossen Freunde
(1966)

Wieland Schmied, surveying developments in German art in this century, put the case as follows: '[Baselitz] was trying to create pictures with an inherent monumentality which would fit in with the history of significant Western painting and yet be contemporary in every detail' (Schmied 1985: 66–7), but there is a much more revealing view. Baselitz does fall into the category of neo-expressionism at this point because the theme of his work is the hero. In Baselitz's pictures, however, the hero has become bewildered and displaced. This is the European condition of revolutionary Russia or Germany in 1945: a soldier wandering from place to place in disarray, a world-shattering atomic physicist whose life is spared for a packet of cigarettes, very much post-Nietzschean figures. Baselitz was being simultaneously pedagogic and ironic in the manifesto which accompanied *Die grossen Freunde*. His final words, in the manifesto, are: 'The picture is free from all doubts. The painter has, in all due responsibility, held a social parade.' But, of course, the picture is full of doubt, and the focus of this doubt is the broken subject.[13] The diagnosis of the health of the picture, which Baselitz gives us, is subversive, with Baselitz obsessively wondering if the 'healthy' are really diseased. I am hale and hearty, he suggests, and if you are like me, and as fragmented as history, then let me see your regression, your distortion, the multiple conditions of your body, and the disarray of the things you carry with you. As it was put in the Second Pandemonium Manifesto (the second of two iconoclastic statements on art produced by Baselitz and Eugen Schönebeck in 1961 and 1962), 'No impossible leadership without a hidden malady. Constant renewal of the toxins' (Baselitz and Schönebeck 1992: 624). The vision which comes to him as a result of this call is too fragmented to be representable, and too real and specific to be rendered in abstract terms. His art will be simultaneously abstracted and figurative. Baselitz's post-pandemonium production of neo-expressionist art depicts the state of modern subjectivity, and comments on the ended utopian illusions of integration, coherence, adaptability, connectability and completeness.[14]

Let me repeat my question: is Baselitz exploring the fragmentation of the unified, one-dimensional, totalitarian subject; is he telling us that the one subject is gone, and a good thing too!! Or does the work suggest that the one-subject, one-destiny, one-truth, with all else as barbarism and lies, is just in hiding? Is it waiting to spring out from the undergrowth? The answer that we have thus far is that the fracture paintings are explorations of fragmentation as a given. The unified subject is gone, leaked down the

drain. *Die grossen Freunde* and the manifesto accompanying it are out-
growths of splitting, distortion and becoming unwholesomely physical, as
condition of being. To underline this, a comment from *Pandemonium 1*,
written by Baselitz and Schönebeck in 1961:

> In my eyes can be seen the altar of nature, the sacrifice of flesh, bits of food in the
> drain, evaporation from the bedclothes, bleeding from stumps and aerial roots,
> oriental light on the pearly teeth of lovely women, gristle, negative shapes, spots
> of shadow, drops of wax, parades of epileptics, orchestrations of the flatulent,
> warty, mushy, and jellyfishy beings, bodily members, braided erectile tissue,
> mouldy dough, gristly growths in a desert landscape. (Baselitz and Schönebeck
> 1992: 622)

If postmodern art is, at least in part, defined by a weakened subject and
the pluralisation of perspectives which admit of no metanarrative overview,
then, as Anthony d'Offay said in 1985, with Baselitz, 'German painting
stepped unnoticed into postmodernism'. The fracture paintings are a continuation of, and a turning within, work undertaken without the reassur-
ance of either self-identity or teleological history.

The fracture paintings as a source of insights into the contemporary
condition of the weakened subject are, at this point, far from exhausted.
Even though the postmodern subject, as intimated in the paintings we have
considered, is fragmented or fractured, this does not mean that harmony or
reconciliation is out of the question. *Die grossen Freunde* may be a split
image of the same fragmented subject, whose two parts do not fit together,
but they are *Die grossen Freunde*. When Ulrich Weisner interviewed him in
1985, Baselitz put it like this:

> Harmony consists in tension. It requires a variety of elements. And if you
> establish a rapport between these elements, you get harmony. But you can only
> achieve this via disharmony. Everything which you see and which you think is
> right corresponds to this sense of harmony and unison. But as an artist, you can't
> work with harmony: you can't use a harmonious result which someone else has
> worked towards and achieved. You can only use it by destroying it. There are any
> number of books about this: Kandinsky, Malevich, Baumeister and Nay devised
> theories with the aim of achieving harmony through co-ordination. You can read
> their writings. And when you've finished reading them, you have to do something
> entirely different in order to make your own pictures. This means you have to
> destroy these harmonies. The effect of destruction is brief, arbitrary and short-
> lived. What lives on is the result because it establishes a new harmony. (cited in
> Muthesius 1990: 32–3)

Doubtless this statement catches Baselitz in optimistic mood. It does illustrate, however, that acceptance of a fractured self need not lead into
existential nightmare.[15]

At its very simplest, the advent of postmodernity signifies recognition of
an irreparable fracture within the global ontology of the social. The dream
of the great religions, as secularised by Hegel and Marx, that the original
alienation of the subject would be finally repaired with the arrival of a
perfectly coherent state of collective being, is now hardly credible. In actual
practice, postmodern discourse has been developing on the basis that there

Georg Baselitz, *MMM in G and A*
(1962–7)

are multiple fractures, and so a boundless plurality of more or less independent sites of modally empowered cultural difference. If one wished, in these circumstances, to model, in its simplest form, contemporary subjectivity, then the model advanced would be composed of two misfitting parts with an edge between them. Such a model would suggest that the key task is to establish what contingent harmonies could be achieved between the two parts Such a model might form the starting point for a postmodern psychology. Baselitz's exploration of fracture pointed in this direction.

In Lyotard's terms, *MMM in G and A* by Georg Baselitz is clearly a figural work, a painting which resists easy analysis through the application of conceptual oppositions. It is, in other words, an evocation of depth and radical heterogeneity. When something resists conceptual analysis through the rule of oppositions, then we may suspect that what is at issue is a complex object which is multiply and heterogeneously layered. An analytical approach to such complexity will be to seek reduction (as we saw in the case of the philosophy of mind). A *figural* approach is something else. At the very least it will involve two very different orders of things (otherwise there would be no genuine complexity, no real depth). Lyotard writes about art and effectively argues against the imperialism of both sociology and reductive neurobiology, as follows:

> The position of art is a denial of the position of discourse. The position of art indicates a function of the position of the figure . . . the transcendence of the symbol is the figure, that is to say a spatial manifestation which linguistic space cannot incorporate without being overthrown, an exteriority which cannot be interiorized as a *signification*. Art is posed otherwise, as plasticity and desire, curved extension, in the face of invariance and reason. (Readings 1991: 24–5, original emphasis)

In *MMM in G and A*, no simple slide across is going to make these two pieces fit. In fact, a more likely manoeuvre will be to slide the bottom half *forward*, and already we can see that we confront an instance of considerable complexity. There is no camouflage here, no hiding the fact that this is a pared down representation of the simplest postmodern self. The harmony that can be established between these notional halves is not something that can be pre-judged. There is no rule. It is a question of performance, of making the event, of sliding forward and about to see what

Georg Baselitz, *Kullervo's Feet* (1967)

happens. It is a precarious business. Yet this is the simplest case. *Kullervo's Feet* will be that much more complex.

With this painting, we can begin to grasp what is at issue in admitting the impossibility of pre-figuring the future. Who could say what contingent harmonies can be established here? Recognition of the figural means realising that there will be lines that are hard to cross, and that there will be tasks which will never be ended, and that there may be points of zero contact even between contiguous fields. This would be a series of hard political lessons at either micro- or macro-level, lessons which sociologists would be bound to reject.

Baselitz has always claimed that his work is for him entirely existent within the confines of the canvas, and that he has no interest in being symbolic, only in making pictures. He said, 'I have always seen my paintings as independent of meanings with regard to contents – and also independent from associations that could result from them' (cited in Calvocoressi 1985: 894). Despite or even because of this, the horizontal lines through *MMM in G and A* and *Kullervo's Feet* provide an ontological structure for which there was neither warrant nor argument. It is obvious, in retrospect, that the structure would be exceeded in very short order, and so it turned out. Other geometries emerge. Superimposition of layer upon layer adds to the mounting complexity, as we can see with *Woodmen*. It is significant that all of the fracture paintings are paintings on paintings. Baselitz never worked with a blank canvas. Jablonka's commentary on *Woodmen* is relevant:

> Here not only is the function of the edge of the painting illustrated in the centre of the painting by cutting off the image; the edge itself is painted, at the border of the pictorial field, and manifests itself as an interruption of what is painted on the canvas. The initial painting is clearly seen as a thin layer of paint, or else an accumulation of layers of paint. The vulnerability of this layer is made clear in terms of content: the legs of one of the three walking figures seem to pierce through the black paint surface. (Jablonka 1982: 16)

This effect of triple canvassing, of painting on painting on painting, of being on being on being, is so exquisitely connectable to the complex heterogeneity of postmodern being that it is at first hard to understand Baselitz's next move. Let us conclude, at this point, that the fracture paintings of Georg Baselitz are not paranoid, that they do not envisage the

Georg Baselitz, *Woodmen* (1968)

enemy – as a whole, autonomous, self-sufficient but ravaging being – lurking, half hidden in the undergrowth, that the whole and self-sufficient stranger, as either life or death force, is just as much a myth as the supreme self which, when raised to the nth power, founds Western visions of God, that neither God nor the stranger is concealed in the trees. Then, after exploding his *Heroes*, guillotining the *Partisans* and superimposing his subjects on themselves to the point where they burst through themselves, why, from 1969 are the trees (his first inverted painting was titled *The Forest on its Head*), and subsequently the heads and torsos, painted upside down?

Inversion

Baselitz said that it was a matter of retaining content but escaping representation, keeping the subject without being ruled by it:

> The object expresses nothing at all. Painting is not a means to an end. On the contrary, painting is autonomous. And I said to myself: if this is the case, then I must take everything which has been made an object of painting – landscape, the portrait, and the nude, for example – and paint it upside-down. That is the best way to liberate representation from content. (Baselitz cited in Muthesius 1990: 88)[16]

Confused echoes of expressionism are most strong here, since, like his *Heroes*, the artist can no longer have confidence in his faculties. The subject in the second half of the twentieth century, with its socially constructed certainties of touch and accomplishment, has to be disassembled. Here we have the very opposite of Bourdieu's repudiation of the subject: now we are dealing with the arrogance of the twentieth-century subject: an approach to the subject from the other end, so to speak. The fracture paintings express the condition of the subject; the practice of inversion is the artist's response. To liberate his work from the tyranny of the false unity of the perceiving ego, Baselitz will express through his brushes what the object does not express by itself (because self-defeating, disingenuously unified, and blinded subjectivity gets in the way, providing a false clarity founded upon a history of successful interpellations – scientific, political, ethical, aesthetic). He will find a freer form of expression through this attempt to evade the false simplicity of the object. To put this another way, inversion removes the conceit that a broken ego can find unity for just long enough to banish the distance between the world and its representation. Turning the world upside down was an outrageously brilliant step beyond the fracture paintings. While the fractures expressed the condition of the contemporary subject in terms of a psycho-ontology of disconnection, they did not pose the problem of how to be an artist in the lived realisation of that fragmentation, nor how to extend a narrative as a fragmented subject existing over time. The response to both dilemmas is inversion. Mistrust of the fragmented ego as a mirror of the world leads to Baselitz's practice of painting upside down, which allows him simultaneously to mistrust and express, inversion constituting the liberation of representation from the arrogant assumption that a unified ego can grasp its objects entire with an angel's touch. In the second place, inversion frees the painting from the draughtsman's contract but keeps and even extends its potential for narrative: inversion will allow Baselitz seriality without requiring commitment to continuity, causation or succession.

Georg Baselitz, *Portrait of Kasper and Ilka König* (1971)

It was also, he said, a way of giving him the freedom 'to concentrate on painterly problems'. Adriani presents an account of the logic of this inversion which makes the issue of technique just as important as the reduction of the subject. Baselitz would surely approve:

> With reality turned upside down, inversion becomes a way for Baselitz to point out specifically the irreal nature of the picture's meaning . . . Without the usual recognition effect, the motif's relevance is now its painterly and graphic qualities. Although it most definitely has been subject to deliberation in its function as a personal statement, inversion successfully allows it to slip through the clutches of interpretation . . . Inversion, which can be as unspectacular a process as the choice of a meaningless subject, means that certain expectant attitudes cannot get 'hold' of the subject matter in the usual way: the renunciation of illusionism by quasi-illusionistic, figurative means. (Adriani 1994)

The fact that Baselitz found inversion to be a way to focus on painting, and to retain the subjective point of view without simply repeating its illusions, will not be in dispute. Indeed, it is a core argument of this entire book that it is possible to retain the subject without falling prey to its formerly constitutive illusions.[17] But we must test out the ability of inversion as a way of delivering what Baselitz hoped for.

The first alternative account of inversion which offers itself is less than charitable. It is that Baselitz has moved beyond profound, albeit unreflective, exploration of the contemporary subject and its world. This movement, however, has been a regression, a switch into gimmickry which does not transcend the traditional mechanisms of ego's mastery. This critical dismissal comes from a powerful source. In 1982, the American artist Joseph Kosuth presented an exhibition entitled Cathexis at the Leo Castelli Gallery in New York. This was a development from an installation at the Staatsgalerie in Stuttgart in late 1981. Accompanying the exhibition in New York was an essay, entitled 'Notes on *Cathexis*'. Both in Stuttgart and in New York, the key manoeuvre was the presentation of inverted part-images accompanied by didactic text. In the accompanying text, Kosuth wrote:

> When viewed 'normally' the fictive space of the painting permits the viewer an entrance to a credible world; it is the power of the order and rationality of that world which forces the viewer to accept the painting (*and* its world) on its own terms. Those 'terms' cannot be read because they are left unseen: the world, and the art which presents it, is presented as 'natural' and unproblematic. Turning the image 'upside-down' stops that monologue; one no longer has a 'window to another world', one has an object, an artefact, composed of parts and located here in this world. One experiences this as an *event*, and as such it is an act which locates and includes the viewer. (Kosuth 1991: 200)

Kosuth, then, requires an art of inversion to do two things: to break the natural order of automatic understanding *and* to force the viewer to participate in an event. It is clear enough that Baselitz's inversions do the first of these things. It is, however, also pretty clear that Kosuth thinks they do not do the second (Kosuth writes dismissively of those who would see his practice of inversion in relation to Baselitz [1991: 199]). Kosuth's characterization of the difference between them is accurate. Baselitz inverts as a matter of existential and technical exploration; Kosuth did so as an educator, sociologically committed to collective subjectivity, while Baselitz strongly believes that the artist has no social responsibility (Darragon 1996a: 104).

There is a second critique. Doesn't Heidegger's critique of Nietzsche's response to metaphysics provide a model for the elimination of any false hopes that inversion can provide a fundamental advance out of the given structure which itself appears to spawn the need for the desired transcendence? For example, does the structure of oppression change if the roles of slave and master are turned upside down? Heidegger argues that

> as a mere countermovement it necessarily remains, as does everything 'anti', held fast in the essence of that over against which it moves. Nietzsche's countermovement against metaphysics is, as the mere turning upside down of metaphysics, an inextricable entanglement in metaphysics. (Heidegger, 1977: 61)

This double critique of Baselitz's strategy of inversion – that it does not involve the viewer, except by a bedazzling focus on one aspect of a complex problematic, and that inversion merely perpetuates the given structural context, which remains the same before and after the turnabout – must be addressed. The first critique is Hegelian in structure, demanding that the movement of the existential condition can only be grasped totalistically, that it cannot be explored bit by bit, and hence warning that anything short of total breakthrough will leave us where we started – groping in a dark present unilluminated by a cunning history that will speak only of the past. Kosuth recognised the conundrum, telling his viewers from within the frame of *Cathexis 8*: 'That which presents itself, here, as a whole can only be recognised as a part of something larger (a "picture" out of view) yet too inaccessible for you to find *the* location (a "construction" which has just included you)' (1991: fig. 29). At this point the issue may well be axiological: a clear choice between the risks of bedazzlement, due to a solar focus on a recognisably bounded phenomenon, and the perpetual postponements of gnosticism, with its promise of the whole. As for the second critique, does it not miss a crucial practical point, which is that inversion may be used as a strategy for declaring captivity within 'the essence of that over against which it moves'? It is precisely when the performances of oppressor and oppressed are inverted that the structure of oppression becomes starkly visible.

When the work and standpoint of Baselitz are measured in the light of these two criticisms, what becomes apparent is a certain modesty of ambition. This modest witness does not aspire to form or reveal a new totality, nor does he give a series of promises concerning what inversion will achieve. Sometimes the reticence may even be overstated. In 1983, Baselitz said, 'The artist is not responsible to anyone . . . his only responsibility consists in an attitude to the work . . . no communication with any public whatsoever' (Gablik 1991: 61). Suzi Gablik astutely identifies the myth of the autonomous male artist behind this statement, while Shiff's discussion of the apparent contradiction between claiming to be outside of society while at the same time thematising, for example, the destruction of Dresden in a series of twenty works from 1989 entitled *'45*, is inconclusive, ending with the somewhat dogmatic view that the pictorial language game is all that matters (Shiff 1996: 41–3). But there are other perspectives: that of the modest witness, and also that deriving from Spivak's Kantian distinction between critical and dogmatic practice, where 'critical' means 'a philosophy that is aware of the limits of knowing' and 'dogmatic' means the presentation of 'coherent general principles without sufficient interest in empirical details' (Spivak 1991: 25).

What consideration of the two general critiques of inversion shows is that with Baselitz the concern with 'the limits of knowing' characterises the work as it moves from fracture into inversion. If we can now see that Baselitz's focus on the inverted figure draws us, even a shade uncritically, to his shining picture book parade of weak subjects, and if we also know that there is no easy theoretical gesture of refusal available to us, then perhaps we have to engage in a certain form of being that allows being critical in a state of bedazzlement. We have Baselitz's own view:

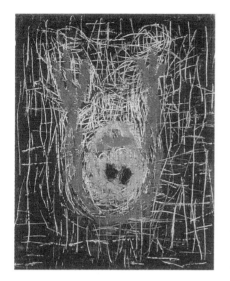
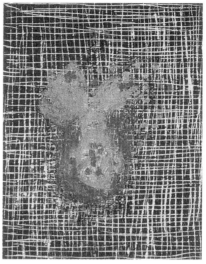
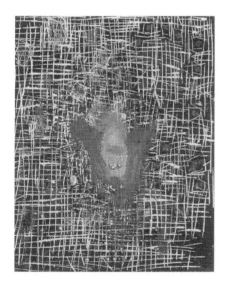

Georg Baselitz, *'45* (panels 1,2,11,12 – 1989)

Baselitz states that he never painted representationally, in the traditional, illustrative sense. His theme is painting itself, and the motifs recognisable in his pictures merely denote a certain already established genre – still life, nude, or landscape. In 1969, Baselitz's procedure led him, quite logically, to rotate the subjects he had retained as a point of departure 180 degrees in order to divest them of content, of conventional significance. Since then he has continually developed new, sometimes dazzling possibilities in shaping his pictorial syntax. 'What matters in painting,' he says, 'is not the content factor, but visual invention . . . the necessity of the pictorial structure.' (Schilling, 1989: 48)

Baselitz and the history of art

How seriously must we take Baselitz's view that his work is just about pictorial structure, that he refuses the significance of content and meaning for his own elaboration of his work? It should first be noted that Baselitz does not comment on the significance of his individual works. He does acknowledge in general that his practice would be inconceivable without some sense of history (Darragon 1996a: 18). He has never said that there is something improper in the search for meaning within the works that he has made. In short, the elucidation of meaning is not the artist's function; it is for someone else. For Baselitz, the work is contained within the realms of the painter's equipment: canvas, paint and mind:

When I crawl around on the canvas and squeeze out the paint, I know what I am doing but I don't know what it is that I am doing . . . What happens on the canvas happens because it is important, and because it has to happen, but I have no adequate explanation for it. (Baselitz cited in Waldman 1995: 202)

The social is locked out of this equation. Art historians have, however, sought to link him to the history of art, seeking, as yet without conspicuous success, to type his work within the conventional narrative of the history of painting schools. As well as the link to expressionism, which we have considered, there have also been attempts to demonstrate his connection to mannerism, to romanticism, and to the Christian iconography of inversion.

The style of art known as mannerism was most influential through the sixteenth century. Kuspit puts the case as follows:

Baselitz's early figures are clearly constructed according to a mannerist aesthetic. The principle of small heads and large, long bodies usually holds . . . The upside-downness of his later heads is . . . a grimmer way of pulling the figure apart, of stretching it on the mannerist rack. And the harsh painterliness is a final mannerist violation of the figure, another way of pushing it to the limit of self-contradiction and of affirming its non-naturalness – its lack of conformity to any normative conception. Baselitz's mannerism articulates a fundamental anti-harmony. (1988: 14)

Mannerism is usually understood as a rather loosely defined distancing from Renaissance clarity which took place in painting in the thick middle of the sixteenth century. Against a background of social and religious unrest, and led by the tentative quasi-expressionist explorations of late Michelangelo, Italian painting became somewhat stylised and dramatic, especially in the

Parmigianino (1503–40), *Lady with Three Children*

work of Tintoretto, Parmigianino and Bronzino. Tintoretto's *The Stealing of the Body of St Mark* (Accademia Galleries, Venice) demonstrates the search for effects of light, as does the work of a painter much influenced by him – El Greco, whose *Christ Driving the Traders from the Temple* (National Gallery, London) also shows the small heads and long bodies mentioned above, a variation of which can be seen in the combination of small head and large body to be found in Parmigianino's *Lady with Three Children* (Prado, Madrid). We also know that Baselitz had declared an interest in the excesses of mannerism in the first of the *Pandemonium Manifestos* (Waldman 1995: 27) and that he spent six months in Florence in 1965, and was influenced by the mannerist work with which he came into contact there. Whether, however, we can say that Kuspit is right, and that mannerism is a matter of violating the figure, so that 'the upside-downness of the later heads' is a mannerist gesture, is not clear. There is certainly a set of links which are of interest, but do they tell us more than the pictures themselves, when set in the context of their contemporary audience? To try and answer this, we should consider the head.

The head is a major theme in the work of Georg Baselitz, but whereas the physicalists in the philosophy of mind deploy the reductionist language of synaptic connections, as the sociologists conceptualise the agent as a matter of social connections, in order to explain and enframe, it is difficult to see Baselitz's approach as similarly demystifying or as having a desire for objective singularity. Baselitz's work is neither portraiture in the great tradition, nor is it consciously philosophical in the way that is represented by Magritte. In terms of painting, it is technically much closer to the work of Bacon, being about the struggle with the medium and its aleatory outcomes, with the expressionist result that conscious method produces results which stand on their own ground. Baselitz commented upon this as follows:

> The first pictures where I used figuration, or shall we say, with concrete visual material, the first that were concrete in my mind . . . weren't heads in the sense of portraits but instead something like pictures with a concoction of colours and in the centre of this a head that became increasingly precise from picture to picture . . . the simplest way to realise an idea is to do a head . . . The head is never a portrait, it is simply the vehicle for my artistic idea. (Baselitz 1987, cited in Adriani 1994)

Georg Baselitz, *Die Elbe* (1990)

This artistic idea is not carefully pre-conceptualised, but when Baselitz says that 'there is only the accident – exclusively' (Darragon 1996b: 48), he goes on to explain that, once having placed himself in a position to be provoked by the accidents inherent in the relationship between himself and his materials, then the accident will be provocative.

If we compare his painting and his sculpture, for example *Self-Portrait I* (1996), the wall of twenty inverted head pictures, shown at Martin-Gropius-Bau in Berlin in 1991, and at the 1996–7 exhibition at the Musée de l'Art Moderne de la Ville de Paris, and two wood sculptures from the Dresden Women series, *The Sick Woman from Radebeul* (1990) and *The Elbe* (1990), what we can see is that inverted painting provides a context for the emergence of the provocative accident, and that emergence in the sculpture is provided for by his tools: axe, chainsaw, knife and paint. We are, to be quite clear, within a context here which is illuminated by the idea of a mannerist aesthetic, by shared notions of excess and distortion of the image, but this capillary art-historical connection requires a highly educated even rarefied hermeneutic to appreciate the comparability of the challenge posed by Pontormo and Parmigianino in their time to Baselitz in ours.

It is certainly possible to philosophise about the difference between the inverted pictures and the conventional elevation of the sculpture. The 'normal', right-way-up orientation of the sculpture disorients the critical-theoretic explanation of the inversions of the painted heads, weakening the neo-Marxist account of inversion that since the world is upside down (with those creating value receiving nothing), the subject must be inverted to gain a proper perspective. Kuspit writes:

> Eristic dialectic involves, in the words of Hegel, entering 'into the strength of the opponent (the petrified or authoritatively given) in order to destroy him from within.' Baselitz's anamorphic scenes and upside-down figures and scenes – extensions of the anamorphic idea, that is, the idea of disturbed, alienated, mad vision that sees the unconscious vision at the moment of seeing it consciously – are inseparable from his eristic, painterly dialectic. The anamorphic image, in its alien flexibility – in its anti-authoritarian character – creates a 'disperspective'

from which the unconscious truth can be 'perceived.' By destroying the point of view and the line of sight, it liberates the perceiver from the control of perspective, emblematic of authoritarian control or social repression in general. (Kuspit 1988: 129)

Here he appeals to a social order to which the subject will belong and which will be the right way up. But this view does not reckon with the sculpture, with the chiselling away of distinctive features of any social order, whichever way up, which laid claim to the subject. The sculpture proclaims that any social order will do violence, and the inverted painting allows him to show the result, while the sculpture allows him to show the process: 'When I took a piece of wood into my hands, I did not want to go in the same direction as the wood, but against the grain. That is fighting back' (Baselitz 1987, cited in Adriani 1994). This 'fighting back', however, is not a political matter (Darragon 1996a: 102). Baselitz thinks that bad art emerges out of the attempt to make a political intervention within the social order, that the 'language' of art and that of politics are separate.

The chainsaws and axes he uses to fashion the wood (Waldman 1995: 97) do not create works of propaganda. It is hardly even appropriate to call what emerges a finished result, although there is a sense of task and goal implied in Baselitz's view that 'Sculpture is a shorter path to express the same problem [of appearance, volume, figure/ground] than painting; it's more brutal and primitive than painting, which has a certain reserve' (cited in Laffon 1996: 15). Waldman even notes that while painting is a matter of illusion, with sculpture there is a more direct connection to the real (Waldman 1995: 107). But *Scheibenkopf* (1986), a wooden head with entirely hollowed through eyes, and *G-Kopf* (1987), a crude, hewn head with 'Death-Star' shuttering, almost on a planetary scale, offer the kind of insight into the formation of the subject which insists that the violence of the process is often unbearable. It is the sculptural equivalent of the ordeal which we will see Julie undergo in *Three Colours: Blue*. This is work on an existential plane. As he says, 'I think that the existential is more important than the cultural' (Darragon 1996a: 82). This does not mean that he is only engaged on the existential level. He has a strong interest in the history of art, shown, for example, in the two paintings bought for the new Reichstag, which were inspired by Caspar David Friedrich (*Friedrich's Frau am Abgrund* and *Friedrich's Melancholie*). Baselitz is also very well aware of what it means for him to be a northern, specifically German, rather than a Latin artist. In the end, however, his major theme is the underfocused, partially formed subject struggling with probably necessary and unavoidable, but nevertheless alien cultural and historical forces. Does this mean that the contemporary labelling of Baselitz as a neo-romantic, then, has something to offer for an understanding of his work? While being quite clear that his notion of romanticism is very far from any conventional school, he does seem to allow some validity to this designation, saying:

In Germany there is an idea of Romanticism which has a quite different sense from what is meant by that term in France, where it is understood as being playful, dreamlike and sentimental. But if we look more closely at Romanticism, it can be seen that there is something revolutionary about it, something very clear and profound. (Darragon 1996a: 82–3)

The public announcement that the works of Caspar David Friedrich, the German romantic painter, had inspired the two works that Baselitz had painted for the new Reichstag seemed to confirm the general understanding within the German art establishment that he does fit into the scholarly definitions of German romanticism advanced, for example, by Willi Geismeier, and this seems borne out when these pictures are set against a painting like Karl Blechen's *Gotische Kirchenruine* and other similar pictures showing a dramatic contrast between the vulnerable but somehow ineffably promising human subject and the giant overpowering forces of nature and/or culture.

If we look to the right-hand panel of Bacon's *Three Studies for a Crucifixion* (see page 104), described by Michael Peppiat as 'a sublimation of personal pain in the most universally recognisable symbol of human suffering' (Peppiat 1996: 191), we find Richard Calvocoressi (1985) linking this reference to inverted crucifixion to Baselitz's 1969 studies from the Masaccio *Crucifixion of the Apostle Peter*, and almost wondering to what extent Baselitz's practice of inversion has its origin in the death of St Peter and other examples of abjection and death through inversion. While it is true that Baselitz painted some of the *Stations of the Cross* in 1983 and 1984, it seems likely that when we look across the whole of Baselitz's *oeuvre*, these images from Christian iconography were more resource for his work than origin of his turn to inversion in 1969. But what does hold these images together is his neo-romantic thematic of weak but abiding and finally triumphant subjectivity in the face of overwhelming forces.

Calvocoressi suggests that it is part of Baselitz's art 'to undermine the individuality of his subject and purge it of any emotional connotation (1985: 894), but this surely cannot be sustained. What Baselitz paints and sculpts are partial subjects faced with solitude as incompleteness and being with others as trial of transcendence (as Baselitz noted whilst engaged in studying the poetry of the gallows: 'One sees differently from up there' [cited in Darragon 1996b: 31]). As a final illustration of the lack of clarity but finally undeniable presence of pure but incomplete human existence, his continuing series of pictures in the 1990s, the *Bild* series,[18] for example *Bildzweiundzwanzig* (1993) and *Bildneunundzwanzig* (1994) overlay the subject with the pain and confusion of being with others.[19] However, as is evident from his published writings and interviews, Baselitz himself, while allowing that these works are in some sense a return to the theme of the *Heroes* of the 1960s, does not feel it to be his proper function to make such claims about the meaning of his work – even to the extent of confirming that *Bildsechzehn* (1993) is a reworking of *Die grossen Freunde* – except through his work, in the form, for instance of *The Background Story* (1996), which finally will have – as Baselitz would want – to speak for itself.

Baselitz and the subject

Georg Baselitz, *The Background Story*, 1996.

Baselitz is caught in the space between expressionism and 'New Objectivity' (*neue Sachlichkeit*) (Waldman 1995: 12). He did not feel that the expressionist tradition as he saw it was meaningful for him, and he was distanced from *neue Sachlichkeit* for just the same reason – its thematisation of exteriority (Waldman 1995: 12). He gives primacy to colour, form, figure and ground, and is self-enclosed in the language game of his own plastic art. It is tempting to say that he also allows his own untutored, uncontrolled self, derailed by inversion, sculptural violence and refusal of detachment, to leak onto the canvas or into the wood. This, however, would be to impute a causal link between Baselitz's subjectivity and his art which he denies, and in this he is quite right to suggest that such an explanation, even if correct, would be beside the point. Imagining, perhaps here moving into the frame of reference shared by sociology and the philosophy of mind, that such links were made, they would not compromise the *sui generis* impact of Baselitz's *oeuvre*, of the subject-affirmation which suffuses his work. Waldman suggests that Baselitz has moved from the tragedy inherent in the world, expressed in his early and provocative work, to the discomfort of necessary assimilation in his work in the 1990s (Waldman 1995: 172). All through, however, there is a sense of side by side, of *Die grossen Freunde*, of the relationship between subject and society as contested adjacency:

> I believe that my work consists in solely letting myself out of myself so that I can work. So I vanish, stand next to it, and leave the field to the person who has been trained by me to work it. This proceeds smoothly and successfully as long as I focus on filling and stopping up all untight places, such as rips and holes in my head, making sure that nothing I think gets lost. However, it's more important to keep my head free of those influences, insinuations, ideologies, doctrines, all the crap that people believe is the connection to the world. I'm downright afflicted with a very strong disbelief. I'm not willing to join the chorus. I think that the artist's asocial behaviour is the only guarantee . . . (Baselitz in Waldman 1995: 234)

That last sentence concludes ' . . . that at least paintings will be saved from destruction.' The spirit of his work, however, from the beginning, is the thought that at least something of himself, and of us, will be saved from social dissolution, from the unspeakably strong forces of social incorporation, which, as far as we can tell, and we should hope, will always conjure up counter-appearance as resistance on the second panel of the diptych.

Notes

1. Can theories of learning be reconceptualised as synaptic reprogramming? The standard neuroscientific position is that they can. An interesting case study might be that of the treatment of phantom limb pain pioneered by Ramachandran, in which control over a phantom limb is restored by getting the patient to place their real limb into an enclosure in which mirrors are used to create the image of the other limb, thereby allowing the patient to alter the configuration of the phantom limb by unclenching a fist (important for some motorcycle accident victims whose physical hand-memory of grasping the handlebars is strongly 'imprinted' in their minds) or repositioning an arm. While the effectiveness of Ramachandran's 'virtual reality box' has been challenged by Ronald Melzack as due to a simple placebo effect, nevertheless other researchers, such as Peter Halligan, in Oxford, are finding that at least temporary relief can be obtained by the use of the mirror box. The relief achieved is welcomed by the subject of the (if this is what it is) synaptic reprogramming.

2. Ramachandran, looking at the condition known as 'Alice in Wonderland syndrome', where patients (usually sufferers from severe migraines) feel they have grown very tall or very small, and speculating that this might be due to partial interruption of blood supply to some parts of the brain but not others, wonders whether this does not indicate that body image is merely a construct, functioning at the end of the day to enable reproduction of the species. This interplay of Darwinism and constructionism has become the default position within neuroscience and the philosophy of mind. The work done with phantom limb patients to ease their pain, in some cases by implanting electrodes under the skull, on the surface of the brain itself, is brilliant medicine underpinned by its usual behaviourist, stimulus–response, cause and effect philosophy. This is not something to criticise, for how can the philosophy of repair work and improvement be otherwise? Thus those who might be sceptical of a return to behaviourism within the social sciences *tout court* might ponder the approach of Talcott Parsons to the question of controlled institutional change in Germany after the Second World War, the work of Durkheim on professional associations, and, in general, the dominant approach to the question of 'social problems'. It is only exaggerating a little to say that the *mechanismo* underlying these examples makes it appear somewhat surprising that the replacement of Kant and Hegel, in the field of social theory, has not already been accomplished (although the next note suggests a reason for this).

3. In the philosophy of mind, the clearest case is that of David Chalmers who argues that consciousness should be understood as a basic level of reality, comparable to the four fundamental forces of physics; and while it is not my concern in this book to meditate very much on the 'linguistic turn' in philosophy, it might be noted that the same kind of move, but this time with regard to language and communication, erecting this perspective to the status of an *a posteriori* fundamental, has been made in many places. The following from Habermas (1992: 25) is not untypical: 'everything that earns the name of subjectivity, even if it is a being-familiar-with-oneself, no matter how preliminary, is indebted to the unrelentingly individuating force possessed by the linguistic medium'.

4. Following a period of military service which began in 1914, Kirchner had a breakdown in 1915 which led to a period in a sanatorium.

5. In 1925–6, Kirchner painted a kind of memorial to *Die Brücke*, with his portrayal of himself and the other three. This picture depicts a mood of accusatory reflection. It hangs in the Ludwig Museum, Cologne.

6. In March 1908, Edvard Munch exhibited with *Die Brücke* in Dresden.

7. Flemish expressionism developed at a slower pace than was the case in Dresden. In particular the work of Frits van den Berghe did not really reach maturity until 1924 (with *Sunday* and then with his gouache, *Cinema*, the following year).

8. The movement away from expressionism was not, however, generally seen as a betrayal. Oskar Schlemmer, for example, wrote: 'If today's arts love the machine, technology and organisation, if they aspire to precision and reject anything vague and dreamy, this implies an instinctive repudiation of chaos and a longing to find the form appropriate to our times' (cited in Richie 1998: 341).

9. Paul Crowther (1993: 168) has quite properly noted that the work of Baselitz (together with the work of Kiefer and Morley) serves to undermine any simple attempt at neat categorisation, while other attempts to identify movements in contemporary art, notably the notions of 'Bad painting' and the 'transavantgarde' have also been thought to include Baselitz (Lucie-Smith 1984: 270). Additionally, Craig Owens made the point that neo-expressionism was not a good label, since expressionism was a modernist movement, while the artists generally gathered together under the heading of neo-expressionism 'are engaged . . . in declaring the bankruptcy of the modernist tradition' (Owens 1992: 147). Continuing in the same vein, Hal Foster argued that the neo-expressionism of the 1980s was complicit with the regressive cultural politics of the Reagan–Bush era (Foster 1996: 36); although I am sure that Foster would be the first to admit that such generalisations are almost always rendered problematic when measured in the light of any individual artist's trajectory. Finally, it is worth pointing out that Baselitz refers directly to the expressionists of *Die Brücke* in three major paintings – *Nachtessen in Dresden* and *Brückechor* both from 1983 (to the former of which, as Waldman [1995: 110] has noted, some of his sculpture is related), and *Das Malerbild* of 1987–8 (Waldman 1995: 162); that his 1979–80 *Strassenbild* – a series of eighteen pictures dominated by the idea of a woman watching the street out of her window – is a precise counterpart to Kirchner's *Berlin Street Scenes*; and that his output of printed work in the early 1980s is very clearly marked by the influence of the expressionist tradition as can be seen in the 1992 Tate Gallery exhibition of printed work.

10. Donald Kuspit recognised from the outset the spinal relation between twentieth-century Euro-American art and subjectivity, but his commitment to a certain existential holism, which can be, for him, sustained despite how the world breaks us apart and reveals our imperfections ('one turns to art to satisfy . . . the need for a coherent, unified sense of self': 1988: 547), does shape his deeply knowledgeable analyses of contemporary German art.

11. This is not the question normally posed by art historians. Waldman, for example, notes that the picture was actually a response to the use of colour and form in Jasper Johns's work (Waldman 1995: 67).

12. Fabrice Hergott has provided a precise chronology, which adds to the overall context. According to this view, Baselitz's first work consists of 'enormous heads and derisory portraits and self-portraits. All these figures live an adolescence dominated by violence and disgust, an existential nausea in which the exterior world and the interior world are confused . . . This violence matches the violence done to himself as a German . . . He has become autistic by making the manipulation of his body the activity that allows him to bear reality . . . This sombre period of his work is the ground from which his future works will grow . . . He then paints the *Heroes*, the soldiers he had seen wandering a few years after the end of the war . . . In 1966, the series of paintings entitled *Friends* splits the *Hero* figure into two. A new dynamism thus appears, a sort of euphoria that replaces the autism of the repressed soldiers and finds itself relieved of the burden of his solitude' (1997: 107–13).

13. Siegfried Gohr has an optimistic view of *Die grossen Freunde*, finding that it symbolises the awakening of creative genius (Waldman 1996: 48). Waldman points out that the theme of the hero inflects all of Baselitz's subsequent work (ibid.: 56).

14. This is naturally not the only way to interpret Baselitz's work. For example, *Die grossen Freunde* is also readable as an effect of the artist's unconscious. Interpreting the picture from this perspective allows us to see the two figures as two different views of an incompleteness, of the case study in irreconcilability which the postmodern self now appears to be. As Julia Kristeva has written: 'The foreigner is within us. And when we flee from or struggle against the foreigner, we are fighting our unconscious' (Kristeva, 1991: 191).

15. A similarly positive approach to the problem of postmodern fracture has been taken by Jean-François Lyotard, who did not regard difference as entirely disabling. Lyotard may have

made a misjudgement, at some time between June 1978 and July 1980, in the thinking that led up to his decision that the only indubitable object of his phrasing could be the phrase itself. His reasoning paralleled that of Descartes: just as the thinking being thinks even when utterly deceived, and thereby finds certainty in the fact of thinking itself, so did Lyotard realise that to doubt that one phrases is still to phrase. However, perhaps a gain in confidence, thereby achieved, allowed Lyotard to develop his concept of the differend. So, while it can be argued that the concept of the differend could have been invested with much more energy had it not emerged from an outdated Cartesianism, the concept of the differend is (just as with Baselitz's notion of harmony) a sign of hope and aspiration in what can be seen as spiritless times.

16. As he put it elsewhere in 1981, 'The sole issue is my possibility of painting a picture. In a nonsupportive culture, a destructive artist is capable of analysis. An object painted upside down is suitable for painting because it is unsuitable as an object. I have no notion about the solidity of the depiction. I don't correct the rightness of the depiction. My relationship to the object is arbitrary. The painting is methodically organised by an aggressive, dissonant reversal of the ornamentation. Harmony is knocked out of whack. A further limit is reached' (in Waldman 1995: 214).

17. Baselitz started in the 1990s, like Jackson Pollock, to paint on the floor. This prevented him from stepping back to see his work in progress in its entirety – another way of refusing illusionistic ego-mastery.

18. This series painted between April 1991 and December 1995 began with *Bildeins*, but Baselitz was unhappy with it and overpainted it. Hence the series begins with *Bildübereins*. As Darragon notes, Baselitz was aware of the fact that he was undertaking some form of meditation on the *Heroes*, but was also locked inside the closed system of this series (Darragon 1996b: 27–8).

19. Waldman's view is more anodyne: that the 1990s heroes have been emptied out and are ready to take on new meanings (Waldman 1995: 190).

5

CARNALITY AND POWER: THE HUMAN SUBJECT IN THE WORK OF FRANCIS BACON

In 1966, Bacon said, 'We are meat, we are potential carcasses. If I go into a butcher's shop I always think it's surprising that I wasn't there instead of the animal' (Sylvester 1980: 46). This is a frequently cited comment, which might be taken in two ways. Either we are all meat, disembowelled, de-veined, sliced into manageable lumps and destined to be grilled or to decompose; as Deleuze puts it in his study of Bacon, 'Have pity for meat . . . everyone who suffers is meat' (Deleuze 1984: 20). Or we are animal, not now in the sense of being herded, slaughtered, plucked and preserved, but as a bundle of muscle, flesh, nerve and sensation. These two registers, of power and submission and of physical flux, are the lines toward an understanding of Bacon's presentation of the contemporary subject. They are sometimes blurred, and, of course, other themes will intervene, but in what follows we will first explore the question of power, and then the issue of flesh. We will find that in Bacon's work the fundamental condition of the human subject is undecidable between these two conditions – that of the primal social scene and that of the mobile body. This undecidability manifests itself as a supplementation, with the physical presence of the body flooding over the boundaries of strictly social relations, and with issues of power emerging to cloud any simple view of the body as muscle and movement. The conse-quence of this ontological undecidability is a certain separation of themes in Bacon's work, a separation which crystallises in particular into portraits which oscillate between torsions of the flesh and the anguish of power, and into primal social dramas which veer from the movements of bone, flesh and muscle to the actions of one body on another. There is no resolution to these tensions: in Bacon's work the bedrock is riven.

The cries of strong swimmers

There are some revealing thoughts in the Sylvester interviews on the 1944 triptych, *Three Studies for Figures at the Base of a Crucifixion*. Bacon said that it was influenced by work being done by Picasso in the late 1920s. He also said the following, about his interest in the theme of the Crucifixion in general:

I've always been very moved by pictures about slaughterhouses and meat, and to me they belong very much to the whole thing of the Crucifixion. There've been extraordinary photographs which have been done of animals just being taken up before they were slaughtered; and the smell of death. We don't know, of course, but it appears by these photographs that they're so aware of what is going to happen to them, they do everything to attempt to escape. I think these pictures were very much based on that kind of thing, which to me is very, very near this whole thing of the Crucifixion. I know for religious people, for Christians, the Crucifixion has a totally different significance. But as a non-believer, it was just an act of man's behaviour, a way of behaviour to another. (Sylvester 1980: 23)

The three panels of the 1944 triptych each show a powerful and distorted figure in deep anguish. Each panel has an orange-red background, and in each case the figure is mounted, set up in isolation (a key move through Bacon's whole *oeuvre*, as Deleuze [1984: 9–10] points out), perched on a table, hunched over a pedestal, and balanced on a stretch of grass. The creatures share a family resemblance. The left figure is female, with hair covering her face and a draped garment beginning below the 'shoulders'. Her head is bowed. The right figure is a screaming reptile–human–dog with great muscular power denied by an impotent cry, or, perhaps better, held in abeyance during a scream of anticipation. The central figure, again possessing an enormous amount of latent strength in its powerfully struc-tured body, is bandaged, recalling Matthias Grünewald's pine panel, *The Mocking of Christ*, which may have formed part of a series of Stations, and which featured Christ with bandages over his eyes (Peppiat 1996: 87). The 1944 triptych was, according to Peppiat, very substantially informed by Picasso's *Guernica* and the preparatory sketches for that work. He also notes that Bacon at the time was intensely interested in Eliot's *The Family Reunion* which was based on Aeschylus' *Orestia* (ibid.: 89), and Bacon confessed that the Eumenides were very much in his thoughts when it was painted.

In spite of their muscle and teeth, the figures at the base of Bacon's first Crucifixion are temporarily helpless, but the triptych is set in the ante-room of retribution and is washed with the sense of time suspended and energies to come. It is, then, hardly surprising that when the triptych was first shown, in April 1945, it was understood against the background of the Second World War. As Russell put it,

> Common to all three figures was a mindless voracity, an automatic unregulated gluttony, a ravening undifferentiated capacity for hatred. Each was as if cornered . . . They were the creatures who gather as ghouls round any scene of human degradation: April 1945 was to see a whole parade of them before the body of Mussolini as it hung from a butcher's hook in the suburbs of Milan. (Russell 1979: 11)

Russell's view was that these ghoulish witnesses could be related to 'uniformed respecters of the law, champions of order and due form, servants of Power' (ibid.). It may be wondered, however, if Bacon's triptych does not go back to a more ancient dialectic of force and retribution; not so much a question of due form and dutiful servanthood (for who could

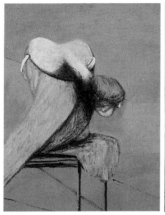  

left panel   centre panel   right panel

Francis Bacon, *Three Studies for Figures at the Base of a Crucifixion* (1944)

imagine these creatures dutiful?), more a matter of a shackled (note the lines of enclosure across all three panels) instinct for striking first or striking back. It is not by happenstance that the Greek name Agamemnon can be roughly translated as 'nemesis awaits', and a deeper understanding of Bacon's triptych can be developed by going back to the *Orestia*.

Aeschylus' trilogy begins with *Agamemnon*, which opens in Agamemnon's palace after the fall of Troy. The Chorus celebrate the victory in song, but they are also witnesses in search of understanding, narrating the sacrifice by Agamemnon of his own daughter to ensure victory against Troy, concerned that the news of the victory given to them by Agamemnon's wife, Clytemnestra, might be false, and then, in dialogue with the herald who confirms the news, referring to the sorrows of absence both at home and abroad when the army is at war. Clytemnestra sends a message to Agamemnon to say that she misses him and cannot wait for his return, and when he does arrive, with Cassandra, the unheeded prophetess who has been taken prisoner from Troy, Clytemnestra publicly affirms her fidelity and love for Agamemnon. She had laid down carpets for him to walk upon into his home. Cassandra, who had remained outside when Agamemnon and Clytemnestra went into the palace, is in deep distress and she foretells that she and Agamemnon will both be murdered by Clytemnestra. Cassandra, accepting her fate, goes inside, and, soon after, Agamemnon is heard to cry that he has been mortally wounded. The Elders force their way into the palace and are confronted with Clytemnestra, weapon in hand, standing over the dead bodies of Agamemnon and Cassandra. She is exultant, declaring that she is now revenged for Agamemnon's sacrifice of their daughter, Iphigeneia. A supplementary stratum of complexity is now revealed, when Agamemnon's cousin, Aegisthos, arrives and says that this is no more than just since Atreus, Agamemnon's father, had responded to his

brother's (Thyestes, Aegisthos' father) challenge for the throne by canni-
balising Thyestes' other children. Aegisthos and Clytemnestra had become
lovers during Agamemnon's absence and had plotted together to kill
Agamemnon. Aegisthos now plans to become king, but the Chorus warns
him that Agamemnon's son, Orestes, will return.

Orestes returns at the beginning of the second part of the trilogy, known
as *The Choephoroe* or *Libation-Bearers*, which recounts the story of Orestes'
retribution. Orestes meets his sister Elektra at Agamemnon's grave. He has
been directed by Apollo to avenge Agamemnon's death, and brother and
sister plan to regain the kingdom. The Chorus, by now full participants
rather than mere witnesses, demand justice for Agamemnon's ignominious
death, and Orestes and Elektra call upon the Gods to aid them in their task.
Clytemnestra had dreamt of giving birth to a snake whose fangs drew her
blood as she went to feed it, and Orestes will now fulfil that dream,
alienated from his mother by her murderous action which is greatly com-
pounded by her secret burial of Agamemnon, the feet hacked off his corpse
so his spirit should not be able to chase her. Orestes disguises himself and
his friend, Pylades, and they approach the city. Once inside, they will claim
they bring news of the death of Orestes. Clytemnestra hears this directly
from the feigned strangers, and after a few words of grief that the city will
not derive future benefit from a man unsullied by the crimes of the past, she
sends the strangers off for refreshment, and bids Orestes' old nurse get
Aegisthos. The distraught nurse, Kilissa, tells the Chorus of her news and
mission. The leader of the Chorus suggests to her that things are not so
clear, and tells her that Aegisthos should be told that all is safe, that his
bodyguards need not accompany him. When the nurse has left, the Chorus
entreat Zeus to keep Orestes safe, and then reply when Aegisthos arrives
inquiring about the death of Orestes that he should see the strangers.
Aegisthos' death is shouted out by a slave beating at the door of the
women's house, and Clytemnestra immediately understands the sense of the
riddle that the dead are raised and the living slain. Clytemnestra pleads with
Orestes for her life, but her arguments are feebly put, and Orestes forces her
into the palace where Aegisthos lies, to kill her on the same spot. Orestes
realises fully now what he has done, and imagines himself hunted by wild
dogs. The Chorus sing that no mortal life is ever free of such pain, but ask
the Gods to watch over him.

The last play, *The Eumenides*, begins in front of the temple of Apollo at
Delphi. Apollo's prophetess has had a horrifying but contradictory vision
of a supplicant prostrate in prayer but holding a sword in a bloodied hand,
and surrounded by a sleeping group of black, shadowy and abominable
Gorgons. These are the Eumenides, the Furies, who deal in wickedness and
sorrow, and Orestes is the prostrate figure. The vision turns into reality as
the temple doors open, but Apollo is standing guard. Apollo tells Orestes
that he must go to Athens to be judged, and so to find peace, reassuring
him that it is with Apollo that the responsibility for the death of
Clytemnestra lies. Apollo calls on Hermes, his brother, to guide Orestes on

his journey. Clytemnestra's ghost wakes up the Furies, who challenge Apollo for causing the death of Clytemnestra. This matricidal destruction of the eternal blood relation cannot go unpunished. Apollo replies that they ignore the sanctimony of matrimony and warns the Furies of the wrath of the Gods if they harm Orestes. The Furies, as a Chorus with a leader, are, however, present at the temple of Athena when Orestes arrives for the judgement which is to set him free, and they demand justice and retribution against Orestes, setting out their case that matricide cannot be tolerated in any circumstances. Athena cannot decide on this alone and determines that there will be a trial by jury. The trial opens with the case, made by the Leader of the Furies, against Orestes, that he killed his mother. Orestes cannot deny this, and calls upon Apollo to defend him. He does so, arguing that Orestes' action was the will of Zeus, and that in any event the proper blood relation is between father and child. The Furies are outraged at this devaluation of the maternal bond. Athena asks the jury of Athenian citizens for its verdict, declaring, after the votes have been cast but before they are counted, that in the event of the twelve votes being split equally, she will cast her vote for Orestes. The result is a draw, and so Orestes goes free, proclaiming as he goes that Argos will forever be faithful to Athens. The Furies will not accept the verdict and threaten ruin for Athens, but Athena offers them a home if they will listen to reason and think again, underpinning her offer with the promise of timeless influence should they agree, and the threat of exile and, implicitly, the displeasure of the Gods should they not. They are persuaded, and in this their aspect changes. Their power assured, their faces will be more gentle as persuasion and consideration become their first response. They will work for the prosperity of Athens, closing the chapter on blood-revenge, finally saying, 'And fear the tides of life no more.'

The forces which are brought to bear on all the characters of the *Orestia* are enormous, and the efforts to establish order and bring peace are almost beyond even the Gods. The blinded power of Agamemnon, Clytemnestra, Orestes and the Furies is evoked by the sightless muscle and mouth of the middle figure of Bacon's triptych. The left figure of Clytemnestra is draped in Agamemnon's winding sheet which is smeared with the blood from his wounds and amputated feet, while the right figure recalls the Furies at the point of their awakening by Clytemnestra's ghost. But the lined structures around them are taking form, as Athena's twin principles of rationality and threat (she was seen as goddess of both reason and war, the latter in its intellectual rather than brutal aspect) begin to enclose and tame the brutal power represented by these visions of muscle, bone and mouth. From the first, then, Bacon gives us a view of the subject as a witnessing of separable worlds of reason and force, the former coming to be enclosed by the latter, by lines not of potentiation but of control. We must wait to see who are the line-makers in Bacon's world, and what forms of distortion will await them.

The Family Reunion by T.S. Eliot is, at least in part, an exploration in a modern context of the mind, feeling and emotion of Orestes. Bacon had been reading the play, but the subtle shadings of Eliot's work (he had, for example, refused John Gielgud the part of Harry, because he thought that Gielgud would not be able to understand his motivations [Ackroyd 1984: 246]) are not found in Bacon's portrayal of the human subject at this time. Bacon's strong, but individually un-nuanced, presentations of the existential condition continue with his studies of papal authority. The ambiguities of Athena – goddess of justice, but also of war, symbolised by the owl but also the snake – have translated into studies of papal heads. But, we find that the inspiration of the cold urbanity and political presence of the Velázquez portrait of Innocent X does not lead Bacon merely to modern studies of massive if violent competence in the wielding of power, but rather that Bacon's depiction of authority is underpinned by the existential ambiguity between suffering and ravenousness, expressed in periods of waiting terminated by the emission of a scream.

Both Bacon and Newman have been greatly concerned with the screaming cry. Their treatments of it could not be more different. In Bacon's work it rises up from the ribcage and out through the throat. It is not a sublime gesture toward the Absolute, such as we find in Newman, but an existential pulse. In their different ways, both artists reject the social. As Philippe Sollers said of Bacon's work, 'Families, religions, philosophies, financial markets are there to divert us from this black presence' (Sollers 1996: 7). It is the innocence of the existential condition prior to the Oedipal struggle with the father which, for Sollers (ibid.: 39), illuminates Bacon's canvases. There is a variant of the right-hand panel of the 1944 triptych (shown at the 1998 'Francis Bacon: The Human Body' exhibition in London), which shows a stream of what could be blood issuing from or pouring into the extended mouth. Feeding or vomiting, the sense of strictly undiverted physical being is plain to see. There also appear to be two flowers, entering or exiting. What is cultivated is foreign. Forced in or forced out, it makes no difference.

Between suffering and preying, in Bacon's papal heads, there is no difference, no elaboration of the base condition. Again we have an archetypal presentation of the supplement. It would be fanciful to imagine that Bacon's 1953 *Study after Velasquez's Portrait of Pope Innocent X* is directly inspired by either the story of Pope Formosus's posthumous trial, when his body was disinterred, placed on a throne, found guilty of various treasons, suffered amputation of the fingers on which holy rings had been placed at his consecration, and then thrown into the Tiber, or by the relentless pursuit of ecclesiastical and family political power by Pope Alexander IV (Rodrigo Borgia). But, even if there is no evidence that Bacon drew inspiration for his studies of papal heads from the history of Rome, that history, whether in the dark years of the 900s or in the era of Machiavelli, both helps to illuminate the intensity of Bacon's images and underscores his lack of subtlety. It should, however, be crystal clear that this is not a criticism – precisely the reverse, for subtlety is a social affair, and Bacon sought the point before such accommodation. To find the social condition,

Francis Bacon, *Study for a Portrait* (1953)

itself a supplement to his studies of preying and suffering, we have to look elsewhere, at the alternations between the witness and the puppet-master in his portraiture.

John Russell's description of the Velázquez portrait of Innocent X reads as follows:

> [T]he most powerful man in the world. Everything points to it: the throne, the robes, the ring, the state paper held in the left hand, and the note of perfectly balanced and incorruptible authority which is set by the relaxed way in which the Pope's arms rest lightly on the throne. (Russell 1979: 42)

We have moved well beyond, in the late twentieth century, such obvious insignia of power. The more appropriate image is now Bacon's *Study for a Portrait* from 1953. Again, everything points to it: the darkened background, illuminating nothing that would provide purchase or context for those who hold our fate in their grip; the judgmental gaze, heedless of explanation or narrative, echoing Bacon's own distaste for the pleas for mitigation inherent in all stories; the formal clothing, revealing nothing but the authority of the wearer; the throne of power framing this instance of imperious superciliousness. This *Study for a Portrait* de-dramatises the scream of authority, representing it as an unnecessary epiphenomenon.

Bacon's exploration of the mythological instance of zero empathy and total command continues with the 1962 *Three Studies for a Crucifixion*, where on the left panel two clothed figures are set against a split carcass in the foreground. The definition of the left of these figures is all in the head and its dispassionate bearing of control (Peppiat [1996: 190] sees the left-hand figure as older and disgruntled, and finds both figures to be of equal weight), while the right-hand figure with its more specific musculature is in retreat from the meat which reflects its own condition. Deleuze describes these two figures as 'witnesses, the one passive while the other one is ready to take flight' (Deleuze 1984: 52), but they are surely much more a part of the existential drama than this. On the other hand, John Russell's reading echoes Deleuze's (ibid.: 52) other suggestion that these figures are dressed like vampires, and finds them to be 'an updated Burke and Hare, a pair of thigh-booted anatomists bent on moving from one indignity to the next' (Russell 1979: 128). Even allowing for Russell's view that 'the two figures on the left are susceptible of so many interpretations' (ibid.: 114) this Crucifixion scene is not the setting for an ordinary crime. The figure on the left has the demeanour of a senior bureaucrat, an auditor-in-chief who has

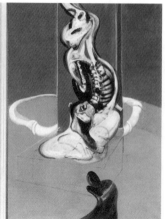

left panel   centre panel   right panel

Francis Bacon, *Three Studies for a Crucifixion* (1962)

arrived to check that things are going as they should. Its head is a study in
observation and soulless satisfaction. Far from passive, as Deleuze suggests,
this is a study in vigilance, marked as the end of a period of waiting by the
motion internal to the scene. This fearsome character may have been at
rest, even reading the newspaper (see *Study for Portrait*, 1970) or listening
to *Missa Solemnis*, enduring the stasis of authority first presented in *Pope I*
of 1951. Now, however, the bemused demeanour of the first Pope is past,
and so too the scream which came as the nature of the office became
clearer. Now the alternations between stasis and activity are remorseless.

If the core of authority is engaged stasis, the status of the witness is
disengaged and therefore mobile. The right-hand figure, in retreat, in the
left panel of the 1962 Crucifixion triptych, exemplifies this inconsequential
movement. This motility is present throughout Bacon's many full-face
portraits. Of these numerous exercises in translating the rootlessness of the
witness into facial anamorphisms, deformations without transformation, as
Deleuze puts it (1984: 40), we can consider the triptych *Three Portraits* from
1973, focusing on the head in particular.

The left panel contains a portrait of George Dyer in right profile. It is one
of the least distorted of Bacon's heads. Dyer had died over a year earlier,
and the treatment is sombre, reflective and far less dramatic than the May–
June triptych which depicts his death. Talking to David Sylvester, Bacon
admitted that he found it hard to do portraits of people whom he knew but
who had died, that having his models around, even while he was working
from photographs (in this case probably John Deakin's well-known right
profile of Dyer), made the portrait somewhat easier to deform (Sylvester
1980: 144–6). The rendition in paint of the essential mobility of a witness
perhaps becomes somewhat contradictory once the person concerned is no
longer in movement. The centre panel is a self-portrait. When asked why he

left panel   centre panel   right panel

Francis Bacon, *Three Portraits (Dyer, Bacon, Freud)* (1973)

had painted so many, Bacon replied, 'It's just expediency' (ibid.: 1980: 144). He was not, he thought, involved deeply in the tradition of self-portraiture. To him, then, the pictures of himself were, again, renditions of the mobile subject, with the movement transferred into the deformations arrived at through the partially aleatory encounter of brush, paint and canvas. The right panel shows Lucien Freud, of whom he had done two triptychs in 1966 and 1969.

The dominant interpretation of Bacon's portraits from 1960, after which the scream does not figure, has focused on distortion as decay, citing, for example, the influence upon Bacon of a book he had acquired in France, of hand-coloured photographs of dental diseases. Bertolucci, filming *Last Tango in Paris*, had taken Marlon Brando to the 1971 Bacon exhibition at the Grand Palais, and said, 'I wanted Paul to be like Lucien Freud and the other characters that returned obsessively in Bacon's work: faces eaten up by something that comes from within' (cited in Peppiat: 1996: 245). Michel Leiris, himself one of Bacon's models, said, 'Bacon's portraits, as if endowed with some prescient power, show their models from the outset as creatures already attacked by decay' (Leiris 1983: 26). Decay, however, was not a dominant theme in Bacon's mind. He was concerned above all with the technical problems of capturing what he called the mystery of appearance:

The longer you work, the more the mystery deepens of what appearance is, or how can what is called appearance be made in another medium. And it needs a sort of moment of magic to coagulate colour and form so that it gets the equivalent of appearance, the appearance that you see at any moment, because so-called appearance is only riveted for one moment as that appearance . . . I mean, appearance is like a continuously floating thing. (Sylvester 1980: 118)

When speaking about two portraits of Michel Leiris, which he did in 1976
and 1978, he further explained that the art of portraiture, for him, was to
make the image more like the subject through a process of deformation:

> I'm always hoping to deform people into appearance; I can't paint them literally.
> For instance, I think that, of those two paintings of Michel Leiris, the one I did
> which is less literally like him is in fact more poignantly like him . . . that is always
> one of the things in painting that is really impossible to explain. And I would like
> to make my pictures more and more artificial, more and more what is called
> distorted . . . (Sylvester 1980: 146–8)

If this process of working at distortion to get closer to the truth illuminates Bacon's art, it also comments on the witness as a key figure in the
elemental social drama, on its movement, its transience, its contestability,
its distance, allowing perspective but denying control, and its temptation to
go closer and partake of the real, to do more than swim along, which might
be hard enough: to go closer and then to scream.

Body and society

Bacon's heads are studies in power. As we move from the papal heads, after
Velázquez, to their full bodies, the bodies are clothed in power, royal purple
to hide the limbs and add to the imperial grimace. This is his social theme,
and it raises the question whether Bacon's art is divided: his treatment
of the body as base materialism, and his treatment of the head as a kind of
Machiavelli-inspired portrait of an elemental social condition consisting in
the exercise of power and its witnesses perennially drawn to the flame. This
is another question of the supplement's existence as flesh and its subordination by others. It is then only a half-truth when Bacon says of himself,
'Perhaps I have no sense of the social' (cited in Sollers 1996: 18). His sense
of the social is perhaps conjured up in a favourite quotation from
Aeschylus that 'the reek of human blood is laughter to my heart' (cited in
Farson 1994: 127), and takes inspiration from Orestes, witness to the death
of his sister and father, and drawn close into the drama of power which is
brought to a climax with his murder of his mother. But these are themes
within the sphere of flesh subordinated. Bacon also dealt with the body
itself, as flesh, as meat, liquid and solid, flowing. However, to approach the
body in itself, as muscle, bone, flesh and blood, all in movement, but
without its social frame, is not so easy. Why is this?

The body is a public matter. Bodies are social phenomena. From the
sociological standpoint, this applies if we take an interior view and consider
our own experience of pleasure, pain, hunger, thirst, touch, smell, sight,
hearing, taste, growth, decay, strength, weakness, movement, or stillness.
The rough and the smooth, the hot and the cold, the wet and the dry, sharp
or blunt: embodied experience is social experience. Birth, sex and death,
infancy, adolescence, maturity and old age: these are social categories,
experienced under licence. As Caroline Bynum, a historian specialising in the

medieval period, puts it, 'Experiences as basic as birthing and being born, working and eating, aging and dying were very different in the fens of England, the forests of Brittany, and the bustling cities of the Rhineland and the North of Italy' (Bynum 1999: 262–3), and these differences arise from the differences of social context. Interiority is, then, it might appear, a franchised operation. From an external point of view, things are even plainer. The experience of the other is apprehended through social categories: father, mother, sister, brother, friend, foe, colleague, rival, stranger, neighbour, biology, psychology, physics, chemistry, thermodynamics, history, literature, anthropology, autobiography – the entire hierarchy of known types and knowledge forms is arrayed beneath the social canopy.[1] The double subjugation of interiority and exteriority within the social realm is pervasive. Our bodies are not our own. This social enclosure is not, however, entirely sealed. There are leakages; there is excess; there is the time of the body, a corporeal time, different from the time of social organisation. What follows on from the leaks and eruptions is a process of recovery, repair and recuperation. This is not exceptional. Another kind of time existing alongside linear time as part of the normal social order of things will not easily be granted; it may survive only through resistance, since the linear time of social organisation represses the time of the body, and refuses time to the subject. The reproduction of the social enclosure of the body, like the denial of any kind of autonomous subjectivity, is a matter of boundary maintenance and of re-corralling what escapes. The re-territorialisation of the body by society, and paradigmatically by sociology, is a networked strategy which parallels the denial of subjectivity within the main traditions of social thought. We can see the extent to which our bodies are not our own, but also the potential for leakage out of this social framing, in any number of instances: birth, love, death and illness are perhaps some of the most obvious points of tension, and we can develop the latter two areas with an example or two.

In March 1998, a sculptor was put on trial for the alleged theft of body parts from the Royal College of Surgeons in London. Not only did Anthony-Noel Kelly stand accused of theft, he was also charged with necrophilia, for being obsessed with what he is not licensed to desire. Brian Masters, who has written books on both Dennis Nilsen and Rosemary West, wrote as follows, in the *Observer*, on 29 March 1998:

> A very destructive kind of necrophilia is the passion for dismemberment, a characteristic of a number of addictive murderers. Nobody has suggested that Anthony-Noel Kelly himself cut up the bodies whose parts he hoarded and then translated into wall-coverings, but the very fact that he went on collecting them and preserving them as artefacts points to a measure of obsession and a degree of comfort derived from ownership of them. There is even something suspiciously 'serial' in the repetitive pinning of body parts on his walls. The necrophilic character of this activity is blatant.

Masters argued that this is poisoned art, an art of death that he also compared to the work of Rachel Whiteread (of her *House*, he writes, 'I felt that the fingers which made it must have been sticky with the stuff of decay') and Damien Hirst (whose work is characterised as 'the empty vessels left when emotion has been siphoned out'). Masters compares this kind of work with what is for him an entirely opposite case, the art of Michelangelo, Rembrandt, even Bosch and Picasso, art which is life-affirming even when it treats of death, and which does not 'gloat on death, nor reduce it to a pile of body parts'. As a would-be spokesperson for 'proper' social values, Masters wants these body parts for himself so that they can be respected for the lives they once were. We should not see the bones, or the flesh, but remember and celebrate the lives. There are laws and customs to ensure that we follow this code. The breaking of such taboos will not be tolerated, either by the courts or by public opinion. The leakage of unlicensed bodies into the public domain is a perversion.

Matters are not, of course, so simple. The day before Masters presented his diatribe to the readers of the *Observer*, the same newspaper group published a magazine article about the archaeological discovery of perfectly preserved 2,000-year-old bodies. This article proclaimed, 'Bog bodies are the archaeologist's dream come true – fully-formed human corpses with skin, bones and internal organs intact. They can bring history alive more directly than any old dusty document ever could. But now, rampant exploitation of the preservative peat in which they are found stands to rob us of this crucial link with the past' (Pitts 1998: 38). While it may seem as if there is something of an antinomy here, between the 'legitimate' fascination with Tollund man, found perfectly preserved and with a noose around his neck, and the condemned necrophilia of Kelly and Hirst, the contradiction is more apparent than real. On both sides of the comparison we find extensive mechanisms of social incorporation. Necrophilia slides easily into the field of art; Damien Hirst's agent, Jay Jopling, speaking of the 1990s generation of new British artists, explains:

> They emerged when there was very little support for art, the museums were not buying art in this country, there were very few private collectors, very little public patronage. So, in the face of adversity, the artists were forced to put on their own exhibitions. At that time, in the late 1980s, early 1990s, the national newspapers didn't pay attention to contemporary art at all. It was into that environment that Marc Quinn emerged with his blood head and Damien with his shark. (Macdonald 1997: 6)

As for hanged men drawn from the marshes, they find a space, ready-made for them, in the field of science, as 'more than 50 scientific specialists contributed to the British Museum's first substantial report on Lindow Man', discovered in 1984 in Cheshire, and also suspected of having been hanged (Pitts 1998: 40). And there are other ways of engaging both whole bodies and body parts than those we find associated with Kelly's sculpture and Tollund man. These too affirm the apparent inescapability of the social.

Caroline Bynum has traced the representations of resurrection from AD 200 through to the late Middle Ages. She finds that the depiction of resurrection as the reconnecting of limbs is frequently encountered right across Europe, from Carolingian depictions of the 'rising dead as bones still in their coffins or regurgitated body parts' (Bynum 1995: 186) through to the Torcello mosaic, in which 'an angel sounds the trumpet, while clothed dead rise from tombs, and beasts vomit up bodies and limbs' (ibid.: 189). As Bynum puts it: 'In monastic prose, the metaphors used for body still saw it as bits and pieces, scattered abroad by death but re-collected at the end of time' (ibid.: 186). The conclusion which she reaches at the end of her study is that, despite the emphasis upon soul and spirit in Christianity, 'a concern for material and structural continuity showed remarkable persistence' (ibid.: 11). She argues that this persistence is the key to understanding some quite bizarre relics, such as entrail caskets and reliquaries for the display of body parts such as arms and hands, and asserts that 'The idea of the person, bequeathed by the Middle Ages to the modern world, was not a concept of soul escaping body or soul using body; it was a concept of self in which physicality was integrally bound to sensation, emotion, reasoning, identity' (ibid.: 11). As Bynum would be the first to point out, this legacy was a social legacy, reinforced by representations of the mouth of hell devouring the bodies of the sinful. The body was always a social and linear affair.

If the work of jurists, moralists, scientists, artists, scholars and art entrepreneurs can so easily re-corral the body and reaffirm its enclosure, affirming the social borders around each potential transgression, can embodied sensation never be presented outside its social frame? This question has been of particular importance in the development of feminist, post-colonial and queer theorising and practice. It has, however, been posed as a double rejection, of a certain social domination, but also of an essentialism of the body. The focus here has been, then, on the politics of the body, on altering rather than trying to remove its social frame. This stance has been adopted within feminist thinking to combat the Kantian elitism which separated rational men from natural women. Margrit Shildrick, in *Leaky Bodies and Boundaries*, puts the position very clearly:

I favour a feminist rewriting of the subject that demands an attention to the corporeal body. Now this sense of embodiment is precisely what has been omitted most often from masculine accounts of subjectivity. One major point of the post-Cartesian notion of the universal, transcendent subject is that *he* is constituted in the radical separation of mind from body. The privileging of the so-called higher faculties of reason, intellect, spirit, and so on, over the material and mundane, grounds a two-tier system in which women, tied as they ostensibly are to their bodies, and most particularly to their reproductive bodies, have been deemed largely incapable of autonomous rational thought. Quite simply, women are deemed to live their bodies in ways that men are not, and this constraint on transcendence is alone sufficient to disqualify them from full subjectivity. The absent body characterises male/moral discourse, and women, being all too solid, are paradoxically situated in that absence. If, then, women are to occupy subject positions not by reiterating the split and practising transcendence, but by reclaiming the unity of body and mind, then we must do so by affirming embodiment. (Shildrick 1997: 168)

As Bynum illustrates and our earlier skirmish with Descartes and Haraway also shows, now elaborated in this statement from Shildrick, the politics and social framing of the body are crucially important. Does that mean, however, that there is just no room for attempts to think about and represent the body outside of its social enclosure? Before returning to Bacon, to explore that question I want to point to a valuable study which powerfully duplicates the sociological rejection of the subject in a sociological rejection of the autonomous body, but then, at one point only, presents a shining suggestion that there might be other perspectives.

When Jackie Stacey was diagnosed with cancer, her first response was to become an expert: 'a bid for control at the very moment it had been taken away from me' (Stacey 1997: 3). She read and rewrote the narrative of her own body:

> almost negligible manifestations were reread as the crucial early signs of the disease. The subsequent and much more dramatic physical symptoms were then also rationalised within this pathological trajectory: I was told that the abdominal pain had been caused by the tumour rupturing, and bleeding into the abdominal cavity resulting in peritonitis . . . The narrative of my body continued to be rewritten at each stage. As I lay recovering from surgery, I tried to find out what had been removed apart from the tumour . . . Since the tumour had ruptured, some malignant cells may have been left behind and therefore chemotherapy might be necessary . . . linearity, cause and effect and possible closures present themselves almost automatically. (1997: 4–5)

As she was completing the introduction to her book, more than four years after her operation, Jackie Stacey still did not know how to think about her body. Was the illness in the past, or did it remain a part of her? An X-ray showed a suspicious mass, which turned out to be a false alarm, but it had the effect of confirming that this narrative of her body was far from closed. Also it could run within two modes, even simultaneously if not without a certain cognitive dissonance in the face of the epistemological contradictions. The mode of science promised, and in this case has at least partially delivered, a cure:

> Teratoma . . . used to be one of the most fatal cancers, killing its victims within eighteen months, its unusually fast-growing cells spreading through the body like wildfire. In the 1990s however it is one of the most treatable cancers; the new discovery of a particular chemotherapy cocktail, which acts effectively on such rapidly dividing cells, has brought an *almost* guaranteed promise of a cure. Bleomycin, etoposide, and cisplatinum provide the magic formula in most cases. From the worst to the best kind of cancer in fifteen years. Thank God for scientific discovery. (1997: 11)

In the mode of science, it is the scientists who are the 'heroes'. Within the discourses of alternative therapies and self-health, it is the patient who becomes heroic, and this entails a different narrativisation of the body and its former behaviour: 'Cancer is interpreted as a metaphor for the self-destructive lifestyle that has since been rejected' (ibid.: 12). Changes in lifestyle, reduction of stress, a better diet, more exercise, relaxation therapies of various kinds may help recovery, and patients do recover.

Stacey's book was written for a whole complex of reasons, but one of her aims was to examine the concepts of self that emerge out of these, sometimes conflicting, narratives of science and self-health. What I am interested to ask of her book is the extent to which it points to the body beyond the social, to the time of the subject beyond linearity. What is already clear from her opening pages is the sealing up of the narratives within the linear and social perspectives. Her gloss on that time fits too well into Bourdieu's double denial of subjective autonomy and of its potential life outside the social; it does not yet disturb the complacent moral outrage of a commentator like Brian Masters, or cause too much disquiet among the religious authorities who have always known that in the final analysis our bodies were theirs. The mere presence of the additions to scientific medicine from alternative therapies is insufficient to quell the doubt that hybridity is not much more than social re-territorialisation.

The single, simple, numinous indication of the body's own time in Jackie Stacey's story concerns a remarkable coincidence. She had gone on holiday to recover, following completion of the chemotherapy:

> As I walked down the main street of Paleachora in Crete, people stared. They always stare, but on this holiday they stared a lot. Not surprising really. I had lost eyebrows, eyelashes and hair, and that does give a person an unusual look. I wore a scarf or a hat in public, but I did look different. Certainly no one else looked like me. That is, until two women walked towards me, one of whom wore a pale blue headscarf wound round in a recognisable turban style. She also had that rather uncannily naked look of someone with no eyebrows or eyelashes. She looked completely familiar and yet totally unfamiliar at the same time. Did I do a double-take, or do I just imagine that I did? How obvious was the shock in my expression? (1997: 19)

The woman in the pale blue headscarf had also come to Crete to recover from teratoma, having had the same treatment, the same operation, suffered the same side effects. She had the apartment next door but one. Stacey refers to the 'insurmountable relief of recognition' and 'The physical relaxation of the emotional connection' (ibid.). Certainly it was a social encounter, but it was also *unheimlich*, a magical meeting without reported personal precedent.[2] Jackie Stacey's encounters with alternative therapies, biomedical language and critical commentary reinforced her view of the strategies deployed in society to deal with the body, which is refused permission to speak of itself, and which will be made to communicate through distorting channels of metaphoricity (as she points out, the discomfort caused by the word 'lesbian' is not too dissimilar to that caused by the word 'cancer'; both are subject to weak taboos, both words run too close to allowing the body to speak in its own language, and there is no social licence for that). What is socially licensed is 'the brave face', 'try not to worry', and sundry other ways of preventing the body from speaking in its own right. This even extends to people who are 'better' but do not look it, and to people who are unwell but look fine. Perhaps the final, possibly quite vicious re-territorialisation consists in the expectation that bodies which have been close to death and are now returned can impart their knowledge to the world: 'The person who has had cancer is presented as a sagacious messenger whose purpose is to remind everyone of the preciousness and the precariousness of life. The so-called "survivors" of cancer are seen to possess knowledge of the secrets of life, as well as the secrets of death' (ibid.: 244–5).

Jackie Stacey's narrative account of the battle between medicine and cancer casts medicine in the role of the masculine hero, plunging into the depths to emerge triumphant to reimpose order upon a recalcitrant world.[3] Whether or not the drive to mark out boundaries is a masculine trait, it is certainly a prime characteristic of social organisations, and of society *tout court*. It may be mistaken, in both an epistemological and a moral sense, to see sociology as a mirror of society in this respect, but it is probable that mechanisms of boundary maintenance, prohibition of otherness and reincorporation are crucial to social reproduction. Embodied subjectivity is a site of weakness in the social carapace, and it is at this complex location that we can see the effort of subject and body denial at work. Such negations as can be seen in the work of Bourdieu and others are testament to the powers of bones and being. The effective imperialism of the sociological perspective, of its control over these powers of the flesh, is illustrated nowhere better than in Jackie Stacey's superb account of changes taking place in her own body, in which there is only one brief moment outside of social control. What Bacon did was to elaborate an exteriority, a non-social, sociology-proof arena in which bodily powers, including weakness, recalcitrance and durability, might be illuminated. It is an arena which is difficult to enter.

Meat

Bacon's *Pope No 11*, 1960, has fixed eyes which look upon a spine with ribs and meat attached; this could be his own meat in both senses. Little wonder that his mouth and lower face are ill-defined as if the ribs had been drawn up out of the throat, or as if pausing for a moment before feeding again. Both themes, the body as meat and the body as power, are present here, just as in the 1962 Crucifixion triptych with the condescending power of the head hovering over the meat and bone on the table and in the adjoining panels. When Bacon expressed it succinctly to David Sylvester, saying, 'When you go into a butcher's shop and see how beautiful meat can be and then you think about it, you can think of the whole horror of life – of one thing living off another' (Sylvester 1980: 48), he conjured up this double thematic: the head as the site of the will to feed off another, therefore the object of the other's resistance, and the body as contingently either means of subjugation or source of satisfaction. Social institutions combine to screen off and effect respite from this base existential condition, but Bacon wanted to go behind the curtains and into the cage. The Pope (a figure which we might now be coming to see as of enormous but immature

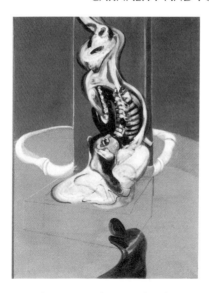

Francis Bacon, *Three Studies for a Crucifixion* (1962), right panel

power), whom he placed on a yellow throne, with de-emphasised limbs, against a curtained background, is screaming for meat. No longer planning the future according to the dictates of the past, this creature is only in the revealed abyss of the present (Sollers 1996: 52), as we will find Ballard to be in *Crash*.

David Sylvester drew a contrast between Newman and Bacon, with the former seen as one of the great exponents of the 'abstract sublime', and the latter presented as 'the one great exponent in our time of the Figurative Sublime' (Sylvester 1998: 21). But this surely must not be taken to mean that Bacon's art is properly the art of flesh transcended, but rather of flesh ascended, traced by its veins and not networks of social power. With Bacon, flesh, one might say, is in our face. It is true that it has volume, and is more than a surface projection of the kind that Baselitz explores. We are not dealing here with figures appearing at a window, their three-dimensionality denied us by a glass screen (although he did work from the depthless dimensions of the photograph, his 'models' were those whose depths he had some insight into). His quest for the thickness of the subject is emphasised in his use of the three-dimensionality of the cage, the voluminousness of curtains, the windows onto the spreading night, the arrows marking out the points of access, and – now in the register of sensation rather than control – above all in his treatment of the body. Must Sylvester not have meant, with his notion of the figurative sublime, that Bacon's treatment of flesh and bone was not distracted by social epiphenomena? He may have spent his private life as if on a film set, acting for the crowds of actors around him, who would in their turn act for him, but on this side of his work there were no social performances. In Bacon's treatment of the body, the body is all.

For Gilles Deleuze, the body is the materiality of the figure. It is not its spatial arrangement, not its structure, but a site of intensities. The figure in Bacon's work does not have a face, with its fixed spatial arrangement and its sites of differentiated functions. It has a head, the treatment of which as animal mass re-presents the face as head, establishing, Deleuze suggests, a 'zone of indiscernibility between human and animal' (Deleuze 1984: 20). This is not, then, a simple transformation, not a combination of forms, but the discovery of what human and animal have in common – their existence as flesh and bone in local confrontation, not as part of a structural configuration, but as meat. This, Deleuze tells us, is how to understand the mouth and teeth in Bacon's works, as a local assemblage of flesh and bone. He points to the inverted Crucifixion, in the right panel of the 1962 triptych, in which, in popular parlance in both French and English, one might say that the flesh falls from the bones. Citing a series of reclining figures, Deleuze finds that Bacon treats the bones as rigging, an acrobat's apparatus for the flesh to hang from and perform around. This interest in descent, as a key trope in Bacon's painting of the body, goes back to the Spinozian formulation of *A Thousand Plateaus*:

> Spinoza asks: What can a body do? We call the *latitude* of a body the affects of which it is capable at a given degree of power, or rather within the limits of that degree. *Latitude is made up of intensive parts falling under a capacity, and longitude of extensive parts falling under a relation.* (Deleuze and Guattari 1987: 256–7, italics in the original)

For Deleuze, the spiritual animation of Bacon's rendition of flesh into colour is pity. The object of this pity is meat. Its locus is the church as a place of prayer and compassion, but also a place of butchery and execution. Both pity and butchery are symbolically re-enacted in front of the Crucifixion. Human suffering is bestial and bestial suffering is human, a profound identity between human and animal. 'What revolutionary artists, politicians, priests or whatever have not experienced this extreme moment when they are nothing other than beasts, become responsible not for the bodies which are dead, but in front of those which are dying?' (Deleuze 1984: 21). Can this sorrowful indiscernibility between animal meat and the human body be transposed into an identity between meat and the head? Can the hard, sculpted skull be evaded? Deleuze thinks that Bacon answers yes to both questions, that in direct line of descent from Rembrandt he gives us the head as flesh freed from the underlying structure of skull and eye socket, in what (and Deleuze does not say this) amounts to an existential and piteous gesture. This flesh and meat is without support yet will bear the world. In Deleuze's view, Bacon's work illustrates an increasingly intimate relationship between meat and the head, to the point where all meat takes the form of a head without a face. One might say, of Bacon's bodies and heads, that they develop to the point where their social identity becomes epiphenomenal, to the point at which they conjure up a general rather than a particular recognition, and the mode of that recognition is pity.

There is a series of oppositions in this reading of Bacon by Deleuze: the head and the face, flesh and bone, human and animal, Crucifixion and butchery, and two terms without a developed other: descent and pity. Whilst agreeing with Polan that the oppositions are not treated by Deleuze in the mode of parodic inversion (Polan 1994: 245), there is little doubt that Deleuze treats the oppositions especially of face and head, flesh and bone, and human and animal within a recognisably Hegelian–Derridean way. His use of the term 'becoming', as in 'becoming-animal', is symptomatic here. This is not a matter for criticism, since the overturning of accepted hierarchically structured oppositions is certainly a way (if not *the* way) of deepening engagement and understanding. It does however raise questions about the hidden opposite terms, the absent partners to descent and pity. To take the issue of the vertical plane first of all, a careful study of Bacon's work shows that while the figures and heads may be in a relationship of superiority or inferiority, as we have discussed above in relation to the question of the elemental social scenes which some of Bacon's work dramatises, the figures and heads themselves are, much more often than not, twisted in a horizontal plane. In other words, Deleuze reads the body in Bacon's *oeuvre* as, to follow his Spinozian formulation quoted above, falling under a relation. Whereas reading Bacon's art as supplementary, as indeterminate between the elemental social relation of power and spectatorship and the pure capacity of the flesh, we will look for and find, in his treatment of the body, torque and torsion, a horizontal tension, a latitude, rather than challenge or submission to gravity.

The question of pity is more profound. Again it falls under a relation, but the term is incomplete. It describes the spirit of the witness, but does not enter into what is witnessed. Perhaps we can see this best in Bacon's *Triptych Inspired by T.S. Eliot's Poem 'Sweeney Agonistes'* (1967). Eliot's *Sweeney Agonistes*, a play he worked on for a very long time and which he never finished, begins with two quotations. The first, from the second part of the *Orestia*, has Orestes hunted by the Eumenides, and declaring that he must move on. The response to terror here is flight, and if there is a witness's pity it is directed to the soul without rest. The body can run, which is in its nature, but the utopia of the soul is repose, and this is denied Orestes, at least until the judgement of Athena. The second quotation is from St John of the Cross, and reads, italicised, '*Hence the soul cannot be possessed of the divine union, until it has divested itself of the love of created beings.*' This is far from an opening to a discourse within which pity has a place. It approximates more nearly to the motto of some mythical serial killer.

The play opens with a conversational prologue between two women: Dusty and Doris. They are discussing two men, Pereira and Sam: 'it wouldn't do to be too nice to Pereira', but 'Sam's a gentleman through and through.' Pereira rings to speak to Doris, but Dusty lies and says she is ill. The interplay of the women continues as Doris begins to read the cards. One of the cards which is cut is the two of spades, the coffin. Even Sam's arrival with some visitors to London does not divert Doris from wanting to know whose coffin it might be. The four arrivals swap comments about their army life, and then compare and discuss attitudes to London, with the two women. The next scene has nine characters: Sweeney, Swarts and Snow have been added to the previous group. There is a playful mood, reminiscent of Noel Coward, as Sweeney tells Doris he will take her off to a cannibal island and eat her. But life would be boring on an island: 'Birth, and copulation, and death. That's all . . .' 'That's no life,' says Doris, but 'Life is death,' says Sweeney, and goes on to say that he 'knew a man once

left panel   centre panel   right panel

Francis Bacon, *Triptych Inspired by T.S. Eliot's Poem 'Sweeney Agonistes'* (1967)

did a girl in'. Doris doesn't like where this is going. She'd drawn the two of spades, and wants the conversation to stop. But the others want to hear, and Sweeney says:

> Any man might do a girl in
> Any man has to, needs to, wants to
> Once in a lifetime, do a girl in
> Well he kept her there in a bath
> With a gallon of lysol in a bath

He explained that this went on for months, the man behaving as if nothing had happened. He paid the landlord, did the shopping, fetched the news-papers. There were no visitors, so perhaps that made it easier. But, really, it wasn't easy. He couldn't believe it. At times he went to the bathroom certain that he had imagined everything, that there was not the faintest chance that there was a body there. At other moments he knew that he was the cadaver, that the body in the bath was his physical metaphor, that all being human came down to was existence in a state of temporarily sus-pended physical decomposition. All the language, all the social stuff, none of it could be denied, but even though it was important, it got nowhere near the root of things:

> Death is life and life is death
> I gotta use words when I talk to you
> But if you understand or if you don't
> That's nothing to me and nothing to you
> We all gotta do what we gotta do (Eliot 1936: 130–1)

Peppiat tells us that Bacon's gallery gave the work its title as a means of identification, since he had mentioned that he had been reading Eliot's verse

play while painting it (Peppiat 1996: 229). Russell thinks that the central
panel refers to a puzzling murder in the 1920s, which took place in a
continental railway carriage (Russell 1979: 148). It is easy to speculate as to
what is represented here, but Bacon denied any interest in narration. As
Peppiat points out, there is just no evidence to link the figures in the left
panel to Doris and Dusty, or the figure on the phone in the right panel to
Pereira, who calls them on the phone but never appears. Two things are
plain, however. First there is no pity in this triple scene. It is forensic rather
than heartbreaking. Second, all we have to go on is what is actually on the
canvas. In the left panel, two naked female figures lie prone and twisted on
a raised circular table. In the foreground, on the front of the table there is
an open package or container of some kind, with its contents spilled out.
They may be razor blades. The bodies may be bloodied, but it is not clear.
There may be evidence of them having been tied up, which would explain
the dark bands around the lower torso of the front figure, and there is also
some similar banding around the shoulder of the rear figure. This does not
account however for the three shark-fin appendages, the same colour as
that banding, on the torso of the rear figure. The bodies are enclosed within
a space mapped out by an incomplete and partially curvilinear cube, drawn
from one side of the mirror, the opposite side of which is drawn across the
further part of the table. Reflected in a mirror, a small chest of drawers
stands with its top drawer open. It appears to have been carefully ran-
sacked, and a couple of small items of clothing are lying on the floor in
front of it. The reflection in the mirror begins with the end of the table on
which the bodies lie, but thereafter is distorted: the room is circular, but the
mirror shows the corner of the room; the floor in the mirror is a different
colour, as are the walls. Whether this is a murder scene or not, the bodies
are voluptuous and vulnerable in a scene without pity, waiting for a process
to finish, or for a team of forensic professionals to record and then erase.

The right panel is set in the same room. The bodies have been moved
slightly. The chest of drawers has been closed. The mirror now reflects
someone making a phone call, a bespectacled figure conveying no emotion.
For the absent figure in the centre panel, the process will finish elsewhere.
The body has apparently been ripped from the carriage, not through the
window, which is pristine, the blind half-drawn, but through the door,
which is broken. Left behind are a blood-smeared pillow, a jacket, a holdall
by the chair, and a writing plinth on which is a piece of paper or a pad of
some kind. One might imagine finding these words there:

> But if you understand or if you don't
> That's nothing to me and nothing to you
> We all gotta do what we gotta do

If pity is in question, as Deleuze submits, then the answer to that question is
a definite shake of the head, a negation expressed in the quotation from St
John of the Cross at the head of Eliot's play, and reaffirmed by the triptych
itself. If the subject is meat, it is not pitiful.

Neither pity nor decay: where else might we find the secret of the flesh? One answer which seems obvious has to do with horror, but the argument against this can be developed in the same way as the argument about pity. Horror is a witness's category, and if we wish to seek out a non-social moment in Bacon's work, supplementary to his treatment of the elemental social scene, we will not find it, either in pity or in horror. Allon White was then quite right to say,

> I believe Bacon when he says that his paintings are not about horror. He reveals himself in each canvas too relentlessly intelligent and too solitary to stage-manage a paint horror-show. The unspeakable phobic texture of the paintings is shocking, but Bacon goes to great lengths to avoid the inflated sensationalising of horror which has become a staple of mass culture. Indeed, Bacon's paintings are all the more disturbing for their fastidious dialogue with mass cultural stereotypes. (White 1993: 160–1)

Pity, decay, horror: these staples of Bacon interpretation merely tour us around attitudes to the body as meat. Perhaps the problem is precisely here, that meat itself is actually not as fundamental a notion as Deleuze, for example, might think. Might it not be the case that meat is a modality of notions like pity and horror and decay? We are posing, in other words, the possibility that meat, with its evocation of consumption, is a part of the elemental social drama. This suspicion can be allayed, however, since in this context meat covers all three aspects with which we might be concerned: the subject of power, the object of power, and the condition of the witness watching the drama unfold. It is this saturation of the social plane that is not easily summoned up by the notion of meat, even though it is there. A slight transposition of terms will make this plainer, if we move from butchery to eschatology, from meat to flesh, and consider the extended use of the term flesh, across the realm of literature from the Bible forward, as metaphor for the human condition. But what this literary and religious usage does not make plain is the potential within flesh for movement, its flexibility and expressivity. At the level of the body in itself, then, what Bacon does is to capture both the volume of the flesh and the fluidity of its meat. Pity and piety take their places beneath the principles of volume and fluidity.

Unlike the vast majority of work within the whole tradition of both painting and sculpture, the figures in Bacon's painting are often captured in movement, conveying a real sense of movement rather than its simulation. Contrasting the treatment of flesh between Bacon and, for example, Lucien Freud or Philip Pearlstein or Robert Mapplethorpe, in the latter three cases there is a clear depiction of the pose. If photography is a crucial reference point for contemporary art, as Bacon argued, then it might be appropriate to say that much contemporary art still duplicates the condition of the posed shot, whereas some of Bacon's work is more akin to the cinematic frame, or, in the case of the heads, to a picture taken of a moving face with a slow shutter speed. Bacon's concern with movement goes back, as is well known, to his studies of the Muybridge photographs of bodies in

left panel   centre panel   right panel

Francis Bacon, *Triptych May–June 1973*

movement (Bacon even titled a picture *After Muybridge*). It can be seen that some of his paintings are interpretations of various frozen moments as captured by Muybridge's lens. Now, while this is plain in *Two Figures* from 1953, Bacon's art of the body captured in movement took some time to develop. After 1962, the fluidity of the subject comes to be captured not only existentially but materially, physically, in some of Bacon's work. While many of the full body portraits do not fully participate in this development, indicating a residual place for a notion of stasis, the role of movement as an essential aspect of the potential of the human subject is especially clear in some of his triptychs. The one which will be singled out here is the *Triptych May–June 1973*, the subject of which is the death of the artist's friend, George Dyer.

George Dyer and Francis Bacon met in 1964. Their undulating relationship was to last until Dyer's death in October 1972. George Dyer was a good-looking small-time crook, and Bacon found him both handsome and exciting, becoming very attached to him and painting his portrait several times. Dyer regularly took money from Bacon, and he gambled, drank and used drugs often to excess. Bacon himself had a masochistic streak, and generally tolerated Dyer's behaviour, which could also be, at least for Bacon, extremely winning. There is little doubt, however, that the relationship was stressful for both; at one time Bacon offered Dyer some £20,000 to go and set up home in Brighton and at another time was obviously relieved to see him off to Tangier. Periodical rows between Bacon and Dyer were interspersed with Dyer's attendance at all of Bacon's major openings, whether in London, Paris or New York, where Dyer took obvious pride in pointing to his various portraits. It was a contradictory friendship, one notable low point being when Dyer denounced Bacon to the police for possessing cannabis – a charge Bacon successfully defended, arguing that the cannabis discovered at his studio could not have been his since as an asthmatic he could not use it. Dyer was in Paris with Bacon at the time of Bacon's huge show at the Grand Palais, and was discovered dead, apparently from an overdose of drugs and alcohol, in his hotel room.

The *May–June 1973 Triptych* shows Dyer's final movements: vomiting blood in a basin, tracking across the bathroom, and then dead on the lavatory. This is not a work to arouse Christian piety nor pagan-carnal pity (indeed it reveals in the attempt to evoke pity that Deleuze's reading of Bacon is ultimately a Christian one, the concept of pagan pity being oxymoronic). Dyer's shadow in the central panel is Eumenidean. The arrows in the lower foreground of the left and right panels may be something of a gimmick, but are pointers to the emphasis on movement and the presence of direction which movement implies. The treatment of the body is of muscled, moving flesh, even when it is heading toward death. Even the figure in the left panel, in death, is a study in the potential of muscle and flesh.

When Bacon said that he 'wanted to give the sensation without the boredom of its conveyance' (Sylvester 1980: 65), that he did not deliberately avoid telling stories, but that he thought that the narrative medium was to be avoided because it is tiresome, he surely knew that he was talking nonsense. In his personal relationships, he loved to know what was going on. In his art, he treated the Crucifixion, the *Oresteia*, and the death of his friend. Perhaps the cleanest way to see Bacon and the narrative form is to say that his mode of narration was the jump cut. Even so, there is something still not resolved in treating the *May–June Triptych* as a jump cut account of the flesh and muscle movement to death of George Dyer. It is the only triptych with a definite temporality: vomit over sink, move to lavatory, die on toilet pan. Why do we have to read this from right to left? Is movement to death a movement backwards? There is some justification for such a view, since flesh and muscle in solitude can be seen as the place where, at least for Bacon, everything begins. Even if this philosophical interpretation is right, however, there is something more going on. Knowing that this triptych has a subject – the death of George Dyer – the last moment is always in the left-hand panel. The direction of the flow is dictated by the centre. Swapping left and right does not reverse the flow of events, and placing the centre on the left opens up the triptych to further events as the moving Dyer heads outwards. Let us say that the right panel of the *May–June Triptych* is the opening to the narrative. We know there just might be grounds for suspecting Bacon's sincerity on topics such as stories, and so forth (bearing in mind that he always maintained that he made no preparatory sketches on paper [see Leiris 1983: 30] before the works which he did on canvas, but then lots of rough work on paper was discovered [see Gale 1999]). The general view is that,

> In most of Bacon's triptychs the three panels do not suggest any particular
> sequence; they can be 'read' in any order, which is what the artist intended, and

the main reason why he had each of them put in a separate frame. Time, the essence of narrative, has been removed, as if sucked away. (Peppiat 1996: 251)

Now we see this is not as certain as has been thought. Might it not be the case that quite a few of his triptychs have an inbuilt temporality, which Bacon sought to disguise by insistently, but without being insistent, placing the opening to the narrative on the right? The 'Beach' triptych of 1974–7 begins on the right with an outward gaze, is followed in the centre by some form of encounter, and then concludes on the left with the umbrella being used as a shield against approaching horse-riders. Is it right to suggest that 'There is no hint of a sequence from panel to panel' (Peppiat 1996: 277) in the case of *Triptych 1976*; at the very least does this triptych not betray a classic before and after structure? Is *Triptych – Studies of the Human Body 1979* not, at least conceivably, the story of the wound to the back of the figure in the left-hand panel?

This might seem a disappointing note on which to end this investigation of the human subject in the art of Francis Bacon. We had almost taken him to the point where he was operating at a level more profound than that of either pity or piety, finding that his engagement with flesh and meat was at base a matter of volume and mobility, then exercised as pure force or within a master–slave dialectic, to which, in either case, is added the crucial figure of the human witness. Have we now to repudiate this analysis? On account that there might be stories? Can we not have both subjects with stories and their existential condition? Is this not what the witness as an ontological category does? Does it not demand that we think at both levels? Didn't Bacon, even while denying it?

Notes

1. Cf. Donna Haraway: 'Corporealization involves institutions, narratives, legal structures, power-differentiated human labor, technical practice, analytic apparatus, and much more. The processes "inside" bodies – such as the cascades of action that constitute an organism or that constitute the play of genes and other entities that go to make up a cell – are interactions, not frozen things. For humans, a word like *gene* specifies a multifaceted set of interactions among people and non-humans in historically contingent, practical, knowledge-making work. A gene is not a thing, much less a "master molecule" or a self-contained code. Instead the term *gene* signifies a node of durable action where many actors, human and nonhuman, meet' (Haraway 1997: 142).

2. In Andrew Webber's interpretation of the *Doppelgänger* figure in German literature, we find the following: 'the Doppelganger is archetypally "unheimlich": a prime figure of the uncanny precisely in that it is an original resident in the "Heim" and embodying a constitutive, domestic split in subjectivity. If it occupies only the closeted space of repression, it is none the less perhaps more properly at home than the host subject. While the phenomenon creates a scandal for the epistemological order of things, it cannot simply be written off as phantasm; it insists upon its place in the real. Even as it is disavowed it demands to be recognised as a projected symptom of profound anxiety in the host subject and the order of things. Indeed, it may ultimately project the reality of the autonomous subject into the phantasmatic anti-order of which it is the symptomatic figure' (Webber 1996: 8).

3. 'What unites modern science with the self-health cultures of the 1990s is the desire for mastery. It is the desire to see, to know, and to control. It is the desire to fix meaning and to make outcomes predictable. It is the desire to prove that one has power over disease, the body and the emotions. In short, it is what has been identified as the masculine "urge to fathom the secrets of nature" . . . The desire for order and control, for permanence and immutability, produces a masculine drive to mark out the boundaries' (Stacey 1997: 238, 240).

PART III
LOCATING THE SUBJECT

INTRODUCTION

There is a supplementary relationship between the pursuit of the subject by the artists whose work we have examined, and the repudiation of the subject within the sociological tradition. Each vision has the potential to overwhelm the other. Each may be a necessary corrective to the other. One of the sites where the two perspectives meet is narrative, and to the extent that cinema is approaching the condition of the contemporary narrative form, reflecting the socially contextualised sensibility of the humanities toward the subject – the development of a value sphere begun in poetics, philosophy, music and literature – we may find telling examples within cinema of the situated adjacency of subject valorisation and subject repudiation. Can cinema bear this weight?

In his discussion of Western reactions to the breakdown of communism in Greater Europe, Stjepan Meštrović asks us to consider 'Balkanization as the breaking up of a unit into increasingly smaller units that are hostile to each other' (Meštrović 1994: ix). If something like that definition was what Bloom had in mind when he wrote, in the closing chapter of *The Western Canon*, that 'the Balkanization of literary studies is irreversible' (Bloom 1994: 517), then there are at least two possible interpretations of his statement. Bloom points us to both of them. Either literary studies is breaking up into mutually antagonistic schools but still at some level remaining within some kind of literary totality, or the aesthetic whole, of which literature has traditionally been a part, is decomposing.

Because language is the common medium between canonical literature and critical response, the literary field has been peculiarly vulnerable. It has become an ideological patchwork. Many analysts and critics have not been driven by aesthetic experience but, argues Bloom, by *ressentiment* and the ideologies of race, class and gender:

> Precisely why students of literature have become amateur political scientists, uninformed sociologists, incompetent anthropologists, mediocre philosophers, and overdetermined cultural historians, while a puzzling matter, is not beyond all conjecture. They resent literature, or are ashamed of it. (1994: 521)

Bloom specifies seven types of literary critic, although he lists only six of them: 'Feminists, Marxists, Lacanians, New Historicists, Deconstructionists, Semioticians' (ibid.: 527). The seventh is typified by his entire approach:

> I think that the self, in its quest to be free and solitary, ultimately reads with one aim only: to confront greatness. That confrontation scarcely masks the desire to join greatness, which is the basis of the aesthetic experience once called the Sublime: the quest for a transcendence of limits. (ibid.: 524)

Bloom thinks that great literature is often difficult, but that the experience can be massively rewarding. The locus of that experience is the solitary reader, an existential figure who can draw hope and consolation from the experience of great literature. He thinks that the same is true of art and music, of Matisse and Stravinsky, for example.

An illustration of the way that the study of literature may be breaking up into antagonistic schools is the recent work on Flaubert by Pierre Bourdieu. The basic field-analytic position from which Bourdieu sets out his account of Flaubert in *The Rules of Art* is functionalist. He criticises the aesthetic tradition for what he regards as its continuous reference to the artwork's absence of function, to the primacy of its form, and to the disengaged nature of art as art. What Bourdieu does is assemble an ideal type of the attempted universalisation of art's essence, and he argues that this ideal type, general though it might once have been, ignores the socio-historical location of the work and its reception. He holds that aestheticism privileges the reader's decontextualised subjective experience of the work of art, and that therefore aestheticism universalises the particular, translating particularity into transhistoric normativity. He concludes that ignoring the historicity of both the work and its reception precludes the development of anything approaching an adequate view of aesthetic experience (Bourdieu 1996: 286–7).

If Bourdieu's demotion and derogation of aesthetic values is symptomatic, then there is indeed sense to that first interpretation of Bloom's balkanisation thesis. In opposition to other forms of literary science, and against aestheticism, Bourdieu's approach will draw attention to the historical context and contemporary function of the literary work, allowing, for example, attention to be drawn to the potential role of literature in advancing transnational values. It will also, however, provide some legitimacy for the struggle between ideologies: of race, gender, class and nation. The replacement of aesthetic formalism with ideological functionalism does not, then, provide us with a certain template for a civilising process – unless, of course, one is arguing from one of the competing standpoints. Indeed it may well be, as Bloom hints, quite the reverse.

In certain respects, the second interpretation of Bloom's balkanisation thesis, that the domain of the aesthetic *tout court* is breaking up, is even more worrying. Bloom suspects that reading is a dying art, that 'the reborn theocratic era will be almost wholly an oral and visual culture' (1994: 519). Geoffrey Hartman, reflecting on contemporary culture, had this to say:

> The substantial effects of film and telecommunications are having their impact. An 'information sickness' caused by the speed and quantity of what impinges on us, and abetted by machines that we have invented that generate endless arrays, threatens to overwhelm personal memory. The individual, we complain, cannot 'process' all this information, this flak: public and personal experience are being moved not closer together but further apart. The arts, it used to be said, aspire to the condition of music; now the 'total flow' of video seems to dominate. Can public memory still be called memory when it is increasingly alienated from personal and active recall? (Hartman 1995: 73)

One aspect of this information sickness is the demand for accessibility, for easy experience, for anaesthesia. It is routinely observed that the contemporary television viewer is inured to tragedy. Our cinematic society means that 'Actuality is distanced by larger-than-life violence and retreats behind special effects' (ibid.: 77). How, Hartman asks, within the anaesthetised culture of the facile, also characterised by suspicion of official pronouncements, can we promote awareness of the historical legacy? (The same question needs to be asked in regard to the fulfilment of future potential.) He cites Spielberg's *Schindler's List* as a successful reconnection to the past, and goes on to suggest that 'Art as a performance medium – art not reduced to official meaning or information – has a chance to transmit this inheritance most fully. When art remains accessible, it provides a counterforce to manufactured and monolithic memory' (ibid.: 80).

The balkanisation of the aesthetic was, in fact, announced by Walter Benjamin, in his famous essay, 'The work of art in the age of mechanical reproduction'. He saw that Abel Gance's enthusiasm for the way that film might revivify 'Shakespeare, Rembrandt, Beethoven' promised liquidation rather than resurrection (Benjamin 1970: 223–4). A part of its destructiveness was the way that cinema imposed itself on the spectator, impacting upon the viewer like bullets, subjecting the audience to a fusillade of moving images. The mind of the viewer is taken over, not allowed to reflect but forced on to the next image. The cinema inaugurates the era of the spectacle, the mass of its communicative power being so much greater than its theatrically located predecessors, and so it is that a film like *Schindler's List* can reconstitute memory; Hartman says that this film works 'albeit by spectacular means', but Benjamin's point would be that it works *precisely* by spectacular means. This is, however, only one part of the contemporary effectivity of cinema. A second aspect concerns the distrust of official discourses in the electronic age of democracy (Hartman 1995: 77–8), and raises the question of the popular distrust of literature (not, it should be noted, of narrative) arising out of its formal educational function, its demonstrably elitist positioning, and its permanent betrayal of values. There is, of course, much to be said here about art cinema, youth cinema, political cinema, and the 'moronisation' of mass audiences by popular cinema everywhere. In general, however, cinema may be seen as the leading contemporary medium of seduction.

Whichever interpretation we make of Bloom's notion of the balkanisation of literary studies, its consequence is a certain suspicion, whether of the indoctrination potential of ideological functionalism or because of the mass rejection of a difficult art that is, in any event, tainted by official approval. Neither of these lines of thought is in any way sufficient for us to celebrate the end of literature (as Armando Petrucci has recently noted, 'Our world today produces a broader variety and a much greater amount of written matter than in 1900 or 1950' [1999: 345]), but both may lead us to underline the serious attention being given to film (its status as the 'seventh art' is far from universally acknowledged) that was formerly reserved for the high terrain of literature, music and art.

We are now, however, immediately faced with the issue of the kind of approach to be adopted, and perhaps a certain anti-balkanism would be in order, treating film as both aesthetic object and as socio-historically located. So far as the formal properties of the medium are concerned, we may take our lead from Noel Burch's comparison of Renoir's *La Règle du jeu* and serial music:

> Even taking the term in its simplest sense, the subject is contained in microcosm not only in each sequence but in almost every shot, on a certain level of analysis at least . . . Serial composers appear to us to have a very similar conception of the relationships between the basic choice of a tone row or tone rows (which provides a musical work with its 'subject,' what classical musicians call the 'theme' of a work, although tone rows function quite differently) and the form of the finished work. Serial composers believe that the entire development of a musical work must be derived from the basic cell or at least be located relative to it, even if the actual cellular unit is never recognizable as such. (Burch 1973: 122–3)

Taking Burch out of context, we can begin to ask if 'the subject is contained in microcosm not only in each sequence but in almost every shot'.

6
KIEŚLOWSKI'S SUBJECTS

Blue

Krzysztof Kieślowski died from his second heart attack on 13 March 1996. His 1993 film, *Trois Couleurs: Bleu*, was the first of a trilogy. The film was co-scripted by Kieślowski and Krzysztof Piesiewicz. They had worked together since the 1984 film, *No End*. They met in 1982 when Kieślowski was filming live in the Warsaw law courts where Piesiewicz was a lawyer, and Kieślowski had turned to him for help in 1984 when he decided to try and make a feature film based on some of the things he had seen in the courtroom. After that, following Piesiewicz's initial thought, they had collaborated as joint scriptwriters on *The Decalogue* – Kieślowski's series of ten films for Polish television, from 1988, which reflect, one by one,[1] on the Ten Commandments, and on the moral dilemmas which, for him, constitute a very significant part of the lifeworld of the contemporary subject.[2] Kieślowski's work – with the qualified exception of *Blue* – does not explore the question of the subject in isolation, as an existential hero in anguish, or as a lone artist struggling with a personal history and a social context. His protagonists define and measure themselves against significant others. Their influences and antecedents are not dissolved in a welter of explanation and causation, but are lived with as they pursue their projects and confront their difficulties. In parallel, Kieślowski's work is developed in partnership, especially with co-scriptwriters, cameramen and, crucially, with actors, who, as his seminar for young directors in Amsterdam in 1994 showed, were a continual test of the intelligibility, coherence and personal impact of his narrative explorations of the contemporary subject (Lint 1995).

The trilogy of films, of which *Blue* is the first, was conceptualised by Kieślowski as follows:

> Blue, white, red: liberty, equality, fraternity. Piesiewicz had the idea that having tried *Dekalog*, why shouldn't we try liberty, equality and fraternity? . . . The West has implemented these three concepts on a political or social plane, but it's an entirely different matter on the personal plane. And that's why we thought of these films. (Stok 1993: 212)

Piesiewicz recalled that, 'One night I saw a Polish composer being interviewed on television. He was with his wife. I said to myself that this woman must have an important role in his life. That was the starting point for "Blue"' (cited in Insdorf 1999: 139). *Three Colours: Blue*, then, deals with liberty on the personal plane. As Nigel Andrews, film critic of the *Financial Times*, put it: '*Blue* is about . . . Liberty from memory, from grief. Liberty from the panaceas of the well-meaning.' What Kieślowski found was that freedom of the will and subjective self-determination are socially constrained; and he discovered the social prohibition and sociological impossibility of willed amnesia, pointing therefore to the underlying sense of 'coming to terms with' and 'learning to live with' as the foundation of all effective post-traumatic therapies.[3]

Julie de Courcy, Patrice her composer-husband and Anna their child are on a car journey. The car has a leaking brake pipe. There is an accident.[4] The car goes off the road at a bend and hits a tree. Julie is alive, but the others are dead. A young man named Antoine is close by and runs to the scene. He can do little, but we will hear from him again. Julie regains consciousness in hospital. Kieślowski tells us he used that moment of regained consciousness to indicate how much inside Julie's experience he wanted to take us:

> We wanted to convey Julie's state of mind. When you wake up on an operating table what you see first is the lamp, the lamp becomes a great white haze and then it becomes clearer and clearer. After the accident, Julie can't see the man who brings her the television set clearly. She opens her eyes and, for a while, she sees a blur. It's typical of her mental state of absolute introversion, of focusing in on herself. (Stok 1993: 222)

The reference to the television set probably referred to an earlier script,[5] since in the filmscript and the film as released it is the doctor who tells her of the death of her family who is seen first in a haze, and then reflected in Julie's eye, and so, strictly speaking, her blurred vision is a pre-figuration of, rather than a symptom of, her inward-focusing. Additionally, 'the man' who brings her the television set is Olivier, as we will see hardly just 'the man' in the sense of 'the man who brought the TV set'. In any event, her first activities are deliberate but beyond her capacities. She breaks a window in the hospital corridor in order to distract the nurse while she takes tablets from a locked cabinet and then attempts to swallow them. Her own body proves much more obdurate than the plate glass window, and it rejects the tablets she tries to swallow, despite her obvious determination.

The estrangement and self-isolation which the film explores has its second major moment (the accident, of course, being the first) with Julie's viewing on television of the funeral of her husband and child. The process of alienation, begun with the accident and then heavily emphasised by Julie's absence from the funeral, is further developed with her matter-of-fact instruction to her lawyer that all her property should be sold. Julie insists that no one must know any details, that the money will go into a numbered account chosen at random, although she is concerned to ensure that her mother will be provided for in her nursing home for as long as she lives. Perhaps the strongest sign of her resolve to erase the past comes with the settling of accounts with her husband's music. A world-renowned composer, he had been commissioned to write a *Concerto for Europe*, which was to be performed simultaneously by twelve orchestras in twelve European cities. It was part-written, and there had been some indication that Julie had been actively involved in the writing of her husband's work – perhaps as an editor, perhaps even more. There is a moral question here: does Julie have the right to destroy this music? Her answer is unequivocal. She visits the agency where the music has been deposited, collects what we take to be the only copy, and hurls it into the jaws of a refuse van which minces the concerto along with the black and purple plastic bags. The film critic of *Variety* suggested that the music in this film is a character in its own right (Nesselson 1993), and Julie's act of destruction has all the symbolic and emotional force of a murder.[6]

The locking away of the past, both as memory and as potentiality, continues with Julie's ritualised consumption of her daughter's second lollipop – Anna had eaten the first on the car journey – and then goes further with her attempt to persuade the key friend of the family, Olivier, who loves her, that she is just unremarkable flesh and will be easily and painlessly forgotten. As she walks away from the house in the morning, with just a bag and a cardboard box tied up with string, she scrapes her knuckles along the rough wall at the side of the road: thirty metres of pain to shift her focus from the past to the present.

She intends to live alone and (with the single exception of her mother who is becoming senile) out of contact completely with everyone from her former life. When she is searching for somewhere to live, the estate agent asks her what she does. He thinks that this will help him judge what kind of property will be most suitable. Her reply is that she does nothing, 'absolument rien': a further mark of the emptying out of identity which is taking place, as she plainly rejects any notion of self-fulfilment other than through the simple fact of her continuing existence.

There are weak points in the carapace Julie is forming about herself. The first of these relates to an exception to her excision of the past. This exception is her mother. She is in a nursing home, and Julie visits her. This may be an act of duty. It may also be safe because her mother will make neither demands nor connections as long as she has her television. However, whether done out of love or duty or magnanimity or irrelevance, there is no need of psychoanalytic theory to establish that this active link to her mother is also a thread back to the past Julie is seeking to escape. A second weakness is demonstrated by her requirement that whatever building she lives in must not have any children living in it: this is her (and Kieślowski's) acknowledgement that the will is not strong enough to resist the normal triggering processes of memory, that the insistent presence of children will be intolerable. The third element she cannot choose to disregard is her husband's music. Kieślowski thought that the music was the one thing she could not get away from. He wrote this about it:

> Music is important in *Blue*. Musical notes often appear on the screen, so in this sense the film's about music, about the writing of music, about working on music. For some people Julie is the author of the music we hear. At one stage the

journalist asks Julie: 'Did you write your husband's music?' And Julie slams the
door on her. So this possibility does exist. Then the copyist says: 'There are a lot
of corrections.' There had always been a lot of corrections. Did Julie only do the
corrections? Maybe she's one of those people who aren't able to write a single
sheet of music but is wonderful in correcting a sheet which has already been
written. She sees everything, has an excellent analytical mind and has a great
talent for improving things. The written sheet of music isn't bad but when she's
improved it, it is excellent. But it's not all that important whether she's the author
or co-author, whether she corrects or creates. Even if she only does do the
corrections she's still the author or co-author because what has been corrected is
better than it was before. The music is cited all through the film and then at the
end we hear it in its entirety, solemn and grand. So we're led to think that she's
played a part in its creation. In this sense the film's about music. (Stok 1993: 224)

The massive presence of the music is inescapable, and is synecdochically
linked to the presence of Patrice and Anna in Julie's life.

Her mother, her aversion to children now, and the music are not the only
things that tie Julie to the past. Her first act when she steps into her new flat
is to open her cardboard box and take out the blue light fitting, the only
thing that remained in Anna's 'Blue Room' of her former house, which she
had ordered to be cleared. As she puts up the blue hanging stone chan-
delier, she is crying. It would, at this point, be an error to think that this
partial preservation of the past is a sign of choice on Julie's part. The
clearing away of all detritus to leave a pure subject, a *tabula rasa* recreated
and ready to be written on again but as if for the first time, was surely
exposed as an impossible dream, most definitively by Jacques Derrida,
writing of the inseparability of repetition and erasure, and of the non-
existence of the subject, 'if we mean by that some sovereign solitude of the
author' (Derrida 1978a: 226). As Derrida put it in *On Grammatology*,

> The outside . . . which we believe we know as the most familiar thing in the world,
> as familiarity itself, would not appear . . . without difference as temporalization,
> without the nonpresence of the other inscribed within the sense of the present,
> without the relationship to death as the concrete structure of the living present.
> (Derrida 1976: 70–1)

For Derrida, the idea of a subject with memory control would be untenable. For Julie, perhaps the choice to take the light fitting forward into her
new life was something over which she had some control; one can say the
same thing about the scrap of music in her bag, but she had no control over
the fact that things would go with her. It is this link between the inside and
the outside, between the subject and its social context, that the film shows
to be outside of the will to power.[7]

Kieślowski will find that not only memory is outside of the will; so too is
social existence. The insistently threatening invasions of everyday life are
announced by a fight outside Julie's flat. She contrives to lock herself out
when she goes to see what is happening, spending the night on the landing
and thereby beginning a process of connection with her neighbours. She
rebuffs the first approach, from a neighbour who asks Julie to sign the
petition to eject one of the tenants because she is a sex-worker. The pressure

upon her is considerable: 'everyone else has signed!' Nevertheless, Julie resists, saying it is nothing to do with her. The fortuitous and the contingent visit her again with a call from the young man who was first on the scene of the accident. He bears the twin gifts of her husband's last words, and the neck-chain which had been lying at the scene, and which we later learn was a definitive sign of Patrice's love. Julie deals with both in a detached way, explaining the words and telling Antoine that he can keep the neck-chain. The third intrusion opens what will be a new path: Lucille calls with a bunch of flowers, to thank Julie for not signing the petition; and soon after that, with a certain inevitability, Olivier, who has been searching for her for months, finds Julie in her local café.

Both the past and the future seem as if they are converging on her, denying any prospect of success to her fight to remain in the present, without links to the past and without debt to the future. Her childhood phobia about mice is revived as she finds a nest in the larder. Her mother thinks she is dead, which is the condition she aspires to, at least in the eyes of the other, but Julie cannot resist correcting her. Kieślowski's construction of the mother presents an image of disconnectedness. If this is an example of what willed amnesia might do, it carries the stigmata of social dysfunctionality, dependence, disease and the pathos of repeated misrecognitions. Even though Julie could surely not want this, she has not yet acknowledged the lesson, and says to herself as much as to her mother, 'I want no belongings, no memories, no friends, no love: they are all traps.' If the condition of isolated subjectivity were an existential possibility, then the increasing pressure from past and future might be resisted, but the successful strategies which Kieślowski gives us are suicide and senility. Julie cannot kill herself (although she goes to the edge of this again, in the swimming pool) nor will herself into oblivion. So she begins to face what has happened and will happen. She borrows (creating a debt) a cat to deal with the mice, and then her submission to Lucille's offer to clean up the mess is more a sign of the strength to enter into reciprocities, than it is of weakness in dealing with a phobia. She is called upon to repay this second debt very soon, as Lucille asks her to come to the club on Place Pigalle where she works. It is 11.30 at night and Lucille needs help. Julie goes. It is for Kieślowski the sign that she is ready to be sutured back into the rest of her life.

At the sex club where Lucille works, Julie sees herself on television. Olivier has obtained a copy of Patrice's unfinished manuscript. He says he is going to try and finish the work. Julie had not destroyed the only copy after all. The media are very interested, and they show a range of still pictures of Patrice as accompaniment to the story. There are some of Patrice and a woman that Julie does not know. This double jolt sends Julie to Olivier. There is an exchange at the heart of their meeting: she gives him the words that are meant to go with the *Concerto* (St Paul's Epistle to the Corinthians 1: 13),[8] he gives her the story of Sandrine, Patrice's girlfriend for several years. Julie meets Sandrine, who is pregnant with Patrice's child. Sandrine says, at the end of their first encounter, 'You want to know if he loved me?' 'Yes,' replies Julie. 'That's the question I wanted to ask, but I know the answer now.' Sandrine is wearing Patrice's neck-chain.

Kieślowski forces Julie to a final decision: suicide or senility. She can neither stay under the water, nor countenance her mother's existence. Thus she turns to Olivier, and considers what fate has done. Had Olivier not removed a dossier from Patrice's desk, Julie would have destroyed it unexamined and the pictures of Sandrine it contained would have been no more. 'Maybe it's better this way,' says Julie, as she turns to the manuscript from Patrice that Olivier is working on to see what he has done so far. They work on it together, but the finale is missing. Then Julie remembers the scrap of sheet music in her bag.

Four moments complete the film. The house will not be sold, and Sandrine and her son, to be called Patrice, will live in it. Olivier refuses to acknowledge the music that Julie has completed unless its writers are named. Julie takes the completed manuscript to Olivier, and they make love on the mattress that he had bought when the possessions from Julie's house were sold. The concerto's main themes are played to their textual accompaniment, with a foreground collage of Olivier, Antoine, Julie's mother, Lucille, Julie and her husband's unborn child.

If we imagine that *Blue* was an attempt to present a credible version of a self isolated from its past, if we understand the film as a failed experiment to construct a subject insulated from its social context, and if we thematise the priority established by the end of the film of love and sociality over self and autonomy, a certain picture of the self emerges. This self is characterised as an essentially social subject with a relatively inflexible identity possessed of a will with quite definite internally determined limitations (such as the inability to control memory). How does this picture of the self compare with our conventional understanding?

The subject in *Blue*

The history of the subject as written from Plato onward moves from the subject as God's creation in his image, through a constrained and physical view of voluntary control over our physical actions in Aristotle, to an Augustinian conception of a unified subject able to choose good over evil, to a Cartesian conception of mental agency as domination over the physical world, to a Kantian view that the agent is inscribed within a world with, broadly, an *a priori* moral structure, to a Freudian view of a composite and imperfectly revealed self, to a postmodern view of fragmented subjectivity. Until the last, Freudian and postmodern, stages, this historical narrative of the self has taken the form of a dialectic of strength and weakness explicating the nature of the unified subject. This will require some further elaboration.

It is generally thought that the notion of free will is specific to Western culture from approximately the fourth century AD.[9] While there are clear forerunners of the notion in Plato,[10] and a developed account of voluntary action in Aristotle,[11] it was Christian thought that gave clear shape to the idea with its elaboration of inner-directed behaviour. Within Christian thought, the significance of free will may be understood as the emergence of inner compliance to the Ten Commandments. It represents a change from external obedience to inner harmony with a moral code.[12] The emerging sense from St Augustine onwards was very powerfully of a unified subject, a clear conception of the human individual as having causal powers and moral responsibility, and as operating as a whole force. The inward turn offered by Christianity provided the foundation for the emergence of this conception, which may still be taken entirely for granted, and which both Freudianism and postmodernism have been questioning.

The Augustinian problematic was built upon the human capacity to dwell within *The City of God*, and in the final analysis the primary reference points of Augustine's thought and teaching were otherworldly. A decisive break, however, is marked by Descartes. In his thought a shift is made from human existence as leading to Heaven or Hell, to what Charles Taylor calls the disengaged subject, whose relationship to the world will now be one of instrumental control, and whose relationship to the self is one where reason controls the passions (a mode of subjecthood explored, as we will see, in Kieślowski's *White*). Partly in reaction to Cartesian dualism, Immanuel Kant argued that there is an *a priori* moral law. (Valentine, in *Red*, has a naïve belief in its existence, which takes the form of thinking that people 'naturally' tend to follow it, while the Judge, in the form of a prodigal returning from a wilderness to take on the maieutic function of undermining both structural determination and egocentrism through the promotion of stronger destinies than those which at first appear obviously laid out, thinks that all systems of rules fail at some point.) That is to say Kant thought that the idea of morality cannot be deduced from experience, but is somehow independent of experience and prior to it, that if there were no *a priori* morality, then the way that we live in the world would be unthinkably different. Kieślowski's examination of the life of the subject within a moral cosmos focuses on the phenomenon of love, both in *Blue*, and in *Decalogue 6*: in the latter film, Magda comes to recognise the consequences, both for herself and for the boy who was 'peeping' at her, of rejecting the ontology of love and care: he cuts his wrists, and she is left with an empty life. For both of them, however, there is the possibility of growth. As the contortionist in *Decalogue 8* implies, it is a question of working at it (Garbowski 1997: 25).

The history of thinking about the self, from Plato to Kant, is a history of religion and morality (or, otherwise put, of politics and duty). Nietzsche's critique of morality was therefore not surprisingly also a critique of the unified moral self. He wrote as follows in 1885:

> Granted that nothing is 'given' as real except our world of desires and passions, that we can rise or sink to no other 'reality' than the reality of our drives – for thinking is only the relationship of these drives to one another . . . (Nietzsche 1973: 48)

This formulation of Nietzsche is more extreme than Freud's view, but the Nietzschean dismissal of God in the human form of conscience is widely regarded as a prime antecedent for the deconstructionist critique of unified subjectivity (Jacobitti 1996: 205). But it is surely Freud's work that under-pins the postmodern thesis that fragmentation is the condition of contem-porary subjectivity. At the same time that Nietzsche was writing *Beyond Good and Evil*, Dr Freud was becoming an authority on childhood cerebral palsy and working under Jean-Martin Charcot, whose lectures on hysteria were gaining wide attention. In 1895 Freud and Josef Breuer published the case study of Anna O. She had right-side paralysis for two years, together with defective vision, intermittent anorexia, a nervous cough, and frequent bouts of delirium. Breuer had seen that during her hysterical attacks Anna would mutter things, and he decided to explore the connotations of these mutterings by putting Anna under hypnosis and questioning her. Her condition improved, and it was Anna herself who referred to this early version of psychoanalytic therapy as the 'talking cure'. Through further work, Freud developed the theory of repression, probably the foundational concept of the whole psychoanalytic edifice.[13] To get a picture of the subject according to Freud, however, it is not enough to understand the mechanisms of id, ego and superego. One must add in his theory of devel-opment, which has five critical moments: first, the shift from auto-eroticism to sanctioned object-choice; second, the movement from polymorphous forms of sexual activity to a genito-reproductive focus; third, the replace-ment of overwhelming fixation on one parent by a stable post-obsessional relation to that parent; fourth, the emergence of a near-obsessional relation to a loved outsider; and fifth, the development from a repressed hostility to the same-sex parent to a non-sexual but affective and affectionate relation to that parent (who is not to be seen as a rival for the love of the newly acquired outsider). This is the normal development path.[14] The subject it describes is social and historical, both inter- and intra-personal. The unconscious energies within the subject may be partly repressed, but are always potentially causally active (often routed from nodes at which the development process has gone awry).

The sense of the subject found here is far off the path which ran from Plato to Kant. Nor is it to be found on the line between Christianity and classical sociology. It may better be regarded as somewhere on a new route, stretching toward the postmodern conception of the subject, described as follows by Nikolas Rose:

> In place of the self, new images of subjectivity proliferate: as socially constructed, as dialogic, as inscribed upon the surface of the body, as spatialised, decentred, multiple, nomadic, created in episodic recognition-seeking practices of self-display in particular times and places. (Rose 1996: 169)

It must be said, however, that despite these various deconstructions of the subject, there remains in most formulations some form of classical and enduring background, against which such movements are seen to take place. Often unexamined, at least when the focus is on the subject rather than the atmospheres in which it moves, the enduring presence of the axiological context of the subject, because of the supplementary inter-animation of subject and ground, establishes a limit beyond which the unstitching of the subject cannot go.[15]

We can now come to a precise question concerning Julie. Where is she? Which path is she on? It is very tempting to say that she is at the cross-over point. But that would be illicit. These paths are the byways of historical hermeneutics, not transports for individual subjects. Kieślowski does not make things easy. Not only does he haze over the end of the film with a powerful, lyrical and typically Polish romanticism, he also has a pretty firm view of his own subjectivity as located on the 'old' path:

> If you don't understand your own life, then I don't think you can understand the lives of the characters in your stories, you can't understand the lives of other people. Philosophers know this. Social workers know this . . . I believe that composers do . . . it's absolutely necessary to those who tell stories about life: an authentic understanding of one's own life. By authentic I mean that it's not a public understanding, which I'll share with anybody. It's not for sale, and, in fact, you'll never detect it in my films. Some things you can find out very easily but you'll never understand how much the films I make or the stories I tell mean to me and why. You'll never find that out. I know it, but that knowledge is only for me. (Stok 1993: 36)

It may be, then, that locating Julie as a divided soul, broken up by the loss of part of her being and gradually coming to terms with the contingency of her fractured subjectivity, goes somewhat against the grain of Kieślowski's inclinations. We do get some unwitting support from him, though. He says:

> For all its tragedy and drama, its hard to imagine a more luxurious situation than the one Julie finds herself in. She's completely free at the beginning because her husband and daughter die, she loses her family and all her obligations. She is perfectly provided for, has masses of money and no responsibilities. (ibid.: 212)

The luxury of Julie's situation is that she has no history as a subject. Kieślowski thought to make her free by killing her significant others, disabling her mother, and allowing her to overcome her only childhood neurosis. He could only do this if he saw Julie as a cipher, an empty vessel to be filled by the flood of history and care welling around her. His achievement was to avoid having this symbol of empty subjectivity seem to decide, to make the choice to be reconnected, to opt to be filled with the *caritas* which the music celebrates; rather it was the flood that surrounded her that pulled her in. In truth, the film was about the flood rather than about Julie. So the question of where Julie might be as a subject is a question to be posed about Julie before the accident, and the answer to that question is clear: she would have been an inhabitant of late twentieth-century Europe, a complex, divided, fragmented self set against, and even at times overwhelmed by, a recognisable if confused background. It was the personal trauma which allowed Kieślowski to empty her out, and site her on the 'old' path.

Angela Pope is a film director whose husband died of leukaemia a short time before she saw *Three Colours: Blue*. She described how her own life had been:

> He was gone. I didn't sell up, move out, move on. Nor did I try to blot out the past. I didn't need to because I couldn't remember it, though I tried hard enough. I wore his clothes, read the books he read, tried to speak as he spoke, think as he had thought. None of it worked; the memories stayed stubbornly erased. (Much later they would come back, without my summoning, and with startling ferocity.) (Pope 1996)

She goes on to describe how her public life at this time was a shell, but that, as if from nowhere, the world flooded in. She felt the film was honest, and saw Kieślowski's sentiment ('Though I speak with the tongues of angels, and have not love, I become as a hollow brass') as profound.

Both the film and its sobering real-world duplication demonstrate that memory is beyond willed control. This is a feature of the subject that the traditional line from Plato to Kant did not much dwell on, and it is a facet of subjectivity that now receives increasing attention, a philosopheme whose time has come. Much recent attention has been paid to the need for memory, the will to remember. Cathy Caruth's edited collection, *Trauma: Explorations in Memory*, thus is concerned with the Holocaust, Hiroshima and AIDS, and Shoshana Felman's lead article in that collection is concerned with what it is to witness, to be a witness, to bear witness. The history of interiority may be said to begin with a book of *Confessions*, nothing other than the making public of memory; and it is no coincidence that Derrida's programmatic explication of the 'Memoirs of the Blind' exhibition at the Louvre (1990–1) explores the relation between drawing and memory and concludes with reflections on Augustine's question to God about the nature of tears (Why are they sweet to those in misery?) and Marvell's question of what tears see (Derrida 1993: 129).

Were we able to erase memories at will then we could become senile and dependent as if by a series of strokes (no matter that we made them happen, since after the fact they would by definition not be recalled), and so the appalling vision is of Julie wishing to abandon her memories and (did she but realise it) become her mother. Memories are required keeping: there may be none that should be wilfully abandoned even were that possible. Their insufficiency, however, is a key theme of Kieślowski's work as a whole.

Three subjects

The existentialist, the Cartesian and the Kantian subjects form a set. In many respects, the witness – a category whose importance we noted when we looked at Bacon's work – and the point of potential we saw in the work of Barnett Newman, as well as the subject merely suffering the world, fall into the existential category, the category of being. It is a substantially empty category filled, whether by pain or wonder, by inessential worldly contingency which it is hard to continue to resist and which is a permanent force for the transformation of the existential condition into the fantasies of Cartesianism (which we will now see explored in *White*) or the tragedies of transcendent principle, hinted at in *Red* and explored more extensively in the *Decalogue*. The Cartesian subject is the one familiar to us from theories of rational action. He or she will change the world to suit their desires, harnessing their strong sense of motive self to a vision of the world. This Machiavellian figure is defined by lack, not an interior dissatisfaction such as might be vaguely felt by the existentialist but an exterior absence rooted in disappointment at the world and those who inhabit it. The vision of the world to which the Cartesian is attached will be strongly felt but may be impermanent, easily capable of being changed as a result of the vicissitudes of the world. We are here on the territory of the agent, and are concerned with the question of doing.

While *Blue*, Kieślowski's film on the theme of liberty, is about the untenability of a free subject wilfully divorcing itself from its memories and social context, *White* finds the subject treasuring its memories, deciding that they are not enough, and then embracing the Cartesian moment of subjective power in order to attain self-satisfaction, but it is achieved only at the level of fantasy. Karol, an international prize-winning hairdresser from Poland, the central character in *Three Colours: White*, is being sued for divorce. He and his French wife, Dominique, live in Paris. They have been married for six months, but Karol is temporarily impotent and the marriage has not been consummated. Karol has been working very hard and needs some time to repair his relationship with Dominique. She will not grant it, and tells the judge that she does not love him any more. Dominique has the upper hand. The legal proceedings are in French, which Karol does not understand well, and after the separation is granted, Dominique leaves him in the street with just a big empty trunk. The only place he can think to go is Dominique's hairdressing salon, where he spends the night. When she arrives in the morning to find him there, she goes to phone the police, but Karol pleads. She feels sorry for him, loves him still in some way, and this empathy turns into mutual desire. Both are excited, but Karol cannot sustain his erection, and now it is even worse than before. Dominique sets fire to the curtains in the salon, saying she will report Karol to the police as an arsonist motivated by spite. He can do little else but run away. Several days later, Karol is begging in the métro station opposite Dominique's flat, playing traditional Polish tunes on a paper and comb. Mikolaj, a stranger, recognises one of the melodies, and stops to talk to Karol in Polish. He has a bottle of malt whisky which they share while Karol explains to Mikolaj what has happened to him. Mikolaj has something of a solution: someone he knows will pay a lot of money for his own death. He wants to die but has not the will to do it himself. Karol does not understand. His own position is as bad as it could be, yet still he wants to go on. He takes Mikolaj outside the métro to show him Dominique's flat.

They can see from the shadows on the back-lit curtain of the first-floor flat across the street that she is not alone. Distraught, Karol phones her from the call-box in the métro station, and she replies by making him listen to her orgasm.

Karol's identity, like Julie's, has been all but emptied out. He does not have, comparing *White* with *Blue*, the luxury of Julie's money: he has lost his passport, has no money, no home, no wife, little language, and few obvious sources of self-esteem. It is from this position that *White* will develop its discourse on equality. Its focus is on the process of getting even, and it explores the relationship between equality and revenge. Unlike Julie, however, whose journey is an internal, existential one, Karol is an 'economic' subject bent on fashioning the external world so that it will conform to his desires and needs. *White* is a pre-Kantian film.

Like Julie in *Blue*, Karol's actions from this point on are wilful and self-possessed.[16] Mikolaj had suggested that Karol should go back to Poland, and Karol has the idea that Mikolaj should take him inside the suitcase. There is just one thing that Karol has to do – steal a bust of a young girl which he had admired in a shop window. He is going to take this fantasy-substitute for Dominique with him to Poland. The idea of travelling baggage-class is successful, even though the case is stolen at Warsaw airport, and Karol is beaten up by the airport workers disappointed with their loot, and left at the bottom of a rubbish tip. Karol goes back to the salon where he used to work. It is now run by Jurek, his brother, who takes Karol in, and gives him time to recover. Soon Karol is working again as a stylist with his old clients, but it is clearly temporary, and he seeks out different work with a black-market money-changer, the husband of a woman whose hair he does. Karol is both inconspicuous and enterprising and is employed as a bodyguard for the money-changer. He will continue with some hairdressing to keep his brother happy, but he plans to exploit some of the opportunities to make money that Poland's chaotic post-communist economy is creating.

Whilst his black-market employment is making Karol some money, he gets his decisive opportunity by eavesdropping on his boss during a business deal. A huge retail complex is in the early stages of being planned. Karol's boss and his partner intend to acquire some of the land and then sell it at a profit, but Karol beats them to it, and using the money he has made so far he buys a plot of land from a peasant for $5,000. He only has $1,000, and he goes to see Mikolaj to see about the other four, remembering the 'job' that Mikolaj had mentioned. The contract is still available and Karol takes it. The victim turns out to be Mikolaj himself, but Karol – resourceful, determined, intuitive and humane (a classic subject profile in 'enlightened' capitalism) – tests Mikolaj's resolve by firing a blank bullet from the gun he had placed over his heart. 'The next one's real,' Karol says. Mikolaj backs down, but insists that Karol take the money. He agrees to take it as a loan, and can now complete the deal with the peasant. By the time that Karol has to face the money-changer, whose deal he has partially stolen, he has acquired more plots of land, and has left them in his will to the Church, an engulfing bureaucracy which will come into play should Karol be harmed. Karol will make something like a quarter of a million dollars if the money-changer swallows the betrayal and treats it as just a piece of business. The principle motivating them both is money, and a deal is struck. Karol will use the money to set up a trading company, and Mikolaj will be his partner. It is time for Karol, who amongst other things has been working assiduously to improve his French, to make contact with Dominique. When he phones her, however, she does not want to know him.

Karol has a plan. He makes a new will, leaving everything to Dominique. He then arranges his own funeral. For his chauffeur, Bronek, buying a dead body is easy in a country where everything now has a price. He obtains one of a man who died a violent death, his head crushed when he leant too far out of a tram window. Mikolaj helps by writing an obituary, and Jurek, it later turns out, is enlisted too. Karol secretly watches the mourners at his own funeral, and sees that Dominique is tearful. He goes to her hotel room that night, and is in her bed when she gets there. 'You cried at the funeral,' he says in good French. 'Because you were dead,' she replies. She does not know what to think, and acquiesces when he asks if he can touch her hand, and if she will sit on the bed so he can lay his head on her lap. They make love. Karol is apparently cured of his temporary impotence. In the morning, when Dominique awakes, Karol is gone. She speaks to Mikolaj on the phone, but he insists that Karol is dead. Then there is a knock on the door. It is the police. They have information that Karol may have been murdered. The obvious motive is money, and the entry stamps in Dominique's passport show that she was in Poland at the time of his death. Dominique is taken away. When the body is exhumed, Jurek and Mikolaj both identify the disfigured corpse as Karol.

Karol now employs a lawyer to work toward securing Dominique's release. The final scene of the film shows Dominique at a prison window, signalling to Karol that they can start again. Karol has tears in his eyes. He has regained Dominique, but, at least for the time being, she remains as far from him as she ever was. Karol can only contemplate his fantasy from a distance, although he has in some way evened the score, and possibly established a new basis from which they can move forward.

Franck Garbarz contrasts *Blue* and *White* in terms of interiority and exteriority. Julie's response to loss is to attempt to exercise control over her own being, to excise her memories and have nothing to do with those things that might remind her of the past or that might repeat its tragedy. Karol seeks equilibrium not through inner strength but through an exterior strategy, taking advantage of social opportunities to restore his lost object of desire. Karol will show that fixed identities, especially within a society ruled by unregulated markets, can be refused, assigned, renegotiated. Garbarz also suggests that *White* is a story about the revenge of the East, that an insignificant hairdresser can lay claim to a pretty French woman, and finally succeed, despite setbacks, in making her the prisoner of his gaze.

Karol, unlike Julie, does not pass beyond his loss; instead he displaces his lost object of desire, first onto a bust, then onto a framed image of Dominique. He does not understand, Garbarz suggests, that an emotional relationship entails giving up something of one's self, to create what Martin Buber called 'the between', 'a third entity separated from the two subjects who love each other' (Garbarz 1994: 133). As Buber might have put it reprovingly to Karol, 'Between I and Thou there is . . . no fantasy . . . no end, no greed, and no anticipation' (cited in Theunissen 1984: 275). It might also be added that there would be, in this conception, no sense of revenge, getting even, or, in that meaning of the term, equality. These considerations go a long way to explaining why the relationship between Karol and Dominique went awry in the first place. Dominique had said to Karol, after their failed lovemaking in her salon,

> You don't understand! You never even tried to understand. If I say I love you, you don't understand. If I say I hate you, you still don't understand! You don't even understand that I want to sleep with you! That I need you. Not even that! Do you understand? No! (Kieślowski and Piesiewicz 1998: 115)

From the standpoint of the intersubjective ideal represented in the thought of Martin Buber, Karol is incomplete. This is also true of Dominique. She rejects Karol because he will not give enough of himself to make a third entity composed of parts of them both. Throughout the film, however, in the sense of her search for transcendence, no one takes Karol's place. She laments Karol not for his sake, but for her own, and when he re-materialises, this energises her own renewed quest for transcendence, which even his betrayal and her imprisonment do not derail. Her hope for a satisfying, self-transcending relationship is at least temporarily misplaced, however, since Karol's achievement of 'equality' is constituted by his own and Dominique's alienation from each other. The final scene of the film, in its presentation of an emotional bond, but at a distance, suggests to the audience that this is the subjective ideal in market society. There is a postscript, however. There remains a series of possibilities to be explored once they are each able to live with their fantasies, in the flesh, as it were, after they emerge together, two out of the seven survivors of the ferry disaster at the end of *Red*.

The two figures of the existential and the Cartesian subject are, of course, idealisations, one-sided accentuations from particular perspectives. The subject is a (Newman?) line through both points and then dropped, like a perpendicular, onto the plane of a world made up of innumerable others interrelated in complex patterns. It is the arctic geometry of this vision, the defining emptiness of the existentialist and the essential impermanence of whichever desires are animating the Cartesian, which makes the certitudes of the Kantian subject, operating inside a world with an *a priori* moral structure, so perennially attractive but also, at times, so devastatingly tragic, as the outcomes of the 'good will', enclosed in its project of upholding values, are dwarfed by the achievements of rational calculation. It is enough, as Blanchot and Benjamin might have admitted, to empower the supplementary seductions of messianism, but perhaps not enough, at least for the Kantian subject itself, for the moral option to be seen as just another point on the line. It is the line itself.

Red is the ontological complement to, and precondition for *Blue* and *White*. *Blue* tells us that we cannot escape our past, while *White* suggests that striving for worldly success can lead to subjective fulfilment only as the perpetuation of a fantasy. If the human subject is imprisoned by its past, and possessed of limited powers, what is the logic that rules its fate? The sociological answer is clear. It is that subjects are agents of multi-structurally networked social institutions, and the extremely complex criss-crossing of these arrangements determines life-chances, and conditions the individual agent's ability and will to exploit them. Kieślowski, however, is no sociologist, and his parables of the subject culminate in a subtle critique of reflexivity, an ambiguous illustration that subjectivity cannot be either perfected or invalidated by knowledge, although it might be made more meaningful by locating it against an *a priori* axiological structure. If *Blue* is a dissertation on the emptiness of the existentialist ideal, and *White* an investigation of the internal relationship between power and fantasy, then *Red* is a Kantian fable.[17]

Valentine is a student at the University of Geneva, a photographic model, and in classical dance training. She has a boyfriend who is away working, and who calls her regularly, but is suspicious that while he is away she might be seeing someone else. Throughout the film, although in a minor key, she has the attitude that this is a condition she has to bear. Valentine has a morning routine of getting a newspaper, going into a café and putting one coin into a one-armed bandit. She is pleased to lose, finding it a good omen for the day ahead. Driving home from a catwalk show, Valentine runs over a dog. She stops. The dog is injured, and Valentine puts her in the back of her car and drives her to the address which is on her name tag. A retired judge, named Joseph Kern, lives there, and he seems not to care about the Alsatian's fate. When she asks him if she should take the dog to a veterinary hospital, he replies that she can if she wants. Angry at his attitude, she takes the dog to the vet. Rita, the Alsatian, is just bruised, but she is having puppies and needs some rest, so Valentine takes her home. In the newspaper the following day there is a front-page photographic spread on drugs in Geneva, where the film is set. She recognises her brother in one of the photographs. He appears to be injecting himself and she is distressed by what she sees. Distracted by this, she puts her coin into the machine and wins.

The following Sunday Rita is much recovered, and Valentine, who clearly loves dogs, takes her to the park, letting her off the leash to run around. The dog runs away. Valentine runs after her but loses her. She wonders if she has returned to Kern's house, and drives there. The dog is there with Kern, who tells Valentine to take her, but the dog is hesitant. Valentine had received 600 francs from Kern through the post, to pay for the treatment, although there was no accompanying note. It was too much, Valentine returns it, and Kern goes into the house to get the right money. After a while, Valentine follows him in, and discovers Kern listening quite unashamedly to a neighbour's telephone call through an elaborate hi-fi system. Valentine is disgusted, but Kern's reaction, far from defensive, is to invite Valentine to tell the neighbour; he points out the house concerned. He has no shame because, for him, at that moment, whatever is done will make no difference. The conversation was between a husband and his male lover. When Valentine knocks at the door, she is greeted by the wife and invited in. She cannot go through with it, and claims that she has come to the wrong address. Valentine goes back to Kern's house and explains that she could not say anything, but asks him please to stop. His response is to affirm the irrelevant condition of the witness:

> Let me tell you how it really is. I can spy on him or not. You could have told them or not. But sooner or later he's going to jump out of that window anyway, or she's going to find out and there's going to be hell. At some stage, someone's going to tell his daughter. Maybe she's the one who's going to jump out of that window . . . What can we do about it? (Kieślowski and Piesiewicz 1998: 234)

'Does this remind you of something?' Kern asks. She is thinking about her brother who was in the paper. When he was fifteen he found out that he was not his father's son. Kern listens to another conversation, but Valentine puts her fingers in her ears, and then Kern points to another neighbour talking on a mobile phone which he cannot listen to. A certain conspiratorial bond develops between Valentine and Kern as he tells her that this neighbour is a drug dealer. Another phone conversation comes through the speakers, between a mother and daughter. The mother says she has no food in the house, but the daughter knows this cannot be right. Explaining further, Kern asks Valentine why she picked up his dog from the street. She replies that it was because the dog was hurt. Kern says that it was to avoid the guilt she would still be feeling if she'd left the dog there:

> So who did you do it for? Don't do that old woman's shopping. She's got everything. What she really wants is to see her daughter. But the daughter doesn't want to. She came here at least five times when her mother was pretending to have a heart attack. When she dies, I'm going to have to call her daughter because she won't believe it any more. (ibid.: 243)

Valentine is upset. She does not believe that people are essentially bad. They may be weak, but not bad. She leaves the house, telling Kern that Rita is going to have puppies, a second piece of news to disturb Kern's moral impassivity. The first was when she told him that the neighbour's daughter already knew about her father's boyfriend: she also was listening to the phone call, on an extension.

Valentine is upset when driving home. She phones her mother, to find that her brother is there. Her mother has not seen the picture in the paper, and thinks all is well. Her brother talks to her on the phone. He won't stay long at his mother's house: he can't stand it. Valentine's phone rings. It is the photographer who has been taking pictures of her. A giant enlargement of one of the shots has been erected at a prominent location in the city. A group of people are celebrating the completion of the assignment, and are having fun at the bowling alley. Valentine joins them. Unknown to her, at the same time in his house, Kern is sending handwritten letters to all the people he has been spying on, confessing what he has done.

Some weeks later, Valentine sees a headline in a local paper which announces, in sensationalist tones, that there is to be a civil case between a group of neighbours and a judge who had been listening to their private telephone conversations for years. Valentine has to go and see him, to tell Kern that she had not told anyone. The judge, of course, knows it was not her and tells her what he has done. Valentine wants to know why he told everyone, and Kern replies that it was because of her, because of her disgust at what he was doing. He thought that she might come to see him when she heard. He wants to tell her some things. In particular he wants her to know that her life is not set. It was a lesson that he himself, as he is coming to realise, had forgotten. His discourse is allusive, and Valentine has the sense that something important is happening, without really understanding what. Kern's first story is about Karin, a neighbour of his, to whom he had been listening. She runs a telephone weather report service, but also has a relationship with Auguste, who is just about to take his final examinations to become a judge. Auguste is Kern's *doppelgänger*. He has been seen regularly through the film, crossing Valentine's path, each unaware of the other. They both live in the same *quartier*, and each also visits someone in Kern's neighbourhood. Auguste has a picture of a black-clad dancer in his flat, loves dogs, and will be attracted by the huge picture of Valentine which he will see later on the billboard. Now, because Kern had confessed what he was doing, a series of events was set in train which led to Auguste's lover, Karin, meeting someone else.

Kern's second story concerns a case he had tried some thirty-five years earlier. He acquitted a sailor, but had recently realised that the man was actually guilty. He had, however, found out that the man concerned had since led a fruitful life:

> I did my own investigation. He got married. Has three children and now a grandson too. They love him. He pays his taxes. All the trees he planted in front of his house have taken root and give fruit every year. (Kieślowski and Piesiewicz 1998: 264)

Kern now realises that while he used to think that his judicial role served truth and justice, now he is no longer sure, and he accuses himself of vanity, a lack of modesty. Underlining his regret at having been a prisoner of his former social role, he and Valentine discuss the feelings that his neighbours have toward him. A stone has been thrown through a window. It is the sixth. He tells Valentine that he is not scared, and that he would probably do the same thing in their place. 'You'd throw stones?' asks Valentine:

> No doubt I would if I were in their place. The same goes for all those I judged.
> With their lives, in their position . . . I'd murder, steal, cheat. Of course, I would.
> It's all because I wasn't in their position. I was in mine. (ibid.: 266)

His regret is the very same regret that a thief or murderer is required to show: remorse. The social position of the accused may explain, but it does not excuse. Kieślowski is telling us that the same is just as true for Kern. This is not something that we are often accustomed to hear: a call for or attestation of remorse for being a teacher, a journalist, a doctor, a judge, for only being that and nothing more, for only being an agent. This is a stage further on than the advocate-candidate in *Decalogue 5*, who when asked why he wanted to be a lawyer, replied that the answer becomes increasingly elusive as time goes on. For Kern, to be locked in the language game of the law now appears to him similar to being locked in the language game of crime or local hatred. If the latter are wrong, so, to some extent, is the former. There is a mute appeal here to something like a categorical imperative – never treat people as ends alone, or 'Do unto others . . .' But Kern does not unambiguously symbolize the filling of the void in contemporary life with a moral imperative; instead the film fills this void with contingency, which is another way of breaching, but then remaking, the compartments of which modern life is made up.

Valentine is going to travel from Geneva to England, to see Michel, the boyfriend who is working away. She will take the ferry, at Kern's suggestion. He phones the weather service the week before she is due to sail to see how the Channel will be. Karin, at the weather service, former girlfriend of Auguste, laughs at the coincidence, because she is going that way at about that time with her new man, on his yacht. Before Valentine leaves, there is a catwalk show. She sends a ticket to Kern. He has to recharge his car battery to drive there, echoing Valentine's concern that the red jeep outside her flat had been left with its lights on – it was Auguste's. She and Kern talk after the show. She wants to know more about a dream of her that Kern had mentioned he had had. In that dream, he had an image of Valentine at fifty, happy and waking up beside someone. 'Will that happen?' she asks. 'Yes,' he replies. He tells her that he often used to come to the theatre that they are in, where the fashion parade was held. He recalls,

> Once, during the interval, my books fell all over the place. They were held
> together by an elastic band. One of them, a thick one, fell down below . . . It was
> just before my exam. The book had fallen open on a certain page. I read a few
> sentences. They proved useful. I was able to answer a difficult question in the
> exam. (ibid.: 278)

He is describing something that had happened to Auguste just a few days before. Like Auguste, also, he had lost the woman he loved:

> She was blonde. Delicate, fair, with a long neck. She wore light-coloured dresses
> . . . Had light-coloured furniture. A mirror in a white frame hung in the hallway.
> In that mirror one night I saw her white legs spread, with a man between them.
> (ibid.: 282)

Auguste had seen the same thing, through the window of Karin's flat. As will Auguste, Kern crossed the Channel in the hope of recovering the woman he loved, but for Kern, as for Auguste, the woman concerned dies in an accident. Kern never got involved with another woman. 'I stopped believing,' he said. 'Maybe I didn't meet you' (ibid.: 282).

His decision to take early retirement was occasioned by the coincidence that he had to try the man who had taken his only love away from him. He was found guilty quite properly, but it was after the 'nice feeling of revenge' that Kern sought to leave his profession. Now he has become what he is: eavesdropper, confessor, foreteller of events, and Kantian principle of communication between too easily closed rooms – veritably a man on the phone. Valentine is leaving the next day, and Kern makes her a present of a bottle of pear brandy. He asks to see her ferry ticket. They press palms either side of Kern's car window in farewell. The next day the ferry sinks in bad weather. A private sailing yacht sinks at the same time. There are just seven survivors: Julie, Olivier, Karol, Dominique, Valentine, Auguste, and an English barman named Stephen Killian.

Notes

1. Garbowski follows the conventional view (although this is not very explicit, either in his book or in critical commentary on the series) that Kieślowski did not make a film based on the second Commandment ('Thou shalt not make unto thee any graven image'), and that the series of ten was closed with a second film based on the tenth one ('Thou shalt not covet . . .'). However, since the tenth film concerns a fabulous collection of images, in the form of a stamp collection so valuable that no one in Poland could afford to buy it, this interpretation is at least open to discussion.

2. The emphasis in Kieślowski's *Decalogue* tends to be placed upon problem confrontation, and it is for this reason that perhaps these ten films are less analytically suggestive at the level of the contemporary subject in general. *Decalogue 8*, which concerns a Jewish girl turned away from the home of a Resistance family in 1943 Warsaw, is symptomatic in this respect. Elzbieta, who is conducting a seminar on 'ethical hell', tells her students that she is not interested in 'prototypes', but in the motivations and assignations of meaning by 'real' characters.

3. Perhaps the key, as Cathy Caruth puts it, is the movement from 'a traumatic repetition [to] the ethical burden of a survival' (Caruth 1996: 108). While *Blue* explores this movement at the personal level, the question of making this movement at the cultural level raises equally huge difficulties, and at the cultural level there is a tendency to remain immersed in traumatic repetition. For a discussion of some of the dynamics here, see Farrell 1998.

4. An obituary contains the following: 'one of the things we talked about was how awkward it was to give the characters in a film names. He agreed, but he took it further and talked about the great danger film makers found themselves in, of playing God with their characters' (Engel, 1996). It is hard to know how the writer of serious fiction can be sure of avoiding that, but Kieślowski's answer is to ensure that his characters' desires are not immediately directed at the eternal, that their existence is shown to be demonstrably bound up with multitudinous mortality.

5. Kieślowski said that he would end up having prepared between five and ten scripts for each film (Lint 1995).

6. Other interpretations are, of course, possible. Contrast this interpretation with the following account from Wittgenstein: 'after Schubert's death, his brother cut certain of Schubert's scores into small pieces and gave to his favourite pupils these pieces of a few bars

each. As a sign of piety this action is *just* as comprehensible to us as the other one of keeping the scores undisturbed and accessible to no one. And if Schubert's brother had burnt the scores we could still understand this as a sign of piety' (Wittgenstein 1979: 5, original emphasis).

7. Just as *Decalogue 1* (in which Krzysztof's son Pawel falls through the ice covering a frozen lake, despite the careful calculations which 'guaranteed' that the ice would bear three times his weight) intimates that the relationship between subject and physical world cannot be plumbed to its absolute depth.

8. As might be expected for a Polish filmmaker working in French, the language of the King James Bible is not followed, and the key word in the text is not *charity* but *love*. It is in other words the sense of love as *caritas*, as giving rather than withholding, which ultimately animates the film and its music.

9. 'We have to wait until Augustine before a theory . . . where the goods of the soul are stressed over those of worldly action, is formulated in terms of inner and outer' (Taylor 1989: 121).

10. In the *Timaeus*, Plato distinguished two kinds of cause, the necessary and the divine, and some scholars (see Vesey 1989) have regarded mind as the essence of the divine, and therefore implied that Plato did have a well-formed view of humans as prime movers. The following passage from the *Timaeus*, however, describes Plato's view of mortals (and suggests that this is merely a foretaste of human causal powers, rather than an early version): '[God] ordered his own children to make the generation of mortals. They took over from him an immortal principle of soul, and, imitating him, encased it in a mortal physical globe, with the body as a whole for vehicle, and they built onto it another mortal part, containing terrible and necessary feelings: pleasure – the chief incitement to wrong; pain, which frightens us from good; confidence and fear; two foolish counsellors: obstinate passion and credulous hope. To this mixture they added irrational sensation and desire which shrinks from nothing, and so gave the mortal element its indispensable equipment' (Plato 1955: 95).

11. See the discussion of voluntariness, purposive choice and practical reasoning in Kenny 1979.

12. The idea of compliance with a complex moral code is, however, as *The Decalogue* shows, intensely problematic. *Decalogue 2*, for example, presents an anguished Dotota pregnant with another's child, with her husband gravely ill. Will he survive? If he does, she will terminate the pregnancy. She demands that the consultant tell her if he will die. If the consultant follows his professional ethic, he will indirectly cause the death of the unborn child. He tells her that her husband will die. She keeps the child, but he recovers. The application of a moral precept, just as with the attribution of a principle of social causation, is far from the end of the story. There is no simple rule. Which is why there can be no single graven image, nor one single exhaustive account of a non-subjective agent. It is a position which is almost sanctified in the closing scene of *Decalogue 4*, where father and daughter together burn the unopened letter which neither of them has read.

13. Freud uses the condition of obsessional neurosis to explore the functioning of repression. He finds that 'obsessional neurosis has as its basis a regression owing to which a sadistic trend has been substituted for an affectionate one. It is this hostile impulse against someone who is loved which is subjected to repression . . . As a substitutive formation there arises an alteration of the ego in the shape of an increased conscientiousness . . . But the repression, which was at first successful, does not hold firm; in the further course of things its failure becomes increasingly marked. The vanished affect comes back in its transformed shape as social anxiety, moral anxiety and unlimited self-reproaches; the rejected idea is replaced by a *substitute by displacement*, often a displacement onto something very small or indifferent. A tendency to a complete re-establishment of the repressed idea is as a rule unmistakably present . . . Thus in obsessional neurosis the work of repression is prolonged in a sterile and interminable struggle' (Freud 1984: 157–8, original emphasis). It is not hard to see how an interpretation of Julie's behaviour might be made to fit quite easily into this syndrome (the inevitably neurotic nature of her relationship with Olivier being obscured by Kieślowski's romanticism).

14. It is necessary to enter a significant reservation here, which is that Freud's categories were developed against a background of nineteenth-century social forms. As we can see from

Blue, even a 'normal' development, in Freud's terms, can never really be regarded as finished, since it creates a series of hostages to fortune, a series of continual trials by contingency which the subject will undergo. Further, however, as social forms change, especially in the late twentieth century, the concrete realities of single parenting, women's rights, and the extension of various forms of support/hostility by parents into the early middle age of their children may soon amount to such a significant shift in the primal social background that the Freudian developmental model may need fundamental alteration. For an early exploration of some of the stresses, see *Decalogue 7*, where Majka's child was taken by her mother as her own, a situation which has been eating at Majka for years, and now comes to a head.

15. See the discussion of 'limit-subjectivity' in Boyne 1998.

16. Kieślowski commented, in an interview with Vincent Amiel and Michel Ciment, 'Chance plays no role in *White*. It is only his will that allows him to succeed, even though at the beginning he had no chance' (Amiel 1997: 144).

17. It has been suggested that film theory has currently little room for the protagonist (or the subject, to use the terminology of this book) as a major category (Garbowski 1997: 14). This is a lack which needs addressing to some degree, since the question of the protagonist is surely central to any cinema of moral weight. The conventional categories of the subject used here to illuminate Kieślowski's work (and vice versa) may be a preliminary, albeit crude, place to begin. They are far from being absolutes. There is, for example, a path of maturation (see *Decalogue 5* for a portrayal of existential immaturity and *Decalogue 7* for a portrayal of Kantian confusion) and then also of decay for each of them.

7

ONLY IN THE PRESENT: SUBJECTIVITY AND TIME

The time of the subject

David Cronenberg's film, *Crash*, like all feature films, creates its own time during its running time of ninety-six minutes. This is screen time. This film, however, is obsessed with the instant of the crash, which is no time as movement ceases. The wheels are going nowhere as they spin in the air, and the occupants are dead: frozen onto film and in the morgue. This cessation of time is a daily loss of reality for the thousands of people killed every year on the roads. It also reflects a global compression of time. The broken glass on the tarmac mirrors a global economy which has compressed time to the zero-point at the centre of the World Wide Web. The economic time of classical modernity, which was ticker-tape time, has become screen time, and what was local time has become as irrelevant to the global economic engine as local time has become to the dead subjects on the motorway. Following a major accident, the television cameras arrive in quick time. Running on live time, they feed into satellite time: paid time and pay time for live time through advertising's prime time as now time. This compression of time also characterises democratic politics. Political time was a time for persuasion, coercion and negotiation leading to decision and action. But increasingly the instantaneity of the crash is now the order of events. Permanent ejaculation rather than slow ascent toward climax is the political condition, as feedback processes created by opinion polls and spin doctors crush the political decision process and the political act into sheer simultaneity. The enemies of the new political epistemology are life, foreplay, duration: 'Speed guarantees . . . the value of all information' (Virilio 1995: 53), at the same time as it kills. The crash is not an accident, but the essential expression of the epoch. Disappearance of temporality, refusal of deferral, engenders all movement – backwards into history, forwards into the future, laterally into other language games – as simulation or crime. Surveillance mechanisms design the future to a pattern which is already familiar.[1]

The design of the social, and the extension of its present, is paralleled by cyborg medicine's designs on the body, as Vaughan puts it, in Cronenberg's screenplay: 'It's something we're all intimately involved in: the reshaping of the human body by modern technology' (Cronenberg 1996: 35). Virilio writes,

the place where state-of-the-art technology occurs is . . . the infinitesimal space of
our internal organs . . . the intraorganic intrusion of technology and its micro-
machines into the heart of the living. (Virilio 1995: 100)

Drugs to take users out of time will be supplemented by technological
prosthetics (Lury 1997) to take bodies out of time as ergonomics becomes
reflexive, and the postmodern form of human design, which learnt its
craft and technique from work with disability, colonises and uplifts the
Cinderella field of prosthetics and places it at the heart of the transplant
revolution. There is no space here even for evolutionary time; Darwinian
temporality is on hold. Quoting Louis Thaler, Virilio tells us:

> It seems to me beyond question that man is today evolving under the influence of
> what I would call a *relaxation of the selection process*. This phenomenon is one of
> the effects of . . . medicine . . . Saving babies in our maternity wards . . . will tend
> to introduce mutations into the population that once would have tended to be
> eliminated. (1995: 115–16)

The entry of evolution into its technoscientific phase may point therefore to
a double transcendence of linear temporality, as the *Neuromancer* image of
buying oneself out of time combines with a fearsome technological over-
determination of human ontology, in a scientific quest to seek the denial of
fundamental temporality, to move to the stilled motion of the crash. This
dynamic stasis of zero would find apotheosis during virtual war, in which a
successful software strike for control over the Global Positioning System
(GPS) would mean movement of strategic forces and installations at the
speed of light: the promise of 'chronographic time's absence of duration'
(ibid.: 106).

In certain respects, then, the time of the subject has stopped, and among
the consequences of these developments in the relationship between being
and time are three upon which we will now focus: the inaccessibility of
history, the spectralisation of the future, and the fetishisation of the present.
We will examine these consequences by considering, respectively, the conceptualisation of the Holocaust by Maurice Blanchot, Derrida's essay on
Marx, and David Cronenberg's cinematic reading of J.G. Ballard's *Crash*.

The inaccessibility of history

At the origin of Blanchot's reflection on the disabilities of *post hoc*
reflection on disaster is the Holocaust:

> The holocaust, the absolute event of history – which is a date in history – that
> utter-burn where all history took fire, where the movement of Meaning was
> swallowed up, where the gift, which knows nothing of forgiving or of consent,
> shattered without giving place to anything that can be affirmed, that can be
> denied – gift of very passivity, gift of what cannot be given. How can it be
> preserved, even by thought? How can thought be made the keeper of the
> holocaust where all was lost, including guardian thought? (Blanchot 1995: 47)

Disaster is a word that can hardly be uttered without betrayal, without false aspiration. It is 'beyond the pale of writing' (ibid.: 7). It is a matter for the stars (*des astres*) and is, says, Blanchot, 'not our affair'. Disaster entails the loss of the future; were it our affair, it would be 'no longer to have any future in which to think it'. It is then, *for us*, a matter of forgetfulness, of the immemorial, of 'motionless retreat'. Beyond the horizon of the disaster, we are 'between being and not-being', drawn from then to now; and now is the time of passivity. Even that term, 'passivity' is insufficient: 'passivity is never passive enough'. Always insufficiently abject, we are ruled and persecuted by events we can never grasp. Attacked and indebted, I am charged with crimes 'which cannot be mine . . . pressed into a responsibility which not only exceeds me but which I cannot exercise' (ibid.: 19–20). With what conclusion, then? For Blanchot, the self is gangrenous, and the overlordship of the other is 'pure affliction'. It is part of this affliction that the suffering of the disaster can only be realised after the disaster has taken place, can only ever be misplaced, come too late: 'the disaster always takes place after having taken place, there cannot possibly be any experience of it' (ibid.: 28). This weakened subject, enervated because of the persecutions of the other, is destined to live a life too late. So Blanchot wonders if 'one ought perhaps to speak of a subjectivity without any subject' (ibid.: 30)? Seemingly able to go neither forward nor back, is it at all surprising that stopped motion and frozen trauma become the metaphors of the era? (Ballard 1995: 4).[2]

If we are the disaster, if the disaster is us, right now, how would we know? In parallel to our disconnectedness from the past, there is our dislocation from what is to come; the meaning of our present is absent, unavailable to us: 'the message which ought to make of us messengers is ahead of us by an eternity' (Blanchot 1995: 37). Both too late and too early, what other sense of being might we make other than to play amongst things stopped in their course, or to fool ourselves that we are historical agents, that we could do otherwise, and to appear to ourselves to cause things to crash to a halt?

There is, however, a hint that our self-deceived burial in the present, even if reaction to the burden of the disasters of the past, and understandable resignation to the deferral of all intelligibility, constitutes a premature engagement with the nothingness of death. As Blanchot puts it, the grave is 'an illusory refuge'. His demonstration of this is both sparkling and profound:

> The quick of life would be the burn of a wound – a hurt so lively, a flame so avid that it is not content to live and be present, but consumes all that is present till presence is precisely what is exempt from the present. The quick of life is the exemplarity, in the absence of any example, of un-presence, of un-life; absence in its vivacity . . . (1995: 51)

The question to be asked, then, is what might the relationship be between the disaster and vivacity (seen now as an all-consuming ache)? Blanchot's answer seems to be that even at the same time that the weight of the past both eludes us and burdens us, it is also there as the body of a sentinel, a vigilance that he supposes to be outside of our ontological order. As he puts it, 'the wake does not occur under the sidereal sky'. It is also that present vivacity is a source of the grief that too keeps watch. So the connection between life and disaster is posed as a mysterious link between the empty but pained singularity of the subject and the watchfulness of the disaster, an echo from its station outside of everywhere that we could be.

How might this combination of inner- and super-ontological surveillance work? A clue is given by Blanchot's edict, 'Do not forgive.' This sounds as if it derives from a vastly different register of thought than the one we have been examining. He means to point out, however, that to forgive is first to accuse, and to accuse is first to disregard the essential uncertainty which accompanies our presumed knowledge of what we cannot know. We are dealing here then with the precise opposite of a philosophy of action,[3] and the ontological warrant for this axiology of non-movement is the 'patience of the disaster' deriving from utter exteriority, and leading us 'to expect nothing of the "cosmic" and perhaps nothing of the world'.

The idea of history is, for Blanchot, both necessary and useless, in the sense that 'We must pass by way of this knowledge and forget it.' To hold the past at such a distance, even if comforted (so to speak) by the vigilance of some exterior guardian determining the limits of the acceptable, leads Blanchot into a somewhat contradictory attitude to Auschwitz.[4] He seems to allow its descriptive power, but not to allow judgement of it. He writes of a young prisoner there:

> he had suffered the worst, led his family to the crematorium . . . he was exempted from contact with dead bodies, but when the SS shot someone, he was obliged to hold the victim's head so that the bullet could be more easily lodged in the neck . . . (ibid.: 82)

This young man was prevented from hanging himself. Rescued from his own death, he is supposed to have said that he drew strength from the 'comportment of men before death'. Blanchot's comment is that he did not believe in the transference of strength. We wish to know, but nothing transfers. We wish to see, but do not, cannot, learn. It would be unjust to say of Blanchot that he celebrated this distance. It was for him an awful truth: '*Calm, always calmer, the undesirable calm*', a question of learning '*to think with pain*' (original emphasis). His account of life, then, finds an exhausting burden placed on the subject, with no compensation to be found in either the ordinary or extraordinary run of things; finally breathing (Blanchot's metaphor for this is *writing*) just has to be enough and so it is: it is still, even in its passivity and pain, *life*, which is not, which is the antithesis of, the wound. Furthermore, the solitude of life is not unrelieved: there is an outside from where we are: a source for the sentinels.

Even allowing for the possibility that, in the light of his personal history, Blanchot's reflections on the Holocaust are self-serving, his depiction of the existential condition as a passive abandonment within the present, without reach either forward or back, but somehow tended by a super-ontological guardianship (the territory of the Messiah?) against total transgression, constitutes a fundamental position from and through which to begin to get some purchase on the contemporary social world. Doubtless it can be challenged: the thesis of extreme passivity within the present is entirely uncongenial to all aspirants for thoroughgoing social change, whether powered by the ideologies of science, religion, secular perfection or ecological balance; while the concept of a mythological sentinel, drawing a line beyond which is the worst, is not to be immune to the processes of acclimatisation, illustrated by Karlheinz Weissman's 1995 history of the Third Reich, which 'portrayed Nazism as a left-wing creed, and devoted no more space to the extermination of the Jews than to film and sport under the Third Reich during peacetime' (Evans 1997), and this is to say nothing of the excesses of cold Cartesianism or existential despair. Nevertheless, Blanchot's apposition of forgetfulness and the extraordinary moment of the messianic surge may describe an Eternal Return. Furthermore, it is a return which will always take place in the present. But it is a complex present. Unlike the intemperate and non-temporal politics which Virilio describes, and unlike Cronenberg and Ballard (although there is much deception and temptation here, as we will see) there is dialectic at work in Blanchot, between the present and utter exteriority, between pain and the Messiah, and, at the root of it all, between life and the wound.

The spectralisation of the future

As Blanchot says, the time of the disaster is a time out of joint. In the subtitle of Derrida's book, *Specters of Marx*, reference is made to the *Work of Mourning*. Now, however, we are not concerned with the mourning of individual deaths, those left behind in the disaster; more widely we are mourning for the loss of a general future. To mourn for lives never to be lived is to engage with a particularly haunting problem, the problem of those ghosts from a realm that is never to come into being: not disembodied but never-bodied ghosts from a time out of joint. One version of this unjointed time is given in the opening lines of *The Communist Manifesto*: 'A spectre is haunting Europe – the spectre of communism.' The spectres of communism are ghosts from the future. The pressure Derrida seeks to exert is not that of Blanchot's unbearable accusations from a past that never was in any simple sense, but from a future that never will be in any simple sense:

> *What is* a ghost? What is the *effectivity* or the *presence* of a specter . . . Let us call it a *hauntology* . . . How to *comprehend* in fact the discourse of the end . . . the opposition between 'to be' and 'not to be' . . . After the end of history, the spirit comes by *coming back* . . . the *Manifesto* seems to evoke . . . the first coming of the silent ghost. (Derrida 1994: 10, original emphasis)

A spectre always appears by coming back, because it is in the nature of a ghost that it returns. But Marx thought to break this rule. The spectre haunting Europe was a ghost that was not returning, but was here or about to come here for the first time. If we are to mourn the passing of this spectre, how can we do so? How can we mourn for a spectre that is not a phenomenon of the return? Where is the body? How can we localise the dead, visit its haunts to remind ourselves? From whose grave would this ghost have emerged? The spectre which never had a body, never had a past, never had a grave, was never with us. Is that what we mourn, the loss of what never has been here? What makes it so real, if it never has been here? 'More actual than what is so blithely called a living presence?' (ibid.: 13). A singular non-presence, one might say. Singularity: the thing as its own principle, its own cause; the spectre as singularity which would never have been here before, whose skull would not be found. For Derrida, and he may be right, we must revisit this spectre that we have never visited before. Unless we do so 'there remains . . . only the necessity of the worst' (ibid.: 29). Somehow, though we are locked in the present, without recourse to either before or after, we have a responsibility to conjure up ghosts that never have been and never will be. It seems that both Derrida and Blanchot partake of the same structure of thought, that their difference of focus, one on the historical that was, and one on the historical to come, is perhaps of little relevance: both will draw strength from the ineffable territory of the other.

Marx's significance as the impossible ghost without a past, whose skull is not to be found, whose present absence is therefore not able to be mourned, has then to do with the messianic, with the coming of the other, the sentinel holding a line just a little ahead of us:

> in the waiting [for] or calling of . . . the messianic: the coming of the other, the absolute and unpredictable singularity of the *arrivant* . . . We believe that this messianic remains an *ineffaceable* mark . . . of Marx's legacy. (Derrida 1994: 28, original emphasis)

This spectre, which was never here before, beckons us into the future. The call from behind its visor is that we should somehow disengage if only to some small extent from the present. But there are few prepared to go with the ghost. We prefer the accidents that have defined our lives, rather than the leap that might re-make our future. This invitation to the future, this call for us 'to turn *ourselves* over to the future . . . without concept or certainty of determination' (ibid.: 29) and to embrace the 'violence that interrupts time, disarticulates it, dislodges it, displaces it out of its natural lodging, [takes it] "out of joint"' (ibid.: 31), this spectral interpellation, is repudiated. A classic form of this repudiation can be found in the academy: the return to Marx. As Derrida says, 'the *return* is acceptable provided that the *revolt*, which initially inspired uprising, indignation, insurrection, revolutionary momentum, does not come back' (ibid.). We are, then, faced with a multiple spectre: the spectre of communism is a ghost that was never here before, but that of revolt has its history, its bodies and its burial grounds. There is, then, more than one ghost. Some spectres are unwelcome: the magical power of the state to turn base metal into gold, to value by means of a spectral measure – money. Marx not only conjured up the spectre of communism, but also tried to conjure away the spectres of the state. Which ghosts, then, should call forth our rituals of exorcism?

There is a dominant discourse in politics, the media, the academy. This relegates the threat of Marxist revolution to the past, and celebrates the survival of our present form of market-led democracy. In Derrida's view,

> this triumphant conjuration is striving, in truth, to disavow, and therefore to hide from, the fact that never, never in history, has the horizon of the thing whose survival is being celebrated (namely, all the old models of the capitalist and liberal world) been as dark, threatening, and threatened. (ibid.: 52)

His conclusion is that we must assume the inheritance of Marx, in the sense of the spirit of Marx: 'Inheritance is never a *given*, it is always a task' (ibid., original emphasis).

Derrida is aware that to speak of the death of Marxism as part of a dominant discourse is somewhat paradoxical, since the notion of dominant discourse is within the Marxist frame. But he thinks that the spectre of Marxism does not force us always to a class analysis, nor even that we are forced to accept that strength and force are the key criteria in every case. He is taken by the notion of 'weak messianic force', which is perhaps a sense of a weak future (the sense of which is to be found by contrasting it with Ballard's 'ever-voracious present', or by comparing it to Blanchot's implicit philosophy of life in spite of the wound), and he therefore does not think that to adopt the problematic of economic and political domination means that everything has to be understood always in its terms.

Fukuyama is the noisy, successful celebrant of the death of Marxism and the end of history. *The Last Man* is, says Derrida, a gospel. Fukuyama preaches that Heaven is liberal democracy, and we are just about there. But there are two unspeakably large errors, empirical howlers, in his thinking. He neglects the conflict of ideologies which remains intense, and he ignores the desperation which marks his presumed liberal utopia at every point. From Fukuyama's perspective (but also, and this, of course, is the point, from the perspectives of Cronenberg, Ballard and Virilio) the time of Jerusalem is out of joint. The Middle East is the site of three warring eschatologies – all contesting the future, all engaged with the future, all rejecting the present, all dancing – in their ways – with the ghost of Marx. Fukuyama thinks that liberal democracy is triumphant, but neglects to reflect both on the Christianity of his vision and on the empirical disproofs of a view that liberal democracy is instantiated in Europe and North America in a way that even might approach adequacy to the ideal Heaven he promises. Just look at this list, Derrida tells us: (1) unemployment; (2) homelessness; (3) economic conflict; (4) unmanageable global markets; (5) foreign debt; (6) the arms trade; (7) nuclear proliferation; (8) ethnic wars;

(9) the black market 'states' of *Mafiosi* and Colombian drug operations; (10) the irresolutions of international law; and his postcard, whether destined to arrive or not, does not even mention famine, disease, environmental damage, everyday crime, intergenerational conflict, and the confetti of communities without hope spread across the world. Such phenomena put the work of Fukuyama (and that of Ballard, Cronenberg and Virilio) in perspective: their clarion calls and crash tactics should not persuade us, Derrida seems to say, that the world is entirely stopped; this stilled vision is a very partial one. It is not enough, however, to say that. There are many, and they have weight, who reside in the stilled tableau, feasting at the crash sites: what about them, what about us?

Derrida's question, then: what can we learn from the composite spectre of Marxism? In particular, if the evocation of this spectre is our work, then what should be the nature of our conjuration? The spectre draws us toward a double strategy. First, the spirit of Marxism will point us to the task of reducing the gap between the empirical and the ideal. Fukuyama's complacent idealisations are granted a certain weight, but confronted with every shortfall, and in this critical spirit of Marxism, the hauntological task is defined by the necessity of always attempting and succeeding in closing the gap bit by bit. Second, the ideal is denied. In Derrida's words:

> It would be a question of putting into question . . . the very concept of the said ideal. This would extend, for example, to the economic analysis of the market, the laws of capital, of types of capital (financial or symbolic, therefore spectral), liberal parliamentary democracy, modes of representation and suffrage, the determining concept of human rights, women's and children's rights, the current concepts of equality, liberty . . . fraternity . . . It would also extend . . . to the concept of the human. (1994: 87)

The relation between these two spectral strategies is, for Derrida, precisely, undecidable:

> Here are two different reasons to be faithful to a spirit of marxism. They must not be added together but intertwined. They must be implicated with each other in the course of a complex and constantly re-evaluated strategy. There will be no re-politicisation, there will be no politics otherwise. Without this strategy, each of the two reasons could lead back to the worst, to worse than the bad, if one can put it that way, namely to a sort of fatalist idealism or abstract and dogmatic eschatology in the face of the world's evil. (ibid.: 87)

Refusal to conjure up these spirits of Marx consigns us to (using Derrida's term) 'fetishist phantomaticity', and it is exactly this fetishism which is presented to us by Virilio, Ballard and Cronenberg. For Derrida, the end of ideology theorists, now in the latest guise of the work of Fukuyama, are purveyors of *Crash* theory. Both Cronenberg and Virilio demonstrate the worst because of the absolute absence of ghosts from their vision: for them there is no other.

Crash theory

Psychoanalytically, fetishism is a substitute for power. The lack of power – whether to understand drawn from the past – or to act determinately upon the future, gives rise to a fetishistic substitution. Words can be fetishes. Derrida says as much when he refers to the academic subtleties of refusing the call of the spectre by developing a discourse of the return, and perhaps Blanchot puts too much faith in writing.[5] But here we are concerned with our fetishisms, which derive from our loss of power over past and future. Our loss of all temporal horizons leads to the proliferation of fetishised objects and events in the present. These fetishes are the displaced ciphers of our lost projects, the ghosts of past journeys across much richer temporal dimensions than we now know.

Kristeva (1996: 200) refers to 'a softening of the logical order' when discussing the relation between the fetish and the word, and there has to be a certain softening of the psychoanalytic order, for the Freudian theory of fetishism is unambiguous. It defines the fetish as a substitute for the mother's phallus. A case study described by Bruce Fink illustrates this well:

> The case is that of a man who, as a young child, has an extremely close bond with his mother, and whose father – though he lives at home with his wife and son – is effaced for most intents and purposes. The mother takes her son, Jean, as her complement in life, for her husband means nothing to her and does nothing for her. Jean becomes that which she is missing and which can make her whole. At first she cares for him when he is ill, but then pretends that he is ill even when he is not (manually heating up the thermometer to make it seem he has a fever), so that he apparently needs a devoted mother's attention. One of the striking things in this case is that, by the kinds of medical treatments she subjects him to, she makes his whole body into a red, swollen, pus-discharging object that the patient himself can only describe years later as a kind of living dildo with which she does as she pleases. To her, he *is* the penis she wants; at the level of being, he *is* the real object she wants to make her whole. (Fink 1997: 181–2, original emphasis)

In softening the psychoanalytic order here, to examine *Crash* as a symptom and exploration of temporal blockage, we do not deny the relevance of the psychoanalytic orthodoxy of the maternal phallus. Indeed the film opens in an aircraft hangar with a woman's naked breast against the riveted surface of an aeroplane. The psychoanalytic field of fetishism is generalised, however, by taking the theory of the maternal phallus as a specific case of the general theory of fetishism, which, put simply, defines the fetish as a substitute for unavailable power. In the case of *Crash*, the deep structure of the film is a substitution of car-crash sexual consumption as compensation and replacement for the loss of past and future, for being locked in a relentless and voracious present. Both Blanchot and Derrida confront this relentlessness and find resources to subvert it; Virilio reduces it to technology, Cronenberg coverts it to semen in a wound.

Cronenberg's film begins with Catherine Ballard having emotionless sex with her flying instructor, and then cuts to Catherine's husband, James, a film producer, who is similarly engaged with a junior member of the crew of the film he is producing. Later, on the balcony of their apartment over-looking a swathe of freeways, they compare notes while being coolly intimate with each other. Possibly that night, or maybe a few days later, James Ballard is driving at night, but is trying to review some papers at the same time.[6] He loses control of the car and leaves the road at about sixty miles an hour, bumping over a kerb and slaloming down a slight bank and onto a slip road bearing traffic coming in the other direction. He avoids one car, then hits another head on. Its driver is thrown through the windscreen and into the front passenger space of Ballard's car. Ballard is injured and so is Dr Helen Remington, the passenger in the other car. Her husband is dead. There is a hospital at the airport, and both Ballard and Helen Remington are taken there. Ballard's leg injuries require a complex caliper, and during his prosthetically enabled walks along the hospital corridors, he briefly meets Helen Remington, and then Vaughan. These two have been talking. Vaughan knows who Ballard is, and looks him over closely. Vaughan, who has a scar on the side of his face and is chewing gum, has some photographs of wounds in his hand.

A day or so later, Catherine is masturbating James under the hospital bedclothes while describing the effect of the impact on the two cars. She wished she had gone to Charles Remington's funeral, but has not visited Helen Remington. She says that she feels too close to her. She is engaged by what has happened, but not disturbed, and is merely intrigued by the prospect of James driving again after he has been released from hospital. He can barely walk, but wants to get back behind the wheel. He goes to the police pound to see his car; Helen Remington is there looking for her husband's car. They leave together in Ballard's new car, exactly the same model and colour as the one which crashed. During the journey to the airport, where Helen Remington works in the Immigration Department, they agree that the intensity of traffic has increased since their accident. Ballard feels oppressed and uncomfortable while driving, something which is heightened when a car pulls out in front of him, forcing him up onto the kerb where the car loses a hubcap. Helen Remington helps him to steer the car to a stop. They drive to an airport garage where it will be quiet, and have urgent sex in the front seat, a coupling which is then duplicated between Ballard and Catherine, less urgently but also in silence.

Helen Remington has known Vaughan since he was a specialist in inter-national computerised traffic systems. She has taken Ballard to watch the reconstruction of the car crash that killed James Dean. They are sitting in a small grandstand watching and listening as Vaughan says into a radio mike: 'The year, 1955. The date, September 30th. The time, now.' They will see a corner-to-corner frontal collision between two cars driven by stuntmen, one of whom, Colin Seagrave, is as obsessed as Vaughan with the re-creation of the fatal car accidents of the famous. Vaughan is Seagrave's passenger in the replica of the Porsche which was driven by James Dean, and continues to narrate into the microphone following some seconds of immobility after the impact. Seagrave has concussion, and is being helped from the Porsche when the authorities arrive. Remington is concerned for his condition and she and Ballard follow Vaughan and Seagrave into the wispy undergrowth at the side of the road. They reach Vaughan's car and head for Seagrave's place, Remington sitting between Ballard and Vaughan, who has one hand on the steering wheel and another between her legs. When they get to Seagrave's house, where Vaughan has a workshop, Seagrave's wife is there, and so is Gabrielle, herself a car crash victim, and part of Vaughan's entourage. Vaughan is anxious to sketch out plans for the reconstruction of the crash that killed Jayne Mansfield, and wants to show Ballard some of his photographs, among which is a picture of Ballard and Remington at the airport garage. He tells Ballard that his project is concerned with the technological reshaping of the human body, but Gabrielle had already said that he makes everything look like a crime.

The first automotive troilism between Vaughan, Ballard and Catherine is tense but inconsequential: three cars on the ordinary road with Vaughan aggressive and dangerous but not quite lunatic. Catherine fantasises aloud about Vaughan, and about Ballard and Vaughan, when she and Ballard are making love back at their apartment. Catherine's fantasies are mirrored by Helen, who in the past has had sex with several different men in cars, each time fantasising that Vaughan was photographing the event as if it were a traffic accident. Helen had been to the Road Accident Research Laboratory, bringing back various scientific reports which Vaughan is reading through at Seagrave's house while the rest (except for Catherine) are watching videotapes of crashes. Helen is intensely engaged with what is on the screen, sexually and emotionally.

Vaughan drives a Lincoln convertible, the type of car Kennedy was in when he was assassinated. He would love to drive a classic crash car, but his general programme is one that he describes as benevolent psychopathology, the liberation of sexual energy created in a car crash. It is a way for him to break through the stasis of the present into somewhere else. It is a theme that is familiar from other Cronenberg films, *Shivers* and *Videodrome* particularly. Vaughan is the dominant figure in *Crash*,[7] involving others, like Ballard, Helen and Seagrave as pieces in his game, even though he uses the word 'partners' of them. Vaughan is not, however, a simple one-dimensional cipher for a simple principle of twisted power. He is naïvely enthusiastic but also intermittently existentially nauseated, as he is just before Ballard, Catherine and he encounter the multiple pile-up caused by Seagrave's private re-run of the Jayne Mansfield crash. Ballard is driving the Lincoln. Vaughan is taking photographs of what for him is a mile-long work of art. Climbing out of the Lincoln to get a closer look, and wandering with his camera amongst the dazed survivors, he sees Seagrave dead, in a blonde wig, with false breasts, and a dead dog in the crumpled vehicle. Back at the Lincoln, Ballard has noticed some blood on the car. The police are looking for a hit-and-run driver, so it is decided to take the car through the car wash. This is not a question of avoiding arrest, more a matter of ensuring that the police do not impound the car. Catherine and Vaughan have heavy-handed sex in the back of the car as it goes through the car wash, with Ballard looking at them in the mirror from the front of the car. Later, in their apartment on their own, Ballard lightly explores Catherine's bruises.

Gabrielle and Ballard visit a Mercedes showroom. Gabrielle wants to see if she can fit into a car which has not been adapted. She gets stuck and her prosthesis tears the leather of the brand new coupé as she tries to free herself, a ripping gesture that is repeated later when Ballard and Gabrielle have sex in the front of his car, as Ballard rips her fishnet stocking to gain access to the vaginal wound at the back of her leg, and further duplicated when Vaughan tells the medical tattooist, inscribing a car motif on his chest, that he wants the tattoo to be 'ragged and dirty'. Ballard also has a tattoo. Each is aroused by the druidic motif on the other's body, and after sex in the Lincoln near a wrecker's yard, Ballard gets into a smashed car which Vaughan then rams twice with his Lincoln, something which he had already done secretly to Catherine's silver two-seater convertible. Later, at night in the rain, James is driving Catherine in her car when Vaughan pulls onto the road after them. Driving as if he was in a stock-car race, Vaughan repeatedly hits Catherine's car in the rear, twice nudging it into the lorry in front of them. He is still in control, but then veers off to the left through the guardrail and down onto the road below, landing on a bus, his car catching fire. Vaughan is dead.

The Lincoln is in the police pound, written off as far as the police are concerned, but still talismanic for Helen and Gabrielle who find it and embrace on the back seat. Ballard and Catherine want to reclaim it and bring it back to life. The final scenes of the film show Ballard in the Lincoln hunting Catherine's two-seater. She releases her seatbelt. He hits her from behind and her car veers off the road and down a bank. The car has flipped over and Catherine has been thrown just clear. When Ballard gets to her, she is dazed and cut, but all right. As Ballard holds her in a sexual clinch from behind, he says, 'Maybe the next one darling, maybe the next one', echoing what Catherine had said to him early in the film when they had compared their experiences in the aircraft hangar and the camera room, and Catherine had said, on hearing that Ballard had been interrupted, 'Poor darling, maybe the next one, maybe the next one.'

Powerless and passive, locked into an interminable present where movement has crashed to a halt, James and Catherine Ballard are drawn by Vaughan into serial car-crash sex. It is a substitute for their impotence *vis-à-vis* both past and present; they have neither past nor future. Their only arena of power comes to be located on the motorways, and the exercise of that power is a fetishised substitute for the past and future that they lack. Exercised on the damaged products of consumer society, their activities intensify in proportion to the pointless speed of the phallic fetishes accelerating all around them, climaxing as the vehicles crash into each other, fulfilling their essential purposelessness. This interpretation of the film is, it must be admitted, a brutally obvious one. Its strength, however, is that

Cronenberg presents no fewer than five avenues out of the impasse which the film inscribes, and then closes off the path on each occasion.

We have already touched upon the first escape road. It is signposted to a future of human–machine hybridity. Donna Haraway famously described the utopian potential of this evolutionary possibility in her Cyborg Manifesto, arguing that the domain of the human–machine has tremendous significance for women, since it will mean the attenuation of the power of biology to determine sex-roles. Haraway's key argument was that cyborgs are sites of cultural ambiguity, transcending the imbalanced dichotomies which have defined sex, race, class and disability. One of the vigorous responses to this vision related to the issue of 'good' and 'bad' cyborgs, and, as Carol Mason (1995: 226) notes, 'good-bad' productions such as *Terminator 2* tended to overwhelm the more open-ended conception which Haraway had developed, according to which cyborgs are, to use Stone's (1995: 178) phrase, 'creatures of cultural interstice'. Against the open textured possibility, Cronenberg/Ballard appears to gesture toward a technological future when James asks Vaughan what he is up to, and Vaughan replies that it is 'the reshaping of the human body by technology'. Some time later, Vaughan shows James two packets of photographs. The first shows movie stars at the height of their appeal, but the pictures are marked with the wounds from which they will later die in car accidents. The second shows the cars in which they died:

> Each photo is marked to show which parts of the cars destroyed or fused with which famous body part: for example, a close up of the dashboard and windshield from the Camus car – Michel Gallimard's *Facel Vega* – is marked 'nasal bridge', 'soft palate', 'left zygomatic arch'. (Cronenberg 1996: 41)

This closure through death and its detailed geography of the possibility of a cyborgic future, even that a 'bad' cyborg might be allowed, is underlined when Vaughan replies to James's comment that he thought the reshaping of the body by modern technology was his project, by saying that this was 'A crude sci-fi project that floats on the surface and doesn't threaten anybody. I use it to test the resilience of my potential partners in psychopathology' (ibid.: 42). As Scott Bukatman points out (1993: 321), *Crash* resists any functionalist assimilation of human and machine. The possibility of a future is indeed evoked, only in order for its destruction to be all the more effective.

The second breach of the present is offered through the medium of cultural history. James Dean, Jayne Mansfield, Albert Camus are all figures from the past. Vaughan might have an exceedingly offbeat interest in cultural history, but nevertheless this does appear to be a reaching into the past, and, what is more, it is done in hermeneutically impeccable, if macabre, style. The roadside re-staging of James Dean's fatal accident finds Vaughan in the passenger seat of the Porsche, driven by stuntman Colin Seagrave. Vaughan announces:

You'll notice that we are not wearing helmets or safety padding of any kind, and our cars are not equipped with roll cages or seat-belts. We depend solely on the skill of our drivers for our safety, so that we can bring you the ultimate in authenticity. (Cronenberg 1996: 28)

Vaughan and Seagrave, then, are historians with access to the past. They appear to have no postmodern concerns about the ownership, definition or inevitable fictionality of the histories that they re-enact; their concern is 'the ultimate in authenticity'. Then Cronenberg/Ballard kills them both: a violent end to the fantasy of reliving the past. Seagrave dies re-enacting the Jayne Mansfield crash. Vaughan responds to the accident by saying that he must record all the details, but when Vaughan dies the documentary imperative dies with him: for James, looking at the wreckage of Vaughan's Lincoln which had plunged on to the top of an airline coach, there is only engagement.

The third potential line out of the bleak stasis of the present takes us to the question of social order, and the role of the police. There is a point in the film when the illegality and pathology of Vaughan's enterprise seems to be admitted. Even if the present cannot be exceeded, perhaps it will be far too extreme to suggest that the figure of the crash is its normal form. We encounter this intimation in the aftermath of the James Dean re-staging. The staging directions are as follows:

> . . . *six police cars, lights flashing and sirens wailing, converge on the lit stretch of road, three from each end. They screech to a halt and dozens of cops pour out of the cars. The crowd panics and streams down from the grandstand onto the road. A loudspeaker mounted on one of the police cars begins to blare . . . Because James and Helen are just in advance of the first wave of spectators, they manage to link up with Vaughan as he helps haul a still-groggy Seagrave off the road and into the woods.* (ibid.: 30–1)

Vaughan's response, however, corrects a view we might first have had that this incursion of the police is a demonstration of the marginality of crash culture. He says, 'It's not the police. It's the Department of Transport. It's a joke. They have no idea who we really are.' It is true that, to use Vaughan's phrase, 'the police were cracking down', but this meant that Seagrave had to stage his final re-enactment despite them, and although the police are supposed to be concerned with two cases of injured pedestrians, they are merely a nuisance and an irrelevance. Furthermore, to underline their complicity with the crash culture, they also supply James with Vaughan's Lincoln, after his death – the vehicle with which James pursues his wife in the final crash scene.

The fourth principle of reason which we are offered, only for it to be snatched away from us, is the principle of science. After the accident in which her husband died, Helen thinks of taking a job with the Road Research Laboratory. They need a medical officer. She is drawn to repeat her car crash, but, apparently, under controlled conditions. The subsequent scene at the laboratory destroys any thought that science might tame the fetishistic energies which the film releases. James, Helen and Vaughan watch a slow-motion replay of a motorcycle colliding with a family saloon with four occupants. Cronenberg's directions read as follows: '*James looks down at the silk-suited wife of a ministry official standing beside him. Her eyes watch the film with a rapt gaze, as if she were seeing herself and her daughters dismembered in the crash*' (ibid.: 40) while Vaughan says, 'Get all the paper you can, Ballard. Some of the stuff they're giving away is terrific: "Mechanisms of occupant ejection", "Tolerances of the human face in crash impacts" . . .' (ibid.: 40). The value-neutrality of scientific investigation is easily turned to Vaughan's account, as, of course, we know, since Heidegger at least, that it can be.

The fifth and final example of closure pertains to Vaughan himself. He is the *daemon*, the fertilising and maieutic figure who crystallises the essence of the present, and impregnates James with its spirit. He is drawn from a tradition of destructive seduction that began with Socrates, but Ballard/Cronenberg does not allow him to function for long as a charismatic figure. His death is matter-of-fact, unremarked except by James's personal excitement: charisma, not routinised, but banalised. The authors allow neither power nor leadership to subsist for more than a short while, just long enough to extend the present, and falling far short of providing a structure that might provide for its transcendence.

If neither science nor the forces of order nor the principle of power threatens the centrality of crash culture within our epoch, there are points in the film where tenderness and love appear to emerge as a potential counterpoint to the celebration of wreckage and death. Ironically, since the film is filled with passionless sex, this is the one avenue which is not entirely blocked. In the car wash, used to wash any remaining blood off Vaughan's car, Catherine and Vaughan have sex. During their 'semi-metallic' coupling, '*Catherine looks into James' eyes in an instant of complete lucidity. Her expression shows both irony and affection, an acceptance of a sexual logic they both recognize and have prepared themselves for*'. On the way back to their apartment, Catherine '*touches James' shoulder in a gesture of domestic affection*'. The subsequent staging instructions run as follows:

INT. BALLARD APT. ELEVATOR – NIGHT
In the elevator, James holds Catherine closely, lovingly.
INT. BALLARD APT. BEDROOM – NIGHT . . .
She watches him with a calm and affectionate gaze as he explores her body and bruises, feeling them gently with his fingers, lips and cheeks, tracing and interpreting the raw symbols that Vaughan's hands and mouth have left across her skin. (ibid.: 51)

It is certainly possible to read such expressions of tenderness (and they are not alone in the script) as after-echoes of the episodes of crash-sex consummation. They can, however, also be read as the single vestige of continuing life in an otherwise unrelenting vista of twisted plastic and stalled movement. When, in the final scenes of the film, James, driving Vaughan's written-off Lincoln, goes hunting for his wife, and hits her sports car, forcing it off the road, down a verge, and then goes to her, to

penetrate her bruised but living body from behind, he affirms the sub-
sistence of love alongside death, as he says, 'Maybe the next one, darling . . .
Maybe the next one . . . ' (ibid.: 65).

Bukatman asserts that Ballard's *Crash* 'represents the ultimate interface
with the realities of a technologized existence' (1993: 192), while Baudrillard
thinks of it as the 'apocalyptic and baroque version' of technology's 'mortal
deconstruction of the body' (111). It is clear that both accounts can be
argued for, but neither interpretation goes beyond its scarifying surface in
the way that Cronenberg's rendition does. In fact Blanchot, Derrida and
Cronenberg are locked together in a perpetual present, and that common
condition seals them, as crash victims, into a relationship of propinquity
which is, in the era of technological and temporal repetition, the only
available certain basis for human interconnection. Blanchot writes of
inevitable passivity in the face of history, Derrida mourns for lost souls who
will never be born, and Cronenberg sets the camera rolling to record their
situation, then edits the result. Could there be any closer bond between
them than that of this, our, community of fate? It is a privileged position
that they have in this disabled vehicle: its underlying tenderness insinuated
by Cronenberg, a benevolent surveillance over it attested to by Blanchot,
and the significance of its interior possibilities sought out by Derrida. It is a
work of fiction, as all crash-victim friendship is, but it does, on the road to
nowhere, create the possibility of remission through relationships. This
condition leads to a conclusion which is quite opposite to the one which
Derrida himself reached in *The Politics of Friendship* (1997), where he
argued that relations of amity might be seeded in democracy. Nevertheless,
Derrida does foreshadow this conclusion in this book, by quoting from
Blanchot on the disaster, as follows:

> And yet, in the proximity of the most distant, to the pressure of the most
> weightless, to the contact of what does not reach us – it is in *friendship* that I can
> respond, a friendship unshared, without reciprocity, friendship of that which has
> passed leaving no trace. This is passivity's response to the un-presence of the
> unknown. (cited in Derrida 1997: 296, original emphasis)

No trace from the past, no reciprocity in the future, being bound together
in metal, plastic and rubber is our permanent fate, and the care and
tenderness of friendship may be the only relief to be found. It is, however,
far from insignificant. As Blanchot put it in his short note on friendship:

> Friendship, this relation without dependence, without episode . . . when the event
> itself comes, it brings this change, not the deepening of the separation, but its
> erasure; not the widening of the caesura but its levelling out and the dissipation of
> the void between us. (Blanchot 1997: 291–2)

Both Blanchot and Derrida have worked on this territory, and both find the
continuing possibility of otherness, of ghosts that have never been, of life
that subsists despite the permanence of the wound; and it seems that even
Crash, for all that the wound is taken as a fetishised object of desire, for all
its false strategies to tempt so as better to emphasise the pulverisation of

hope, cannot quite close the door on the other. This leads us to the view that the fragmented experience of contemporary subjectivity, riven between being, doing and upholding, and locked into a present with problematic access to both past and future, may be further understood if we can only discover the relational modalities between witness and friend and master and slave.

Notes

1. Robert Castel gives the example of active paediatric post-natal protocols which function to ensure that certain forms of the future will not begin, by close monitoring and then acting at the first sign of negative syndrome-formation (Castel 1991: 288).

2. As Ballard put it in his 1995 Introduction to the reissue of *Crash*, 'Increasingly our concepts of past, present and future are being forced to revise themselves. Just as the past, in social and psychological terms, became a casualty of Hiroshima and the nuclear age, so in its turn the future is ceasing to exist, devoured by the all-voracious present' (4).

3. It is interesting to note that the elements of voluntarism that mark Ballard's novel have been largely excised in Cronenberg's screenplay; and one can take Cronenberg's emphasis (1996: 42) on Vaughan's subsequent dismissal, as a crude sci-fi concept, of the project of human–machine hybridity as a repudiation of the actor-based theories of both (in their different ways) Haraway and Latour.

4. Blanchot thought that clarity should not be the principal criterion of thought (Ungar 1995: 91), and it is tempting to set that view alongside his conviction that we cannot properly know the past, seeing both positions, not as illuminating the nature of the epoch, but as self-serving and duplicitous. This case must be confronted, at least briefly, in view of political, theoretical and (apparently) historical affinities between Martin Heidegger, Paul de Man and Blanchot himself. All three had been associated in various ways with right-wing thought during the era of German National Socialism. Heidegger had carried a Nazi party card from 1933 through to 1945, refused almost totally to comment on this for the next forty years, and remains protected by his family and some others, who are responsible for still refusing access to the Heidegger archives in Marbach (Rockmore 1992: 25). Paul de Man had maintained silence, amounting to concealment, with respect to his wartime writings for the Belgian collaborationist newspaper, *Le Soir*, and in the course of these writings he had referred to 'the impeccable behaviour of a highly civilized invader (Mehlman 1995: 114) and had said that 'a solution of the Jewish problem which would envisage the creation of a Jewish colony isolated from Europe, would not entail, for the literary life of the West, deplorable consequences' (Graef 1993: 14). Blanchot has been held to have occupied a position in the French media comparable to Paul de Man's in Belgium. Mehlman fantasised about the three thinkers as follows:

> my first fantasy upon hearing of de Man's writings during the War was of a caricature entitled the Passion of Deconstruction with Derrida on the cross flanked by Blanchot, crucified under the sign Combat, on the one side, and de Man, suffering similarly beneath the rubric *Le Soir*, on the other. As for the Father-who-has-forsaken-him, the cruellest moment of the fantasy would have Heidegger, from whom Derrida received the word 'deconstruction', flashing from above the Nazi membership card he did not relinquish until after the war. (1995: 124)

Whatever position one takes on Heidegger or de Man, it seems relatively clear that the case of Blanchot is rather different. His wartime writings were known and acknowledged. His status as an oppositional thinker meant that his diatribes against weak French governments need not be taken as endorsement of Fascism. They were actually largely ignored, as was pointed out in 1976 in a special journal issue devoted to Blanchot and introduced by Steven Ungar (Holland 1976: 8). Further, an examination of Mehlman's claim that Blanchot be seen as parallel to de

Man shows that his case depends upon some fairly sophisticated and eminently contestable tropological argument, and the extended examination of the philosophical implications of Blanchot's wartime writings, performed by Steven Ungar some nineteen years after the journal issue he introduced, finds somewhat limited fault in that Blanchot, while he warned against German aggression, compared French weakness to the ideological energies of German nationalism, and was not willing to extend the relatively restricted access to his writings of the 1930s and 1940s by organising a new collection of them. In sum, while there is admitted difficulty in arriving at a definitive judgement of Blanchot's early writings, there is a strong case to be made that their animating spirit is oppositional rather than collaborationist. As Allan Stoekl recently put it:

> Politically, like so many leading authors of this century (Orwell, Céline, Bataille, Foucault, Derrida, and even Sartre come to mind), Blanchot seems to have been fundamentally an anarchist, distrustful of all unified authority and codified doctrine; among figures of this type, political commitment, as understood in conventional terms, is always in flux and sometimes takes a dangerous or sinister turn (to the far right, early on, in Blanchot's case; to the Stalinist or *gauchiste* left, later on, in Sartre's, etc.). What remains constant is the anarchism, the *opposition*. (Stoekl 1996: xxviii)

5. 'Why yet another book, where a seismic shuddering – one of the forms of the disaster – lays waste to it? Because the order of the book is required by what the book does not contain – by the absence which eludes the book' (Blanchot 1995: 99). Blanchot seems to be saying that the spirit of writing is structured in much the same way that Derrida sees the spirit of Marxism: writing as the pursuit of the ghost that was never here before and never will be, but nevertheless it must be sought, as the only way to conjure up a weak sense of the future, which is the only sense that we might find.

6. A subliminal intercut of Valentine turning her attention to the car radio, just before hitting Kern's dog, would be quite appropriate.

7. Kathy Acker wrote that 'Ballard's novel is a love letter to Vaughan' (cited in Sinclair 1999: 90).

IN CONCLUSION

How should we now understand the subject? Within the framework of sociological analysis, whether ruled by an objectivist commitment to real structures or by the plastic scepticism of contingent constructionism, the subject is entirely resolved and dissolved into its component social parts. From birth to death, and at all points before, between and after, at every point on both its surface and in its interior, the subject is a social accomplishment. There is no level that is anterior to the social. This is the sociological position and it is unimpeachable. It does not mean that there is no morality or that the sense of the physical is bogus, merely that – just to take these two of many examples that could have been picked – the moral and the physical never escape sociological definition. Sociologically speaking, there has never been a history of the subject which was not first, foremost, and entirely a history of society. Thus, if conceptions of the subject have moved from Platonic replicas of the Gods through various stages to current conceptions of Freudian splitting or postmodern fragmentation, this narrative of the subject is a sociological phenomenon and its stages can be sociologically analysed. None of this, however, authorises the conclusion that the subject is therefore only an agent of wider social forces, or that it does not exist, or that the drive to give cultural expression to the ache and conscious persistence of the human is either inferior or without significance. It does not mean that the exploration of alienation to be found in, for example, the films of David Cronenberg or Robert Bresson does not catch something of the eternal condition of the subject, nor does it enable the refusal of contemporary lessons concerning the poor fit of the moral rags clothing the subject given to us by Maurice Blanchot or Krzysztof Kieślowski. In short, the inevitability of the social takes its place alongside the inevitability of the subject. Neither precludes the other. Sociological explanation is only one perspective on the human world, and even if it does account for the subject to the point of its dissolution, this is just not the case for other perspectives, such as the aesthetic, axiological or dramatic. These in their turn may exclude the sociological. This may be a lesson that sociologists still have to learn, that reflexivity will operate to relativise, that it will perform a function of de-domination.

It was Barnett Newman's self-appointed task to attempt to portray the struggle of the subject without reducing that struggle to a narrative. He wanted to suggest the scale of the phenomenon: infinitely reproduced, infinitely varied, closely united but unspeakably separate, sociologically deniable yet existentially apodictic, beyond and within. Baselitz wished to show the subject uncontaminated, not now by the sociological perspective, but by his own. He was led in a number of directions: fragmentation, inversion, sculptural brutalism, and an obsessively myopic neo-romanticism. Between these artists, we see a contrast of sacred and profane: Newman trying to see and then to express what it is about the subject that is set apart, Baselitz attempting in different ways to approach, without the transport of his own subjectivity – an impossible task, of course – the sheer materiality of the subject. This contrast between Baselitz's figure and Newman's ground, between a dogged phenomenology and a rapturous idealism, is, needless to say, a fundamental alternation in the current of the subject itself. It was then for Francis Bacon to add a third term: a witness to the subject and a witness as subject, a line of inquiry into the conditions of the subject which has hardly begun, but which might suggest a third ontological category to be added to those of master and slave. That the twentieth century was the time of the witness, debarred from but close to the action, admitting both good and evil done to and by others, locked in a present circumscribed by alien histories and inaccessible futures, of great weight but without specific powers, is a thought that is already very familiar. It takes us, it might be thought, into the cinema.

Kieślowski's trilogy suggests to us that there may be three basic ideal types of subject. The existential subject is caught in the night at that point when the only presence to consciousness is the sound of one's breathing and the slightly irregular pulse of the heart. From a base of unadorned bodily existence, unanswerable but insistent questions of meaning arise. This is not a willed condition. Nor is it pristine. It is accompanied by an emotional response: fear, disgust, self-pity, for example. The existential subject is crystallised out of an intersubjective existence, and experienced in language against a ground of significant macro- and micro-others. The Cartesian subject is a creature of instrumental reason. He or she is a construction well known to economists, military commanders, works managers and police forces, to name just some of the more obvious instances. Without elements of calculation, the human subject cannot survive within any context. However, an entirely Cartesian subject is not human, but robotic, controlled by the instructions of others. We are here within what has been called on many occasions the realm of means. The Kantian subject has an answer to the existentialist's question of meaning (an answer which is entirely lost sight of once inside the existentialist mode, but which, from the Kantian standpoint, never leaves one's side, as the musical expression of *caritas* never leaves Julie) and that answer, expressed as a set of shared values, a grammar of collective life, provides an overall framework for the subject's conduct, both instrumental and non-instrumental, *vis-à-vis* him- or herself and others. We are here, as will already be clear and familiar, within the realm of ends. To these three ideal types, it is now necessary to add a fourth: the subject as witness. The three imperatives above of being, doing and care are all of them underpinned, as each is by the others, by the inescapability of testimony. Perhaps this is where the power of sociology lies, as well as the characterisation of the twentieth century, but be that as it may, Bacon, Kieślowski, Ballard (tempted from observation into participation), and no doubt many others, affirm that it is time to give the witness its due, and to begin to work out its implications.

REFERENCES

Ackroyd, P. (1984) *T.S. Eliot*. London: Sphere Books.

Adams, N. (1995) *The Stations of the Cross*. Manchester: St Mary's.

Adriani, G. (1994) 'On re-presentational pictures' in *Georg Baselitz: Printed Works 1965–1992*. Stuttgart: IFA.

Aeschylus (1952) *The Complete Plays*. London: Allen and Unwin.

Alexander, J.C. (1995) *Fin de Siècle Social Theory*. London: Verso.

Alphonsus, St (1965) *The Stations of the Cross*. London: Catholic Truth Society.

Amiel, V. (1995) *Kieslowski*. Paris: Éditions Payot et Rivages.

Amiel, V. (ed.) (1997) *Krzysztof Kieslowski*. Paris: Jean-Michel Place, Positif.

Andrews, N. (1993) 'Struggles for liberty'. *Financial Times*, 14 Oct.

Ariès, P. (1981) *The Hour of our Death*. London: Penguin.

Augustine (1945) *The City of God*. London: J.M. Dent.

Bacon, F. (1985) *Francis Bacon*. London: Tate Gallery and Thames and Hudson.

Bahr, H. (1992) 'From *Expressionism*' [1914] in C. Harrison and P. Wood (eds), *Art in Theory 1900–1990*. Oxford: Blackwell.

Ballard, J.G. (1995) *Crash*. London: Vintage.

Baselitz, G. (1995a) 'Notes on *Nude Elke*'. www.guggenheim.org/baselitz/elke.html.

Baselitz, G. (1995b) 'Notes on *B for Larry*'. www.guggenheim.org/baselitz/larry.html.

Baselitz, G. and Schönebeck, E. (1992) *The Pandemonium Manifestos* [1961] in C. Harrison and P. Wood (eds), *Art in Theory 1900–1990*. Oxford: Blackwell.

Bataille, G. (1997) 'The torment' in F. Botting and S. Wilson (eds), *The Bataille Reader*. Oxford: Blackwell.

Baudrillard, J. (1994) 'Crash' in his *Simulacra and Simulation*. Ann Arbor: University of Michigan Press, pp. 111–20.

Benjamin, W. (1970) 'The work of art in the age of mechanical reproduction' in *Illuminations*. London: Jonathan Cape.

Berlin, I. (1973) *Essays on J.L. Austin*. Oxford: Oxford University Press.

Black, J. (1991) *The Aesthetics of Murder*. Baltimore: Johns Hopkins University Press.

Blanchot, M. (1995) *The Writing of the Disaster*. Lincoln: University of Nebraska Press.

Blanchot, M. (1997) *Friendship*. Stanford: Stanford University Press.

Bloom, H. (1994) *The Western Canon*. London: Macmillan.

Bois, Y.-A., Crimp, D. and Krauss, R. (1984) 'A conversation with Hans Haacke' in A. Michelson, R. Krauss, D. Crimp and J. Copjec (eds), *October: the First Decade, 1976–1986*. Cambridge, MA: MIT Press, 1987.

Born, G. (1995) *Rationalizing Culture*. Berkeley: University of California Press.

Bourdieu, P. (1984) *Distinction*. London: Routledge.

Bourdieu, P. (1987) *Choses dites*. Paris: Minuit.

Bourdieu, P. (1988) 'Vive la crise', *Theory and Society*, Vol. 17, No. 4: 773–87.

Bourdieu, P. (1991) 'Epilogue: on the possibility of a field of world sociology' in P. Bourdieu and J. Coleman (eds), *Social Theory for a Changing Society*. Boulder, CO: Westview Press.

Bourdieu, P. (1996) *The Rules of Art*. Cambridge: Polity.

Bourdieu, P. (1997) *Meditations Pascaliennes*. Paris: Seuil.

Bourdieu, P. (1998a) 'A reasoned utopia and economic fatalism', *New Left Review*, No. 227, Jan./Feb.

Bourdieu, P. (1998b) *Acts of Resistance: Against the New Myths of Our Time*. Cambridge: Polity.

Bourdieu, P. and Haacke, H. (1995) *Free Exchange*. Cambridge: Polity.

Bourdieu, P. and Wacquant, L. (1992) *An Invitation to Reflexive Sociology*. Chicago: Chicago University Press.

Boyne, R. (1998) 'Postmodernism, the sublime and ethics' in I. Velody and A. Still (eds), *The Politics of Modernity*. Cambridge: Cambridge University Press.

Bukatman, S. (1993) *Terminal Identity: the Virtual Subject in Postmodern Science Fiction*. Durham, NC: Duke University Press.

Burch, N. (1973) *Theory of Film Practice*. London: Secker and Warburg.

Butler, J. (1998) 'Merely cultural', *New Left Review*, No. 227, Jan./Feb.: 33–44.

Bynum, C.W. (1995) *The Resurrection of the Body*. New York: Columbia University Press.

Bynum, C.W. (1999) 'Why all the fuss about the body: a medievalist's perspective' in V.E. Bonnell and L. Hunt (eds), *Beyond the Cultural Turn*. Berkeley, CA: University of California Press.

Calas, N. (1995) [1967] 'Subject matter in the work of Barnett Newman' in G. Battcock (ed.), *Minimal Art*. Berkeley, CA: University of California Press, pp. 109–15.

Callon, M. (1986) 'Some elements of a sociology of translation: domestication of the scallops and the fishermen of St. Brieuc Bay' in J. Law (ed.), *Power, Action and Belief*. London: Routledge.

Callon, M. and Latour, B. (1981) 'Unscrewing the big Leviathan: how actors macro-structure reality and how sociologists help them to do it' in K. Knorr-Cetina and A.V. Cicourel (eds), *Advances in Social Theory and Methodology: Toward an Integration of Micro- and Macro-Sociologies*. London: Routledge and Kegan Paul.

Callon, M. and Latour, B. (1992) 'Don't throw the baby out with the Bath School! A reply to Collins and Yearley' in A. Pickering (ed.), *Science as Practice and Culture*. Chicago: Chicago University Press.

Calvocoressi, R. (1983) 'Introduction' in N. Serota and M. Francis (eds), *Georg Baselitz: Paintings 1960–1983*. London: Whitechapel Art Gallery.

Calvocoressi, R. (1985) 'A source of the inverted imagery in Georg Baselitz's paintings', *The Burlington Magazine*, 894–99.

Caruth, C. (ed.) (1995) *Trauma: Explorations in Memory*. Baltimore: Johns Hopkins University Press.

Caruth, C. (1996) *Unclaimed Experience: Trauma, Narrative and History*. Baltimore: Johns Hopkins University Press.

Castel, R. (1991) 'From dangerousness to risk' in G. Burchell, C. Gordon and P. Miller (eds), *The Foucault Effect*. Hemel Hempstead: Harvester Wheatsheaf.

Churchland, P.M. (1995) *The Engine of Reason, the Seat of the Soul*. Cambridge, MA: MIT Press.

Clark, T.J. (1997) 'In defence of abstract expressionism' in R. Krauss, A. Michelson, Y.-A. Bois, B.H.D. Buchlon, H. Foster, D. Hollier and S. Kolbowski (eds), *October: The Second Decade, 1986–1996*. Cambridge, MA: MIT Press.

Collins, H.M. and Yearley, S. (1992a) 'Epistemological chicken' in A. Pickering (ed.), *Science as Practice and Culture*. Chicago: Chicago University Press.

Collins, H.M. and Yearley, S. (1992b) 'Journey into space' in A. Pickering (ed.), *Science as Practice and Culture*. Chicago: Chicago University Press.

Cronenberg, D. (1996) *Crash*. London: Faber and Faber.

Crowther, P. (1989) 'Nietzsche to neo-expressionism: a context for Baselitz', *German Art Now: Art and Design*, No. 5 (December): 76–83.

Crowther, P. (1993) *Critical Aesthetics and Postmodernism*. Oxford: Oxford University Press.

Danto, A. (1999) 'Bourdieu on art: field and individual' in R. Shusterman (ed.), *Bourdieu: a Critical Reader*. Oxford: Blackwell.

Darragon, E. (1996a) *Baselitz Charabia et Basta: Entretiens avec Eric Darragon*. Paris: L'Arche.

Darragon, E. (1996b) 'Baselitz à Paris' in S. Pagé, J. Laffon and O. Burluraux (eds).

Deleuze, G. (1984) *Francis Bacon: Logique de la sensation* (2 vols). Paris: Editions de la différence.

Deleuze, G. and Guattari, F. (1987) *A Thousand Plateaus*. Minneapolis: University of Minnesota Press.

Derrida, J. (1976) *Of Grammatology*. Baltimore: Johns Hopkins University Press.

Derrida, J. (1978a) 'Freud and the scene of writing' in *Writing and Difference*. London: Routledge.

Derrida, J. (1978b) *Edmund Husserl's 'Origin of Geometry': an Introduction*. New York: Nicholas Hays.

Derrida, J. (1982) 'The ends of man' in *Margins of Philosophy*. London: Harvester Wheatsheaf.

Derrida, J. (1987) *The Truth in Painting*. Chicago: University of Chicago Press.

Derrida, J. (1992) *The Other Heading*. Bloomington: Indiana University Press.

Derrida, J. (1993) *Memoirs of the Blind*. Chicago: Chicago University Press.

Derrida, J. (1994) *Specters of Marx: the State of the Debt, the Work of Mourning, and the New International*. New York: Routledge.

Derrida, J. (1997) *The Politics of Friendship*. London: Verso.

Dube, W.-D. (1972) *The Expressionists*. London: Thames and Hudson.

Durkheim, E. (1952) *Suicide*. London: Routledge.

Dyke, C. (1999) 'Bourdieuean dynamics: the American middle class self-constructs', in R. Shusterman (ed.), *Bourdieu: a Critical Reader*. Oxford: Blackwell.

Eliot, T.S. (1936) *Collected Poems 1909–1935*. London: Faber and Faber.

Eliot, T.S. (1962) *Collected Plays*. London: Faber and Faber.

Elster, J. (1981) 'Snobs', *London Review of Books*, 5–18 Nov.: 10–12.

Engel, A. (1996) 'Krzysztof Kieslowski: human touch of a master'. *Guardian*, 14 Mar.

Evans, R.J. (1997) 'Watch on the Rhine'. *Times Higher Educational Supplement*, 7 Nov.

Farrell, K. (1998) *Post-traumatic Culture: Injury and Interpretation in the Nineties*. Baltimore: Johns Hopkins University Press.

Farson, D. (1994) *The Gilded Gutter Life of Francis Bacon*. London: Vintage.

Felman, S. (1995) 'Education and crisis, or the vicissitudes of teaching' in C. Caruth (ed.), *Trauma: Explorations in Memory*. Baltimore: Johns Hopkins University Press.

Fink, B. (1997) *A Clinical Introduction to Lacanian Psychoanalysis: Theory and Technique*. Cambridge, MA: Harvard University Press.

Foster, H. (1996) *The Return of the Real*. Cambridge, MA: MIT Press.

Freud, S. (1984) 'On repression' in *On Metapsychology*. Harmondsworth: Penguin.

Fukuyama, F. (1992) *The End of History and the Last Man*. New York: Free Press.

Gablik, S. (1991) *The Re-enchantment of Art*. London: Thames and Hudson.

Gale, M. (1999) *Francis Bacon: Working on Paper*. London: Tate Gallery.

Garbarz, F. (1994) '*Trois Couleurs Blanc*: inégalité sociale et égalité en amour'. *Études cinématographiques*, 203–10: 129–39.

Garbowski, C. (1997) *Krzysztof Kieślowski's Decalogue Series*. Lublin: Maria Curie-Sklodowska University Press.

Geldof, K. (1997) 'Authority, reading, reflexivity: Pierre Bourdieu and the aesthetic judgement of Kant.' *Diacritics*. Vol. 27, No. 1: 20–43.

Gellner, E. (1968) *Words and Things*. Harmondsworth: Penguin.

Gellner, E. (1998) *Language and Solitude: Wittgenstein, Malinowski and the Habsburg Dilemma*. Cambridge: Cambridge University Press.

Georg Baselitz: Paintings 1964–1967 (1985) Anthony d'Offay Gallery. London.

Georg Baselitz: Prints 1964–1990 (1992) Geneva/Valencia/London: Tate Gallery.

Georg Baselitz: Retrospektive 1964–1991 (1992) Munich: Hirmer-Verlag.

Gohr, S. (1996) 'Toile ou tableau? Considération sur la catégorie "image" chez Georg Baselitz' in S. Pagé, J. Laffon and O. Burluraux (eds).

Gottlieb, A., Rothko, M. and Newman, B. (1992) 'Statement 1943' in C. Harrison and P. Wood (eds), *Art in Theory: 1900–1990*. Oxford: Blackwell.

Graef, O. de (1993) *Serenity in Crisis: a Preface to Paul de Man 1939–1960*. Lincoln: University of Nebraska Press.

Gray, A. (1990) *Lanark*. London: Harvest Books.

Habermas, J. (1992) *Postmetaphysical Thinking*. Cambridge: Polity.

Haraway, D.J. (1989) *Primate Visions*. London: Verso.

Haraway, D.J. (1991) *Simians, Cyborgs and Women*. New York: Routledge.

Haraway, D.J. (1992) 'The promises of monsters: a regenerative politics for inappropriate/d others' in L. Grossberg, C. Nelson and P. Treichler (eds), *Cultural Studies*. London: Routledge

Haraway, D.J. (1997) *Modest Witness @ Second Millennium*. London: Routledge.

Hartman, G. (1995) 'Public memory and its discontents' in M. Brown (ed.), *The Uses of Literary History*. Durham, NC: Duke University Press.

Heidegger, M. (1977) 'The word of Nietzsche: "God is dead"' in *The Question Concerning Technology and Other Essays*. New York: Harper and Row.

Heidegger, M. (1978) 'Letter on humanism' in D.F. Krell (ed.), *Martin Heidegger: Basic Writings*. London: Routledge.

Hergott, F. (1997) 'The interior surface' in *Baselitz*. Milan: Edizione Charta.

Hess, T.B. (1972) *Barnett Newman*. London: Tate Gallery Publications.

Holland, M. (1976) 'Towards a method', *Sub-stance*, No. 14: 27–38.

Insdorf, A. (1999) *Double Lives, Second Chances: the Cinema of Krzysztof Kieslowski*. New York: Hyperion.

Jablonka, R. (1982) *Ruins: Strategies of Destruction in the Fracture Paintings of Georg Baselitz 1966–1969*. London: Anthony d'Offay.

Jackson, F. (1982) 'Epiphenomenal qualia'. *Philosophical Quarterly*, Vol.32: 127–36.

Jacobitti, S. (1996) 'Thinking about the self' in L. May and J. Kohn (eds), *Hannah Arendt: Twenty Years Later*. Cambridge, MA: MIT Press.

Joachimides, C.M., Rosenthal, N. and Schmied, W. (eds) (1985) *German Art in the Twentieth Century: Painting and Sculpture 1905–1985*. Munich/London: Prestel-Verlag and Royal Academy of Arts.

Kandinsky, W. (1977) *Concerning the Spiritual in Art*. New York: Dover.

Kenny, A. (1979) *Aristotle's Theory of the Will*. London: Duckworth.

Kieślowski, K. and Piesiewicz, K. (1998) *Three Colours Trilogy: Blue, White, Red*. London: Faber and Faber.

Knox, S.L. (1998) *Murder: a Tale of Modern American Life*. Durham, NC: Duke University Press.

Kosuth, J. (1991) *Art after Philosophy and After*. Cambridge, MA: MIT Press.

Krens, T., Govan, M. and Thompson, J. (eds) (1989) *Refigured Painting: The German Image 1960–1988*. Munich: Prestel-Verlag.

Kristeva, J. (1991) *Strangers to Ourselves*. Hemel Hempstead: Harvester Wheatsheaf.

Kristeva, J. (1996) 'Is sensation a language?' in J. Lechte (ed.), *Writing and Psychoanalysis*. London: Arnold.

Kuspit, D. (1988) *The New Subjectivism: Art in the 1980s*. New York: Da Capo Press.

Laffon, J. (1996) 'Introduction' in S. Pagé, J. Laffon and O. Burluraux (eds).

Latour, B. (1983) 'Give me a laboratory and I will raise the world' in K.D. Knorr-Cetina and M. Mulkay (eds), *Science Observed: Perspectives on the Social Study of Science*. London: Sage.

Latour, B. (1990) 'Drawing things together' in M. Lynch and S. Woolgar (eds), *Representation in Scientific Practice*. Cambridge, MA: MIT Press.

Latour, B. (1993) *We Have Never Been Modern*. London: Harvester Wheatsheaf.

Latour, B. (1997a) 'On recalling ANT' in *'Actor Network and After' Workshop*. Keele University: Centre for Social Theory and Technology.

Latour, B. (1997b) 'On actor-network theory: a few clarifications' in *'Actor Network and After' Workshop*. Keele University: Centre for Social Theory and Technology.

Law, J. (1994) *Organizing Modernity*. Oxford: Blackwell.

Leiris, M. (1983) *Francis Bacon*. London: Phaidon.

Lévi-Strauss, C. (1976) *Tristes Tropiques*. London: Penguin.

Lint, E. (dir.) (1995) *A Masterclass for Young Directors*. Amsterdam: Kunst Kanaal Video.

Lucie-Smith, E. (1984) *Movements in Art since 1945* (new revised edition). London: Thames and Hudson.

Lury, C. (1997) *Prosthetic Culture*. London: Routledge.

Lyotard, J.-F. (1988) *The Differend*. Manchester: Manchester University Press.

Lyotard, J.-F. (1990) *Heidegger and 'the Jews'*. Minneapolis: Minnesota University Press.

Lyotard, J.-F. (1991) *The Inhuman*. Cambridge: Polity.

Macdonald, M. (1997) 'Shark operator', *Observer Life*, 31 Aug.: 4–6.

Machiavelli, N. (1961) *The Prince*. Harmondsworth: Penguin.

Mason, C. (1995) 'Terminating bodies: toward a cyborg history of abortion' in J. Halberstam and I. Livingstone (eds), *Posthuman Bodies*. Bloomington: Indiana University Press.

Masters, B. 1998 'This bust was cast from a decaying corpse. Whose work does it most resemble: Damien Hirst's or Jeffrey Dahmer's?', *Observer Review*, 29 March.

Mehlman, J. (1995) *Genealogies of the Text: Literature, Psychoanalysis and Politics in Modern France*. Cambridge: Cambridge University Press.

Meštrović, S. (1994) *The Balkanization of the West*. London: Routledge.

Muthesius, A. (ed.) (1990) *Georg Baselitz*. Köln: Taschen.

Nagel, T. (1997) 'What is it like to be a bat?' in N. Block, O. Flanagan and G. Güzeldere (eds), *The Nature of Consciousness: Philosophical Debates*. Cambridge, MA: MIT Press.

Naifeh, S. and Smith, G.W. (1992) *Jackson Pollock: an American Saga*. London: Pimlico.

Nesselson, L. (1993) 'Trois Couleurs: bleu', *Variety*, 20 Sept.

Newman, B. (1966) *The Stations of the Cross: lema sabachthani*. New York: Solomon R. Guggenheim Museum.

Newman, B. (1992) *Selected Writings and Interviews*, ed. John P. O'Neill. Berkeley: University of California Press.

Nietzsche, F. (1973) *Beyond Good and Evil*. Harmondsworth: Penguin.

Nietzsche, F. (1974) *The Gay Science*. New York: Random House.

Owens, C. (1992) *Beyond Recognition: Representation, Power, and Culture*. Berkeley: University of California Press.

Pagé, S. (1996) 'Préface' in S. Pagé, J. Laffon and O. Burluraux (eds).

Pagé, S., Laffon, J. and Burluraux, O. (eds) (1996) *Georg Baselitz: Musée d'Art Moderne de la ville de Paris*. Paris: Éditions des musées de la ville de Paris.

Parsons, T. (1954) 'The problem of controlled institutional change' [1945] in *Essays in Sociological Theory* (revised edition). New York: Free Press.

Pasternak, B. (1988) *Doctor Zhivago*. London: Collins Harvill.

Peppiat, M. (1996) *Francis Bacon: Anatomy of an Enigma*. London: Weidenfeld and Nicolson.

Perreault, J. (1988) *Philip Pearlstein: Drawings and Watercolors*. New York: Harry N. Abrams.

Petrucci, A. (1999) 'Reading to read: a future for reading' in G. Cavallo and R. Chartier (eds), *A History of Reading in the West*. Cambridge: Polity.

Pitts, M. (1998) 'The living dead', *Guardian Weekend*, 28 Mar.

Plato (1955) *Timaeus*. Harmondsworth: Penguin.

Polan, D. (1994) 'Francis Bacon: the logic of sensation' in C.V. Boundas and D. Olkowski (eds), *Gilles Deleuze and the Theater of Philosophy*. New York: Routledge.

Pope, A. (1996) 'In Memory', *Sight and Sound*, Vol. 6, No. 8, Aug.: 65.

Ramachandran, V.S. and Blakeslee, S. (1999) *Phantoms in the Brain: Human Nature and the Architecture of the Mind*. London: Fourth Estate.

Readings, W. (1991) *Introducing Lyotard: Art and Politics*. London: Routledge.

Richie, A. (1998) *Faust's Metropolis*. London: HarperCollins.

Rockmore, T. (1992) *On Heidegger's Nazism and Philosophy*. Hemel Hempstead: Harvester Wheatsheaf.

Rose, N. (1996) *Inventing Our Selves*. Cambridge: Cambridge University Press.

Roskill, M. (1992) *Klee, Kandinsky and the Thought of Their Time*. Urbana: University of Illinois Press.

Russell, J. (1979) *Francis Bacon*. New York: Oxford University Press.

Safranski, R. (1998) *Martin Heidegger: Between Good and Evil*. Cambridge, MA: Harvard University Press.

Sartre, J.-P. (1965a) *Nausea*. Harmondsworth: Penguin.

Sartre, J.-P. (1965b) 'The humanism of existentialism' in *The Philosophy of Existentialism*. New York: Philosophical Library.

Schilling, J. (1989) 'Metaphors: positions in contemporary German painting' in T. Krens, M. Govan and J. Thompson (eds), *Refigured Painting: The German Image 1960–1988*. Munich: Prestel-Verlag.

Schluchter, W. (1996) *Paradoxes of Modernity: Culture and Conduct in the Theory of Max Weber*. Stanford: Stanford University Press.

Schmied, W. (1985) 'Points of departure and transformations in German art 1905–1985' in C.M. Joachimides, N. Rosenthal and W. Schmied (eds), *German Art in the Twentieth Century: Painting and Sculpture 1905–1985*. Munich/London: Prestel-Verlag and Royal Academy of Arts: 21–74.

Schor, G. (1996) *The Prints of Barnett Newman 1961–1969*. Ostfildern-Ruit: Verlag Gerd Hatje.

Scott, J. (1996) *Stratification and Power: Structures of Class, Status and Command*. Cambridge: Polity.

Serota, N. and Francis, M. (eds) (1983) *Georg Baselitz: Paintings 1960–1983*. London: Whitechapel Art Gallery.

Serrano, A. (1996) 'Letter to the National Endowments for the Arts' [1989] in K. Stiles and P. Selz (eds), *Theories and Documents of Contemporary Art*. Berkeley: University of California Press.

Serres, M. (1995) *Angels: a Modern Myth*. Paris: Flammarion.

Shiff, R. (1996) 'Strates' in S. Pagé, J. Laffon and O. Burluraux (eds).

Shildrick, M. (1997) *Leaky Bodies and Boundaries*. London: Routledge.

Sinclair, I. (1999) *Crash*. London: BFI.

Sollers, P. (1996) *Les Passions de Francis Bacon*. Paris: Gallimard.

Spivak, G.C. (1991) *Outside in the Teaching Machine*. London: Routledge.

Stacey, J. (1997) *Teratologies: a Cultural Study of Cancer*. London: Routledge.

Stoekl, A. (1996) 'Introduction' in M. Blanchot, *The Most High*. Lincoln: University of Nebraska Press.

Stok, D. (ed) (1993) *Kieslowski on Kieslowski*. London: Faber and Faber.

Stone, A.R. (1995) *The War of Desire and Technology at the Close of the Mechanical Age*. Cambridge, MA: MIT Press.

Stoullig, C. (1992) 'Picasso, De Kooning: a passion for drawing' in Picasso et al., *The Body on the Cross*. Montreal: Montreal Museum of Fine Arts, pp. 124–9.

Stratton, J. (1996) 'Serial killing and the transformation of the social', *Theory, Culture and Society*, Vol. 13, No. 1: 77–98.

Sylvester, D. (1980) *Interviews with Francis Bacon*. London: Thames and Hudson.

Sylvester, D. (1998) *Francis Bacon: the Human Body*. Berkeley: University of California Press.

Taylor, C. (1989) *Sources of the Self*. Cambridge: Cambridge University Press.

Theunissen, M. (1984) *The Other: Studies in the Social Ontology of Husserl, Heidegger, Sartre and Buber*. Cambridge, MA: MIT Press.

Ungar, S. (1995) *Scandal and Aftereffect: Blanchot and France since 1930*. Minneapolis: University of Minnesota Press.

Vesey, G. (1989) 'Responsibility and free will' in A. Phillips Griffiths (ed.), *Key Themes in Philosophy*. Cambridge: Cambridge University Press.

Virilio, P. (1995) *The Art of the Motor*. Minneapolis: University of Minnesota Press.

Wacquant, L. (1993) 'From ruling class to field of power: an interview with Pierre Bourdieu on La Noblesse d'État', *Theory, Culture and Society*, Vol. 10, No. 3: 19–44.

Waldman, D. (1995) *Georg Baselitz: Art on the Edge*. New York: Guggenheim Museum Publications.

Waldman, D. (1996) 'Notes on *B for Larry*'. www.guggenheim.org/baselitz/larry.html.

Ward, S. (1994) 'In the shadow of the deconstructed metanarratives: Baudrillard, Latour and the end of realist epistemology', *History of the Human Sciences*, Vol. 7, No. 4: 73–94.

Webber, A.J. (1996) *The Doppelganger: Double Visions in German Literature*. Oxford: Clarendon Press.

Weber, M. (1947) *The Theory of Social and Economic Organisation*. New York: Free Press.

Weber, M. (1948) 'Class, status, party' in H.H. Gerth and C. Wright Mills, *From Max Weber*. London: Routledge and Kegan Paul.

White, A. (1993) 'Prosthetic gods in atrocious places: Gilles Deleuze/Francis Bacon' in *Carnival, Hysteria and Writing*. Oxford: Oxford University Press, pp. 160–77.

Wilson, E. (1988) 'Picasso and pâté de foie gras: Pierre Bourdieu's sociology of culture', *Diacritics*, Summer: 47–60.

Wittgenstein, L. (1979) *Remarks on Frazer's 'Golden Bough'*. Retford: Brynmill Press.

Woolgar, S. (1992) 'Some remarks about positionism: a reply to Collins and Yearley' in A. Pickering (ed.), *Science as Practice and Culture*. Chicago: Chicago University Press.

Wright, E.O. (1997) *Class Counts: Comparative Studies in Class Analysis*. Cambridge: Cambridge University Press.

INDEX